# Auguste Blanqui and the Politics of Popular Empowerment

Also Available at Bloomsbury

*Resistance, Revolution and Fascism: Zapatismo and Assemblage Politics*,
Anthony Faramelli
*Spaces of Crisis and Critique: Heterotopias Beyond Foucault*, edited by
Anthony Faramelli, David Hancock, and Robert G. White
*Hegel and Resistance: History, Politics and Dialectics*, edited by
Rebecca Comay and Bart Zantvoort
*The Ethics of Resistance: Tyranny of the Absolute*, Drew M. Dalton
*The Reasoning of Unreason: Universalism, Capitalism and Disenlightenment*,
John Roberts
*On Resistance: A Philosophy of Defiance*, Howard Caygill

# Auguste Blanqui and the Politics of Popular Empowerment

Philippe Le Goff

BLOOMSBURY ACADEMIC
LONDON • NEW YORK • OXFORD • NEW DELHI • SYDNEY

BLOOMSBURY ACADEMIC
Bloomsbury Publishing Plc
50 Bedford Square, London, WC1B 3DP, UK
1385 Broadway, New York, NY 10018, USA
29 Earlsfort Terrace, Dublin 2, Ireland

BLOOMSBURY, BLOOMSBURY ACADEMIC and the Diana logo are trademarks of
Bloomsbury Publishing Plc

First published in Great Britain 2020
This paperback edition published in 2022

Copyright © Philippe Le Goff, 2020

Philippe Le Goff has asserted his right under the Copyright, Designs and Patents Act,
1988, to be identified as Author of this work.

For legal purposes the Acknowledgements on p. vi constitute an extension
of this copyright page.

Cover design by Charlotte Daniels
Cover image © Daria Botieva / EyeEm / Getty Images

All rights reserved. No part of this publication may be reproduced
or transmitted in any form or by any means, electronic or mechanical,
including photocopying, recording, or any information storage or retrieval
system, without prior permission in writing from the publishers.

Bloomsbury Publishing Plc does not have any control over, or responsibility for, any
third-party websites referred to or in this book. All internet addresses given in this
book were correct at the time of going to press. The author and publisher regret any
inconvenience caused if addresses have changed or sites have ceased to exist, but can
accept no responsibility for any such changes.

A catalogue record for this book is available from the British Library.

A catalog record for this book is available from the Library of Congress.

ISBN: HB: 978-1-3500-7679-2
PB: 978-1-3500-7680-8
ePDF: 978-1-3500-7681-5
eBook: 978-1-3500-7682-2

Typeset by Newgen KnowledgeWorks Pvt. Ltd., Chennai, India

To find out more about our authors and books visit www.bloomsbury.com
and sign up for our newsletters.

# Contents

Acknowledgements — vi
List of Abbreviations — vii

Introduction — 1
1  Intelligence — 23
2  Conflict — 55
3  Actors — 83
4  Volition — 113
5  History — 147
Conclusion — 183

Notes — 193
Bibliography — 241
Index — 251

# Acknowledgements

This book is based on a doctoral thesis submitted at Warwick University in 2015. During the subsequent process of revising, correcting and refining my initial arguments and conclusions, I have benefited enormously from the help and support of many people.

I am grateful to Liza Thompson, Lucy Russell and Lisa Goodrum at Bloomsbury for their immediate enthusiasm for the book, for their help in bringing it to fruition and for their patience along the way. An earlier and shorter version of Sections I–III of the Introduction was published in the 'Introduction' to *The Blanqui Reader* (London: Verso, 2018). Thanks to Verso for their kind permission to use both this material and the quotes that serve as epigraphs in Chapters 1–5.

I would like to thank Alex Corcos, Peter Hallward, Victoria Hirst, Jussi Palmusaari and Stefano Pippa for their incisive comments on various chapters and sections, and the anonymous readers for their useful responses to the book proposal and the final draft. I owe special thanks to Nick Hewlett, who not only carefully read the entire manuscript but whose support and friendship have meant a great deal these past few years. Needless to say, I alone am responsible for any remaining errors and misunderstandings contained in the following pages.

As this project has slowly taken shape, the sound advice and steady encouragement of colleagues and students at Warwick's School of Modern Languages and Cultures and Kingston's Centre for Research in Modern European Philosophy have been extremely valuable. Many conversations about many things with Robert Lines have shaped my thinking in more ways than both he and I probably realise.

My thanks, finally, to Victoria, for her understanding, for her love.

# Abbreviations

| | |
|---|---|
| BR | *The Blanqui Reader*, eds. Peter Hallward and Philippe Le Goff (London: Verso, 2018). |
| CS1, CS2 | *Critique Sociale* (Paris: Félix Alcan, 1885), 2 volumes. |
| MF | *Maintenant, il faut des armes*, ed. Dominique Le Nuz (Paris: La Fabrique, 2007). |
| MSS | Manuscript volume, catalogued as NAF 9578 to 9598 (Paris, Bibliothèque Nationale, manuscript collections). |
| ND | *Ni Dieu Ni Maître* (Brussels: Éditions Aden, 2009). |
| OI | *Œuvres I: Des origines à la Révolution de 1848*, ed. Dominique Le Nuz (Nancy: Presses Universitaires de Nancy, 1993). |

# Introduction

Few individuals in the history of revolutionary politics have proved so controversial as Louis-Auguste Blanqui (1805–1881). Remembered, when remembered at all, for the ill-fated coups of May 1839 and August 1870, today Blanqui's name is generally synonymous with conspiratorial organizing and putchist action, with authoritarian elitism and impatient adventurism – with the 'Blanquism', in other words, that led him to emphatic failure during his lifetime, and that has brought him enduring infamy well beyond it.

The damning judgement of posterity was by no means inevitable, however. A leading figure of the radical left in nineteenth-century France, Blanqui's political prestige grew across the major popular uprisings that spanned the course of his long and remarkable life. The insurgent in the anti-government riots of November 1827 and the 'Three Glorious Days' of July 1830, who suffered a near-fatal bullet wound to the neck during the former and was awarded the 'Decoration of July' by the new Orléanist regime in recognition of his role in the latter, once again took to the streets in the insurrection of 31 October 1870, when Parisians attempted to establish a new government capable of salvaging the war effort against Prussia. The orator of the early 1830s, whose passionate speeches were reproduced and circulated among the republican opposition, once again became a powerful voice in the fierce debates between the French exile community in the early 1850s, when his declarations and letters, penned from the island prison of Belle-Île, made their way across Europe. The leader of perhaps the most important radical club in 1848, who insisted on the mass mobilization and organization of the people as the means by which to pressure the Provisional Government into undertaking revolutionary measures, once again called for a similar strategy during the Prussian siege of Paris in the winter of 1870–1, when he briefly served as head of the 169th battalion of the

National Guard. Only imprisonment or illness could hinder a lifelong political and intellectual struggle against the established order – a struggle that was as uncompromising in its commitment to the principles of equality and justice as it was unrelenting in its efforts to realize them. A complex and intriguing character, who left behind a wealth of unpublished writings, by the time of his death Blanqui had become arguably the century's preeminent neo-Jacobin: one of the foremost, and certainly one of the most forceful, proponents of popular power to emerge in the wake of the French Revolution.

And yet, since his death the radical left has, on the whole, not merely overlooked and neglected Blanqui – especially his writings – but often turned him into an object of derision, a byword for theoretical misconception and practical misadventure. Posthumous marginalization and dismissal have eclipsed a lifetime of admiration among friends and notoriety among foes. Received wisdom, founded on the perceived futility of the political enterprise, is willing to concede little more than laudable dedication to a just cause. With few advocates or defenders, much less any followers or disciples, Blanqui's project has all but fallen into the historical and political abyss.

This book seeks to challenge the conventional and prevailing interpretation of Blanqui's political theory and its place in modern political thought. It seeks to show that Blanqui's politics are not merely reducible to 'Blanquism', that his body of thought and political experience are far from irrelevant or inconsequential. It seeks to suggest that returning to this widely underappreciated figure raises some fundamental questions about the politics of popular empowerment that persist to this day.

# I

Often described as the link between Babeuf and Bolshevism,[1] Blanqui occupies a peculiar position in the history of revolutionary politics. He rejected the toothless mutualism of Proudhon, and he defined himself against the limited republicanism of Ledru-Rollin and Louis Blanc. He cannot be pigeon-holed as either a 'utopian' or a 'scientific' socialist, and he was certainly not influenced by Marx. Instead, inspired largely by the legacy of the most radical aspects of the French Revolution, he is perhaps best understood as a neo-Jacobin communist or a forward-looking *sans-culotte*, a political militant of social equality. If he looks backwards to the Enragés and Hébertists of 1792–3, he also anticipates some of the priorities of a whole range of thinkers in the twentieth century, from Lenin and Luxemburg through Guevara and Gramsci to Badiou and Bensaïd.

To appreciate the central concerns of Blanqui's project it must first be situated in a historical landscape shaped by the fallout of the French Revolution, and by the long reaction that sought to stifle memories of 1789. In the first decades of the nineteenth century, the legacy of the Revolution divided France into four main political groupings. The right was split between more moderate royalists who recognized the need to make at least some concessions to the Revolution's legal and economic achievements, and ultra-royalists who sought to reverse any such concessions, to reinstall a royal prerogative, and thereby to return to the structures of the *ancien régime*. Of the two Restoration monarchs, Louis XVIII (who ruled from 1815 to 1824) fell into the former category, while his younger brother Charles X (king from 1824 to 1830) fell into the latter. On the left, meanwhile, there was a growing number of liberals who sought a return to the moderate reformist programme epitomized by the old constitution of 1791, but in ways now designed to forestall any renewal of mass participation in politics, and to block any revival of the Jacobin radicalism that prevailed in 1792–4. The liberals were outflanked, finally, by a small cluster of far left activists who remained committed to precisely such participation and such radicalism, and who dreamed of following in the footsteps of Hébert or Babeuf. Blanqui became one of the foremost representatives of this last grouping. The simplest way to describe his entire project is as an attempt to continue and revitalize, for the nineteenth century, the militant egalitarian legacy of the *sans-culottes*, and to persevere in the tradition of the great popular insurrections (most notably of 10 August 1792 and 31 May 1793) that they organized in order to impose their will upon the governments of the day.

To most of Blanqui's contemporaries, or at least to most members of the political class, such an attempt seemed utterly Quixotic, especially in the late 1820s, when thirty years of imperial and then royalist reaction had all but buried the revolutionary heritage he sought to reinvigorate. On the margins, heroic shadowy figures like the Carbonari helped to preserve an alternative conception of politics, as did veterans of the 1790s like Philippe Buonarroti, whose defence of Babeuf (in his *Conspiracy of the Equals*, published in 1828) provided an important source of inspiration and continuity for a new generation of republicans. But as Blanqui understood more acutely than most, the fact that history is always written by the victors colours both the present and the past. Pending a change in the balance of forces, and a change in the whole understanding of politics and government, the Revolution would be forever dismissed as a short-lived deviation from the natural and established order of things, and a criminally violent one at that.[2]

Although Blanqui dedicated his life to trying to change the material balance of political forces in favour of the exploited and the oppressed, he was more successful in helping to change the way such forces were understood. In the most schematic terms, the broad outlines of his thought might be summarized as follows. Blanqui assumes that all fields and facets of any given established order, from social relations and economic production to popular morality, are subordinate to the primacy of politics. If the decisive political battle culminates in the contest for control of state power, the ideological sphere of thought and ideas defines the broader terrain of the political battlefield. Blanqui takes consciousness to be both constitutive and primary: to be human is to think, and it is the way people think that largely shapes the way they live, and not the reverse. Ways of thinking and living are polarized between principled dedication to notions of justice and equality on the one hand, and the enduring persistence of domination and exploitation, deceit and duplicity, manipulation and opportunism on the other hand. However principled it might be, mere thought in isolation, of course, cannot influence or change society; it must be translated into action. The social sphere, in short, is largely shaped by struggles either to fulfil or to thwart the realization of basic political principles.

Blanqui's general outlook is shaped by a further dualism that separates this variable psychopolitical domain from a natural or cosmological domain governed by regularity and necessity. 'The works of nature are fated or fatal, and are carried out according to immutable laws. The works of human thought are changeable like thought itself, and depend on will, on energy or on weakness.'[3] This dualism blocks any straightforward synthesis or conflation of man and nature, of human affairs and natural processes. Society does not conform to any sort of divine authority or underlying historical tendency, and Blanqui rejects any philosophical system in which 'people figure as nothing more than the blind and involuntary instruments' of God or of any other 'inevitable force'.[4] The shape of a society is ultimately determined not by supposedly objective forces, be they economic or religious, but by our own choices and actions, which are essentially *political* choices and actions.

By the same token, ignorance is the precondition of exploitation in all its forms because it suppresses our capacity for conscious volition, and with it our collective capacity for sociopolitical self-determination. The struggle between emancipation and oppression must be resolved through mass education. Both economic injustice and religious domination are symptoms of popular ignorance that can only be ended through popular enlightenment. Education – 'that is to say, knowledge, the development of intellectual faculties, the growth of human understanding'[5] – enables the fulfilment of the self. Through education all humans can realize themselves, both individually and collectively, as self-determining, autonomous beings. 'Historical experience has shown,' Blanqui repeatedly insists, 'that education is the sole agent of progress.'[6] The long-term conclusion follows as a matter of course: 'No more ignorance, no more oppression!'[7] In the short term, responsibility for initiating processes of mass education falls on the only group of people in a position to undertake them – the *déclassés* intellectuals who align themselves with the atheist workers, artisans and students concentrated in Paris.

More generally, to reject any form of historical necessity within the realm of human affairs is to advance social progress as forever politically possible – so long as people are prepared to do what it requires. 'We can do it,' as Blanqui put it in 1832, 'if we will it!'[8] The collective capacity to realize freedom and equality is tied at every step to the process of collectively willing this realization. 'Words without deeds to back them up are nothing but an empty sigh. Deeds without words to justify them are nothing but crimes. Let us never separate these two elements of justice.'[9] Together these elements combine to sustain the only 'passion' of the revolution – the achievement of its emancipatory 'idea', 'the triumph of [its] principle'.[10] 'Serious politics can be done through the pen and through action', Blanqui continues. 'If it is through the pen, then let it be mighty, dominating, galvanising. If it is through action, let us organise the people so as to lead them into battle. In both cases there is a visible goal, a positive result.'[11] And in both dimensions, revolutionary politics seeks 'to overthrow what currently exists, not aimlessly or for the benefit of intrigues, but by virtue of settled principles, with the firm resolution to build the future on the new foundations that will be provided by enlightened socialism, developed and determined by the events that occur'.[12]

## II

Appreciation of some of the formative events and salient features of Blanqui's life can help us make greater sense of this political project.[13]

Louis-Auguste Blanqui was born on 8 February 1805 in Puget-Théniers, a small town in the Alpes-Maritimes department in south-east France. At the age of 13 he was sent to Paris to enrol as a boarder at the Institution Massin. He soon gained a reputation as a brilliant student and would go on to graduate from the Lycée Charlemagne in 1824. He began to study both law and medicine at the Sorbonne in 1826 and became increasingly politically active as the 1820s progressed, joining the Carbonari in 1824 and participating over the course of 1827 in a series of popular protests against Bourbon rule that left him injured on three separate occasions.

In the evolution of Blanqui's political perspective, however, the 1830 revolution eclipsed all that went before and remained the point of departure for all that followed. The *Trois Glorieuses* of 27–9 July 1830 signalled the return of the people to the political stage: no longer passive objects but the active subjects of their own history. In Blanqui's eyes July was first and foremost 'a sudden and fearsome revelation of the power of the masses'.[14] He witnessed first-hand, in the streets of Paris, not only the capacity of a people to overthrow a repressive regime but also the kinds of manipulation and fragmentation that can stifle any subsequent process of mass empowerment. As the July Monarchy replaced the Bourbon Restoration, and the newly crowned Louis-Philippe sought to legitimize his so-called republican monarchy, Blanqui aimed to bring theoretical clarity to the unfolding political situation. The conclusions he drew from the July Revolution and its aftermath – on questions concerning both the constitution and the containment of popular power, and the consolidation and concentration of established forms of class power – would inform his entire project. Indeed, both the victory and the betrayal of July 1830 cast a long shadow over the whole of Blanqui's political life. 'It is honourable to be fooled,' he admitted in 1846, looking back on the event, 'so long as you are only fooled once.'¹⁵ In defeat lessons were learned, resolutions were made. The unmaking of a revolution was the making of a revolutionary.¹⁶

If Blanqui first rose to prominence during the period in the early 1830s that became known as *le temps des émeutes* ('the time of riots'), his understanding of revolutionary politics evolved in tandem with his recognition of the inadequacy of mere riots or uprisings as a means of challenging the established order of things. In a situation in which this order was protected by political censorship, police surveillance and ruthless armed force, like many of his contemporaries Blanqui concluded that only disciplined conspiratorial insurgency offered any real prospect of revolutionary renewal. Following imprisonment in 1832–3 and again in 1836–7, Blanqui patiently rebuilt the secretive Société des Saisons, which he led in an ill-considered coup attempt on 12 May 1839; the rising was crushed after two days of street battles. Although he evaded capture for several months, in January 1840 Blanqui was convicted and sentenced to life in prison. The brutal conditions of the Mont Saint-Michel prison did indeed nearly end his life on more than one occasion, until his qualified release on medical grounds, shortly before the revival of revolutionary energies in Paris in February 1848.

The subsequent course of Blanqui's brief return to the political stage mirrored the sequence of events over that climactic year: March 1848 saw him rapidly established as an influential figure, at the head of an enthusiastic political club, the Société Républicaine Centrale; in April he was faced with government attempts to discredit him, on trumped-up charges (implied by the so-called Taschereau document) that he had betrayed other participants in the May 1839 insurrection in exchange for a reduced prison sentence; following pressure from his supporters, 15 May found him leading a doomed march on the National Assembly, for which he was again arrested and jailed, just weeks before the disastrous June Days revolt. He would not be released for another ten years.

The cycle of engagement–imprisonment–liberation thus established over the first-half of Blanqui's life continued until his death in early 1881. Having spent no less than 33 of his 75 years behind bars, imprisonment may appear as their defining theme: a bleak and invariable background punctuated only by repeated political failures. *L'Enfermé* ('The Prisoner'), as Gustave

Geffroy entitled his 1897 biography, certainly seems an apt epithet for a man imprisoned by all the post-Restoration regimes of the century (July Monarchy, Second Republic, Second Empire, Third Republic). No matter how long the term or severe the conditions, however, prison never succeeded in breaking Blanqui's political commitment. Deprived of the freedom to act and organize, he devoted his energies – as far as his chronically poor health allowed – to the written word. Like Lenin or Che after him, Blanqui went to extraordinary lengths to unite 'in himself', as Fidel Castro later said of Che, the revolutionary ideas, the revolutionary action and the revolutionary virtues that form the three pillars of his political project.[17] Again rather like Che, it is the way that Blanqui lived his political dedication as an enduring and unconditional commitment, to the point of self-sacrifice, that accounts for the loyalty he came to inspire among younger activists in particular.

A new generation of Blanquist supporters emerged in the 1860s. Blanqui spent most of the preceding decade in political limbo, interned in Belle-Île prison, off the coast of Brittany, while Napoleon III consolidated his grip on power and memories of the compromised Republic of 1848 faded away. As in the early 1830s, in the early 1850s Blanqui once again sought to learn the lessons, and clarify the political consequences, of a defeated revolution. In texts such as 'Warning to the People' (1851) and 'Letter to Maillard' (1852), which were widely circulated within the French exile community across Europe (the former was translated into German and English by Marx and Engels),[18] he poured scorn on Louis Blanc, Alexandre Ledru-Rollin and the other leading republicans from the Provisional Government for having betrayed and mislead the people, delivering the revolution into the hands of its enemies. Despite the decimation of the revolutionary party, and with no prospect of his own liberation from Belle-Île, Blanqui nonetheless reaffirmed both the goal of egalitarian emancipation and the politics of principled conviction and commitment that such a project would require.

Upon his release in August 1859 following a general amnesty, Blanqui quickly decided that propaganda and clandestine political publications, rather than conspiratorial action, would provide the best means of sustaining and renewing a revolutionary project in the face of widespread resignation to the status quo. Imperial censorship, however, just as quickly condemned Blanqui to another prison term. Confined again at Saint-Pélagie in Paris, to his surprise

Blanqui found himself surrounded by a small group of young and enthusiastic followers, which came to include people like Gustave Tridon, Emile Eudes, Eugène Protot, Raoul Rigault and Jules Vallès. The veteran had a crucial influence on these students. 'Blanqui transformed us, corrupted us all,' Paul Lafargue explained. 'To Blanqui falls the honour of being responsible for the revolutionary education of a part of the youth of our generation.'[19] During the late 1860s, some of these young radicals – many of whom would go on to play key roles in the 1871 Paris Commune – began to form an increasingly organized and influential Blanquist party. Some of them also helped Blanqui to escape, disguised, from the Necker prison hospital in Paris in August 1865, and secure his safe passage to Brussels. Apart from a few clandestine trips back into France to meet with his supporters, Blanqui's exile would last until 1869, when a further general amnesty allowed him to return to Paris. Exile afforded Blanqui the freedom to read and write in a more sustained way than in prison or under Bonaparte's Imperial regime, and the late 1860s became one of his most prolific periods as a writer. As well as his *Instructions for an Armed Uprising* (1868) and many of the writings that were posthumously published in the two-volume *Critique Sociale* (1885), Blanqui elaborated on the philosophical underpinnings of his project, producing reams of unpublished notes and essays covering topics from freedom and necessity to religion and materialism.

The mass anti-government demonstration on the occasion of Victor Noir's funeral in January 1870, which Blanqui helped to organize, marked his return to direct political agitation. It was the outbreak and consequences of the Franco-Prussian War later that year, however, that shaped the final decade of his political life. Seeking to tap into popular discontent with the floundering war effort, Blanqui was again pushed by his more impetuous followers to lead an abortive attempt at insurrection, on 14 August, in La Villette, north-east Paris.

This immediate failure nevertheless anticipated an imminent shift in the balance of power. After Napoleon III surrendered to Bismarck at Sedan, mass pressure led to the hasty proclamation of a new Republic on 4 September. Blanqui's response to this rapid change in the political landscape was to set up *La Patrie en Danger*, a newspaper and associated club. He used the columns of the newspaper to attack the provisional Government of National Defence for its inadequate and ineffectual military reaction and to call for popular resistance to the Prussian siege of Paris, which continued through the winter and into the following January. On 31 October, he played a prominent role in another popular uprising, which was again snuffed out after a brief moment of political uncertainty.

On 17 March 1871, on the eve of the further mobilization that would lead to a slightly less ephemeral political result, the establishment of the Paris Commune, Blanqui was again arrested, for his role in the 31 October insurrection. In late May 1871, as in June 1848, the Parisian working class was crushed by the established regime, and the Commune was defeated. By then Blanqui was already immured at the Château de Taureau prison in northern Brittany, oblivious to the massacre taking place in the capital. It was there that he wrote his peculiar meditation on humanity and the universe, *Eternity by the Stars* (1872), a long-standing project whose origins can be traced back to the early 1840s.[20]

Nine long years later, another amnesty campaign finally secured Blanqui's release from prison in June 1879. Despite his age and poor health, he launched himself into a last round of political activity, co-founding the journal *Ni Dieu Ni Maître* and speaking out at venues across France against the establishment of a standing army and in favour of a general pardon for the surviving Communards. Blanqui died of a stroke on 1 January 1881. Perhaps as many as one hundred thousand people joined his funeral procession through the streets of Paris to Père-Lachaise cemetery, where he was buried.

### III

In his own lifetime Blanqui was a symbol of hope and fear, inspiring respect and revulsion in equal measure. For the Marx who narrated the fate of 1848's *Class Struggles in France*, whereas utopian or doctrinaire socialism remained the socialism of the petty bourgeoisie, 'the *proletariat* rallies more and more round *revolutionary socialism*, round *Communism*, for which the bourgeoisie has itself invented the name of *Blanqui*'. This genuine form of socialism, Marx continues, is willing to embrace 'the *class dictatorship* of the proletariat as the necessary transit point to the abolition of class distinctions generally, to the abolition of all the relations of production on which they rest, to the abolition of all the social relations that correspond to these relations of production, to the revolutionizing of all the ideas that result from these social relations'.[21] In Blanqui, 'the noble martyr of revolutionary communism',[22] Marx recognized both the intellectual and political leadership of the French proletariat. Hence the ill-fated march on the National Assembly on 15 May 1848 had, in Marx's eyes, 'no other result save that of removing Blanqui and his comrades, that is, the real leaders of the proletarian party, from the public stage for the entire duration of the cycle' that ended with Louis-Napoleon Bonaparte's coup in December 1851.[23]

Almost thirty years later, an ultimately successful campaign to elect the still-imprisoned Blanqui as a parliamentary deputy for Bordeaux received the support of Giuseppe Garibaldi, who endorsed Blanqui as 'the heroic martyr of human freedom'.[24] Shortly after that, at his funeral, Blanqui's memory was celebrated as much by the proto-anarchist Louise Michel as by the proto-Bolshevik Pyotr Tkachev. The prolific writer Eugène de Mirecourt, by contrast, reflected more 'settled' views when in 1857 he described his subject as 'the most cynical of all the fiends plotting the downfall of modern society'.[25] Conceding Blanqui's 'talents as an organiser' and 'his brilliantly cultured mind', de Mirecourt poured scorn and vitriol over this Machiavellian fanatic, this 'formidable demagogue'.[26] More measured observers likewise chose to highlight 'the form of terror that is attached to the name of Monsieur Auguste Blanqui'; 'his name is an axe', concluded Hippolyte Castille.[27] Heinrich Heine agreed. The 'most honest [*bravste*] fellow under the sun' was, he wrote, 'terrorism incarnate'.[28] It is not surprising that Walter Benjamin later acknowledged Blanqui as 'the most dreaded adversary' of nineteenth-century French society.[29]

Contemporary accounts indeed betray a sense of political, moral and physical repulsion at a disturbing, alien figure. Alexis de Toqueville, recounting Blanqui's dramatic appearance on the rostrum of the National Assembly on 15 May 1848, declared that 'the memory of him has filled me with disgust and horror ever since. He had sunken, withered cheeks, white lips, and a sickly, malign, dirty look like a pallid, mouldy corpse; he was wearing no visible linen; an old black frockcoat covered his lean, emaciated limbs tightly; he looked as if he had lived in a sewer and only just come out'.[30] For Victor Hugo, this 'sinister figure' was a man of 'great ability, no hypocrisy; the same in private as in public. Harsh, stern, serious, never laughing, receiving respect with irony, admiration with sarcasm, love with disdain, and inspiring extraordinary devotion. ... At certain moments he was no longer a man,' Hugo suggested, 'but a sort of lugubrious apparition in which all degrees of hatred born of all degrees of misery seemed to be incarnated'.[31] On the basis of such portraits, one would be hard pushed to refute Paul Lafargue's claim that Blanqui was 'the man of whom the bourgeoisie had made a monster, as it had of Marat'.[32]

Needless to say, many people today are only too ready to dismiss anyone who identifies 'the future of society' with communism as a relic of a bygone age. Dismissal of Blanqui, however, is as easy to find on the left as on the right of the political spectrum. Marxian writers have rarely deviated from Engels' late critique of Blanqui's legacy.[33] Here was an Idealist pre-Marxist communist who, though deserving of admiration for his courageous and unwavering devotion to the cause of revolution and for grasping the basic nature of class struggle, was compromised by his inability to understand and adopt the 'scientific' theory of socialism. So followed his failure to explain socio-economic processes and to take proper account of historical context and material conditions, his privileging of conspiratorial action over popular mobilization by means of mass propaganda and mass political organization, and his reliance on obsolete and authoritarian organizational forms.[34]

The actual validity of this account was seldom considered. Rosa Luxemburg for one did recognize that the question of whether or not Engels' characterization of Blanqui 'is perfectly just can still be discussed. For in 1848', she explained, 'Blanqui did not foresee his club forming a "small minority" at all; on the contrary, in a period of powerful revolutionary upsurge, he was certain that, upon his call, the entire working people – if not in France, then at least in Paris – would rise up to fight the ignominious and criminal policies of the bourgeois government. ... Nevertheless,' she continued, arriving at the crucial point, 'this is not the main question. What concerns us is whether, as comrade Plekhanov strives to demonstrate, Engels' description of Blanqui can be applied to the Bolsheviks'.[35] At stake, then, was not the extent to which 'Blanquism' represented an accurate description of Blanqui's own politics and project, but the term's function as a category in contemporaneous political disputes to denote – and thereby condemn – voluntarist adventurism, substitutionist vanguardism and anti-democratic elitism.

Luxemburg's proposed discussion over the received view of Blanqui never really took place. Remembering him as nothing more than a conspiratorial 'putschist', even those thinkers who in some ways might be described as similar to Blanqui (for instance Lenin, Gramsci, Castro or Che) never self-identified with him.[36] All subscribed, often implicitly, to Lenin's own unambiguous refrain: 'We are not Blanquists, we do not stand for the seizure of power by a minority. We are Marxists, we stand for proletarian class struggle.'[37] Dismissed by moderates and disavowed by radicals, a wedge was driven between Blanqui and socialism. For socialists of all stripes from the Second International onwards, the names 'Blanqui' and 'Blanquism' spelled adventurist naivety at best, cynical despotism at worst. As Walter Benjamin observed, back in 1940, it took less than a generation 'to erase the name of Blanqui, the rallying sound that had reverberated through the preceding century'.[38] Not much has changed since then. 'Blanqui, "the Imprisoned one" [*l'Enfermé*] of capitalist society', writes Maurice Dommanget, Blanqui's foremost biographer, 'is also "the Forgotten one" [*l'Oublié*] of socialism.'[39]

## IV

So why should we remember Blanqui today, nearly 150 years after his death? Why does Blanqui matter? The answer, I suggest in this book, is twofold.

Historically, Blanqui should be restored to his rightful place both in the political sequence that extends from the 1789 French Revolution to the 1871 Paris Commune, and in the wider Jacobin and neo-Jacobin revolutionary tradition alongside other activist-thinkers like Robespierre, Saint-Just, Lenin, Gramsci, Fanon and Che who, in their own times and in their own ways, likewise conceived emancipatory politics first and foremost in terms of collective will and popular empowerment.

Blanqui and his followers helped shape the political history of nineteenth-century France – of this there can be no question. To understand the popular revolts of 1830, 1848 and 1870–1 and their fallout, the emergence of socialism as a sociopolitical principle and an organized sociopolitical movement, is it necessary to engage with Blanqui. His attempt to revive and renew radical republicanism in the wake of the historical defeat of 1794 through searing critiques of Comtean positivism and historical determinism, of unprincipled opportunism and 'utopian' or merely speculative forms of socialism, established him as arguably the foremost neo-Jacobin thinker of the nineteenth century. No less noteworthy is the style of these writings. The urgency, power and passion of Blanqui's early work remain undiminished in his late texts. A master polemicist, across his life Blanqui penned uncompromising denunciations of adversaries both political and intellectual, from Louis Blanc to Auguste Comte, that were replete with sardonic rhetoric and acerbic wit. The sense of formulation, the economy of expression, the breadth of references and allusions (literary, classical, scientific …), the journalistic flair and the military precision – all hold an undeniable allure.

Beyond illuminating this wider political and intellectual history, it does not take any specialist interest to appreciate that Blanqui's life – a life animated by a remarkable sense of purpose and an unyielding resolve that neither continual defeat nor lengthy imprisonment could abate or break – was itself, by any measure, one of the most extraordinary lives of the nineteenth century. In his own time it earned Blanqui a unique status. 'Before Lenin,' Benjamin argues, 'there was no one who had a clearer profile among the proletariat.'[40] Recognition of this profile is long overdue.

Politically, meanwhile, Blanqui should be rediscovered for both his theoretical contribution and his practical example. Indeed, my basic (and most consequential and contentious) move is to approach Blanqui as serious political thinker whose body of thought warrants sustained critical engagement. Blanqui's enduring contribution to radical thought, I argue, is his insistence on the capacity of conscious and organized collective political action to bring about radical social change, and the force and consistency with which he articulated this view. It is, then, his lucid analysis of the struggle for popular power – an analysis that is posited on the insurgent force of the people – that I seek to foreground.

The most important notion in Blanqui's political theory is conscious volition – that is, the individual and collective practical exercise of 'intelligence and will,'[41] of reasoned choices and deliberate action, from which emerges a theory that seeks to account for the role of human agency in human history. If his philosophical writings amount to a sustained effort to understand and explain the development and potentialities of human consciousness and voluntary activity, his political project is rooted in the collective action of conscious and organized popular forces. All his work, I suggest, can be filtered through this notion of conscious volition. More generally, and to borrow Gramsci's characterization of Machiavelli and Marx, I seek to show that Blanqui is most fruitfully read as 'a theorist of militant politics, of action'.[42] Blanqui's central preoccupation is with the practical exigencies of popular empowerment. His entire project revolves around one fundamental question: how do an oppressed people identify the sources of their oppression, and what must they do to overcome and end it? At stake in Blanqui's thought, in other words, is the process by which an oppressed people free themselves and remain free.

When approached in these terms, two thinkers in particular will help to frame my analysis of Blanqui's project: Niccolò Machiavelli and Jean-Jacques Rousseau.

What is necessary in order to seize and then to retain power? Such is the basic question Machiavelli poses in *The Prince*. The answer, Machiavelli suggests, presupposes an ability to delineate the fundamental principles and practices of decisive political action, to recognize the means by which the struggle for political power is waged and won. 'Since my intention is to say something that will prove of practical use to the inquirer,' Machiavelli explains in the key chapter of the text, 'I have thought it proper to represent things as they are in a real truth, rather than as they are imagined.'[43] To be politically effective is to understand the existing balance of forces and the socio-economic interests that underpin it; it is to identify the problems that a project to seize and retain political power will face and to recognize how, practically, to negotiate and overcome them.

Such concerns permeate what Trotsky suggestively calls Blanqui's 'military revolutionary realism'.[44] Blanqui's 'practical socialism'[45] is conceived directly against the 'utopian socialism' of Saint-Simon, Fourier and Cabet, indeed against any socialists who, 'only willing to wage a war of words', are condemned never to escape 'failure' and 'futility' so long as 'they do not understand that force is the sole guarantee of freedom'.[46] Few of Blanqui's contemporaries were so insistent on Machiavelli's basic assumption that 'all armed prophets succeed, whereas unarmed prophets fail'.[47] After Machiavelli, Blanqui ascribes political primacy to arms and organization – to an oppressed people's capacity, in other words, to overcome their oppressors by means of their own organized collective power.

In the wake of 1848 and yet another popular defeat, Blanqui doubled down on this first principle. Responding to criticisms in the press of his 'Warning to the People', which had been published in February 1851 to much outcry, Blanqui, like Machiavelli, presented himself as 'a man who is sincere, who puts aside this fantastic mirage of programmes, these fogs of the kingdom of Utopia, who leaves the domain of fiction so as to return to reality'. Like Machiavelli's advice to new princes – recall that Machiavelli is not writing for established princes and established orders, but for a new prince capable of founding a new order – the measures Blanqui outlined for new revolutionary governments – 'Disarm the bourgeoisie, arm the people' – were written and to be read as 'a serious and practical statement', 'the primary requirement, the sole guarantee of the salvation of the revolution'. And yet 'the most basic words of common sense', as Blanqui described his strategic prescriptions, were instead met with outrage and condemnation.[48] Political realism, however, as Machiavelli first documented, dictates that all actions are to be '[judged] by the result'[49] – and by this metric the popular movement in 1848 failed to do what needed to be done, Blanqui concluded. His subsequent attempt exactly two decades later to produce, with the requisite technical precision and detail, a systematic account of these essential practical steps certainly seems to be inflected by Machiavelli's dictum that a prince 'must have no other object or thought, nor acquire skill in anything, except war, its organisation, and its discipline'.[50] With its injunction 'to learn ... the profession that gives our oppressors all their force, and that would put our revenge and their punishment within our reach',[51] Blanqui's *Instructions for an Armed Uprising* are indeed perhaps best read through one of the central axioms of *The Prince*: 'The first way to lose your state is to neglect the art of war; the first way to win a state is to be skilled in the art of war.'[52]

A profound paradox is at work here, of course: Blanqui's insistence on the necessity of seizing and retaining power is coupled with his complete failure to do so over the course of his life; an obsession with the conditions of enduring victory is coupled with a lifetime of recurrent defeat. Or to put it simply: Blanqui's political project was, by his own standards, a total, unambiguous failure. In a sense, this internal contradiction makes him an even more curious and intriguing, perhaps tragic, figure.

Alongside this form of Machiavellian realism, the political philosophy of Jean-Jacques Rousseau is equally crucial when seeking to understand Blanqui's most salient assumptions.

Rousseau's point of departure, set out in the *Second Discourse*,[53] is well known. The advent of private property dispossessed the common people from their land and founded a social order of mass exploitation and poverty that is organized to serve the interests of a privileged few. This initial conquest, and the degradation, enslavement and corruption it begets, was enshrined in law and consolidated by successive regimes by means of force and deceit. In order to achieve social justice, society as presently constituted, that is, on the basis of servitude and inequality, would therefore have to be reconstituted on the basis of freedom and equality. This was the problem Rousseau sought to resolve. How can a people establish a just form of social organization out of one of organized injustice? What will this process demand of those who undertake it?

Rousseau's social contract seeks to offer 'a form of association which will defend and protect, with the whole of its common force [*la force commune*], the person and property of each associate, and under which each of them, uniting himself to all, will obey himself alone, and remain as free as before.'[54] Against the Malthusian doctrine of 'everyone for themselves', Blanqui will add, almost paraphrasing Rousseau, 'the goal of societies is precisely to eradicate the consequences of ... individual inequalities, to place all weaknesses under the protection of the common force [*la force commune*], superior to the isolated and abusive forces.'[55] In order to overpower these forces, which act in the name of the private interests of the rich, the task facing the people is 'to create, by combination, a totality of forces sufficient to overcome the obstacles resisting them, to direct their operation by a single impulse, and make them act in union.'[56] Everything hinges, in other words, on Rousseau's concept of the general will.

Here again Rousseau's prescription is familiar. 'Each of us puts his person and all his power in common under the supreme direction of the general will,' he explains; 'and we as a body receive each member as an indivisible part of the whole.' 'Immediately,' Rousseau goes on, 'this act of association produces, in place of the individual persons of every contracting party, a moral and collective body, which is composed of as many members as there are votes in the assembly, and which, by the same act, is endowed with its unity, its common self, its life, and its will.'⁵⁷ That civil association is a voluntary act is crucial. What makes Rousseau's thought so distinctive and so radical is precisely that the people themselves constitute the sovereign power through their own collective action. Where for Hobbes rational individuals collectively submit themselves to an absolute authority in return for protection, for Rousseau the collective that is formed of actively unified individuals is itself the sole source of authority and law. The people, as the sovereign, exercise authority over themselves. Collective self-rule means that there is no passive submission to an external master; the sovereign is in no way superior to or distinct from the people, it cannot be represented or transferred, precisely because it '[consists] solely of the persons which form it'.⁵⁸ Popular sovereignty is a matter of voluntary participation, active association and direct empowerment. At the heart of Rousseau's thought, then, is the radically egalitarian insistence on the capacity of all, of ordinary people without wealth, privilege or power, to determine freely and collectively their social arrangements on the basis of the common interest.

As one would expect of a nineteenth-century middle-class Frenchman schooled in the classics and the national canon, this was all very familiar to Blanqui, too (he once claimed to know Rousseau's work, alongside that of Voltaire, Helvétius, Paul-Louis Courier, La Fontaine and Cervantes' *Don Quixote*, 'more or less by heart').⁵⁹ And although direct and explicit reference to Rousseau is only occasionally found in Blanqui's writings – far less than in those of the preceding generation of Jacobins, who consciously styled themselves as disciples of Rousseau, Robespierre at their head – his influence can be clearly seen across them. Many of Blanqui's underlying views, be they on inequality, property or morality, draw heavily on those found in the *Discourses* and the *Social Contract*. Taken as a whole, Blanqui's project is indeed fundamentally Rousseauist in orientation. No other figure in nineteenth-century France did more to develop and promote a Rousseauist conception of egalitarian popular power based on 'the full, integral association' of ordinary people acting out of their 'full and free will'.⁶⁰ The 'government of the people by the people' is 'founded on equality', Blanqui explains, in a highly Rousseauist register; it 'imposes on everyone equal duties and grants the same rights'. Under this republic the people 'indicate their will … through the law, which is nothing other than the expression of the general will'.⁶¹ After Rousseau, Blanqui sees freedom as a matter of collective political practice, of individuals '[gathering] themselves together through association',⁶² through a process based on the free and equal participation of all, so as to realize their individual freedom collectively, which is the only means by which it can be truly realized.

This Rousseauist approach to political action might be summarized in three basic principles: (1) the existing social order, deliberately structured to serve the interests of a privileged minority, is in no way necessary or inevitable; (2) only the conscious and organized collective action of common people here and now can reconstitute society in the common interest; and (3) the concentrated power of this collective actor, if it is to impose itself and endure, will require dedication and resolve in order to overcome the resistance and obstacles it will face.⁶³ For Blanqui as for Rousseau, it follows that a minority, exploiting class – however superior its financial and military resources, however ruthless its resistance to and repression of any challenge to its domination – is 'only capable of defending a power that is not seriously threatened' by an organized popular force with a clear, common goal and the determination to realize it; it is 'equally unable either to maintain or to overthrow a government against the will of the people.'⁶⁴

Questions of continued relevance and lasting legacy should inform any study that seeks to account for the significance of a political thinker. My reading of Blanqui is no different. I seek to situate him within his own historical context, to understand him within his political and intellectual environment, but not confine him to this. His writings are at once a product of, yet not reducible to, the specific sociopolitical conjuncture of their composition. Underpinning this approach is an attempt to reflect on the manner in which his political theory might speak to contemporary politics and contemporary political theory in general, and to questions concerning collective action and popular power in particular. Across the following chapters, I aim to show that Blanqui provides important resources for thinking through three issues above all: that of political temporality (the privileging of political possibility over historical necessity within an understanding of human history as open and contingent), of political agency (the primacy of an actor's sense of purpose, resolve and commitment) and of political strategy (the insistence that effective social struggles presuppose political organization). The Conclusion will offer the most sustained discussion of these three themes.

Of course, that is not to deny the manifest shortcomings of his project. Even the most enthusiastic reconsideration of Blanqui's legacy will need to grapple with at least two apparent limitations. There is, first of all, a tension between the importance ascribed to enlightened consciousness and processes of popular empowerment. To choose commitment to the cause of justice, Blanqui assumes, presupposes consciousness of the initial choice itself; pending their necessary re-education, those who have been systematically mis-educated and deceived seem to remain incapable of exercising the form of collective self-determination that governs a free and equal society. Although he is right to insist on free and informed discussion as the prerequisite to arriving at free and informed decisions, Blanqui's conception of conscious volition too often overstates the gap between knowledge and ignorance, between who has and who lacks the intellectual capacities that decisive voluntary action demands. It leaves him unable to formulate a convincing account of politics as *self*-emancipation and occasionally leads him to embrace substitutionist forms of political organization, whereby a vanguard group might act on behalf of the people rather than with them.

Blanqui's politics certainly serves as an important antidote to any form of economic determinism that might scorn the significance of organized collective action here and now. His own account of the objective socio-economic context and conditions in which subjective political forces operate, however, is undeniably thin. If the image of Blanqui as a blind adventurist indifferent to the constraints of circumstance is unfounded, it is true that he sometimes emphasizes the significance of political action at the expense of an understanding of the historical grounds on which people act.

## V

In the following pages I seek to answer some of the most frequently asked and pressing questions about Blanqui: Why, and to what extent, did he persist with conspiratorial politics? To what extent was his conception of revolutionary change elitist, anti-democratic and authoritarian? To what extent was he guilty of parochialism and nationalism on the one hand and impatient adventurism on the other? What was his relation to Marx and Marxism?

My engagement with these and other related questions will span five chapters. Chapter 1 establishes the foundational role of intelligence in Blanqui's thought. I show that Blanqui's entire project can only be understood in light of his basic assumptions regarding enlightened intelligence and the political consciousness it confers.

Blanqui's insistence, as a matter of principle, on the unequivocal taking of sides is the focus of Chapter 2. I consider the manner in which his analysis of property, the state and contemporary sociopolitical struggles informs his view of politics as inherently and invariably conflictual. I also examine his emphasis on the principled commitment to an ideal and how this informs his politics more generally.

Chapter 3 then explores one of the most significant consequences of the preceding chapter, namely a conception of the people or the proletariat (synonymous terms for Blanqui) as a subjective position. Here the proletariat both presupposes and articulates a political choice, a political principle. But I also explore the term's sociological dimensions, arguing that socio-economic concerns remain crucial to Blanqui's thinking on this point.

Chapter 4 outlines the role of individual and collective volition in Blanqui's understanding of how a popular mobilization begins, how it continues and the subjective resources it will demand. I reflect on what seems to me as a major problem and limitation of Blanqui's politics: the overprivileging of enlightened consciousness as a precondition of collective self-determination. Insofar as those deemed unconscious and unenlightened are incapable of genuine voluntary action, Blanqui, I claim, displays a certain lack of confidence in the mass of the people as voluntary political actors.

Chapter 5 examines Blanqui's understanding of history and human progress. Considering the anti-determinism that pervades Blanqui's thought, I show the extent to which all his writings, including – and contrary to the claims of Walter Benjamin's influential reading – *Eternity by the Stars*, are rooted throughout in the insistence on political possibility over historical necessity.

I conclude with two points that frame the book as a whole. First, I work through and reconstruct the findings of the preceding chapters – the manner in which Blanqui's assumptions about intelligence and consciousness inform his politics of social conflict and principled choice, and how this in turn underpins his conceptions of agency, volition and history – outlining what I take to be the fundamental and most consequential features of Blanqui's political theory, as well as its major ambiguities and shortcomings. Second, I turn to the question of the meaning and relevance of Blanqui for emancipatory politics today, with a reflection on some of the enduring questions he raises and critical insights he provides. My overall aim, therefore, is to show that Blanqui makes a vital contribution not only to an understanding of political thought in the past but also to the way in which we understand politics today.

1

# Intelligence

*Revolutions must take place in the mind before they can be carried out in the streets.*[1]

Across his writings, Blanqui consistently affirms intelligence as the central source of emancipation and education as the decisive site of sociopolitical struggle. From his very first texts in the early 1830s he declares that education is 'most holy and sacred', for it 'makes the man and the citizen'.[2] Around twenty years later he repeats that, since 'man is an intelligence',[3] 'education is a force, a power, the power that governs the world'.[4] A further twenty years after that he is no less insistent that 'the instrument that frees us is not our arm but our brain, and the brain lives only through education. An attack on this guardian mother of thought is an attack on the thinking being itself; it is a social crime'.[5]

Human thought and consciousness, for Blanqui, are ultimately determinant of sociopolitical arrangements. Enlightened instruction and the – politically decisive – intelligence and reason it alone confers are thus crucial components of his project. Blanqui's voluntarism is, to be sure, conceived in the strictest terms as *conscious* volition. Political subjectivity presupposes intellectual consciousness. Individual enlightenment is the essential precondition of both collective voluntary action and collective political power. The implications this has for Blanqui's wider enterprise, and for its reconsideration today, necessarily demands our attention and careful consideration.

In this first chapter, then, we must go right to the heart of Blanqui's theory, establishing the foundational role of intelligence and the manner in which it underpins his conception of politics. Through reconstructing this core element of Blanqui's thinking, a task that will require a certain amount of descriptive exposition and extensive quotation, my aim is to provide a basis from which to analyse in greater depth his project as a whole in subsequent chapters.

## Revolution of the intellect

### Blanqui's dualism

Blanqui's project is broadly underpinned by a dualism according to which nature and its governing laws are separate from human thought, activity and volition. 'The word "law" only means something in the domain of nature', he writes, in direct opposition to the 'utopian' socialism of Saint-Simon and Fourier and its conflation of natural and human laws. 'Whoever speaks of "law" speaks of an invariable, immanent and fatal rule – something that is incompatible with intelligence and will.' There is no such thing as political, social or economic laws, for in the human realm there is only 'caprice and arbitrariness … phenomena that vary according to human whims and passions'.[6] Unlike the natural or cosmological realm, the human realm is not defined by cumulative progress and perpetual evolution. Unlike the natural or cosmological realm, the human realm is contingent; it is open to movement and change, to chance and possibility, to reason and volition. So crucial is this dualism – it would underpin *Eternity by the Stars*, most notably – that elsewhere it finds expression in a characteristically economical aphorism:

> The supposed inevitability of the economic laws that govern society. Pure impertinence. Nothing could be as arbitrary and irregular as the march of human things, which varies according to the whims of billions of caprices. Nothing could be more different from the immutable and inevitable order of natural things.[7]

Appeals to historical necessity, economic imperative or divine authority are thus rejected as a matter of course. Blanqui indeed opposes any philosophy that might 'reduce man to a puppet whose strings are pulled by God', to 'a marionette manipulated in the wings'[8] by a supposedly objective force, be it Providence or the market. That is not to say, however, that humans and human activity are strictly independent from and completely undetermined by the material world. Humanity is certainly constrained by impersonal natural forces but not absolutely. As Blanqui explains,

> People are in no sense the same as plants, whose development is the exclusive work of matter's blind and indifferent forces. To be sure, human beings also depend a great deal on these forces, but not exclusively. Part of what they do depends on personal action, by means of intelligence and will. To fail to make use of this part would be to fail the organism that they are by nature, and that pushes them – though by their own means – towards their progressive improvement.[9]

How, then, are we to understand the open and contingent realm of humankind, with its constituent battle of wills, interests and ideas, as distinct from the immutable realm of nature and natural laws? How can humans work towards their own 'progressive improvement' and development? How does this inform Blanqui's conception of political action and social change?

## Mankind is thought

'Mankind is thought,' Blanqui states; 'without thought mankind is nothing.'[10] Humans and animals, to be sure, share the physical capacity and manual dexterity to build and craft. Blanqui notes how the masterly skill, geometric precision and exacting calculations of birds' nests, bees' honeycomb and spiders' webs emulate if not surpass humans' ability to manipulate material. Hence, what define humanity first and foremost are its cerebral, not manual, capacities. Thought and ideas alone are what make mankind.[11]

At a social level Blanqui takes this assumption to its logical conclusion. 'It is philosophy that governs the world,' he writes. 'All other sciences only affect how a society is run by modifying or reforming its philosophy.' Since 'every society that has existed on earth has been governed by a philosophy', it follows that 'it is the difference in philosophies that determines the difference in social organisations'.[12] In direct contrast to the basic tenets of Marxism, which maintains that 'neither legal relations nor political forms could be comprehended whether by themselves or on the basis of a so-called general development of the human mind, but that on the contrary they originate in the material conditions of life',[13] Blanqui believes that the 'life of a people is not in the works of its hands, but in what it thinks. Material life is nothing but a reflection of this thinking'.[14] Here lies the foundational gesture of Blanqui's project, the implications of which are felt across all his actions and writings. Let us therefore reflect on this point a little further before moving on.

Comparison with Marx is indeed particularly instructive here.[15] Consider the well-known passages from the 'Preface to *A Contribution to the Critique of Political Economy*' (1859), which outline the fundamental assumptions behind the historical materialist view of history:

> In the social production of their existence, men inevitably enter into definite relations, which are independent of their will, namely relations of production appropriate to a given stage in the development of their material forces of production. The totality of these relations of production constitutes the economic structure of society, the real foundation, on which arises a legal and political superstructure and to which correspond definite forms of social consciousness. The mode of production of material life conditions the general process of social, political and intellectual life. It is not the consciousness of men that determines their existence, but their social existence that determines their consciousness.[16]

It is this last sentence above all that establishes a clear divide between Marx's materialism and Blanqui's idealism. Where for Marx 'the anatomy of civil society has to be sought in political economy',[17] for Blanqui it is 'ideas alone that make man what he is',[18] both individually and collectively. Ideas and consciousness condition material life, not vice versa. Ideas and consciousness, Blanqui argues, determine political institutions, economic relations and the overall social existence of humankind. It follows that sociopolitical change occurs through philosophical change, for 'the political manifestation of a people will always be the reflection of the ideas it has been showered with',[19] and 'since 1789 the idea alone has been proletarians' strength and salvation'.[20]

With these claims, we already begin to uncover some of the fundamental limitations of Blanqui's thinking. Insofar as humanity and society are defined principally by their cognitive capacities and collective consciousness, the failure therein to understand and explain the productive forces and social relations that underpin the established order will prevent Blanqui from fully comprehending the objective realities that, while not ultimately determinant, certainly shape the circumstances and processes of political action and social transformation. It will leave Blanqui unable to explain historical change outside the realm of ideas, unable to formulate a militant political project that is properly grounded in the specific, material conditions of its exercise.

'Men make their own history, but they do not make it as they please,' Marx once famously wrote; 'they do not make it under circumstances chosen by themselves, but under circumstances existing already.'[21] Although, as we shall see in the following chapters, Blanqui's essential strength lies precisely in his account of how men make their own history, not least thanks to the absence of a form of historical determinism that at times appears in some of Marx's own writings, his major shortcoming nonetheless remains the failure to sufficiently analyse and account for the historical context and concrete conditions in which this activity takes place.

## Materialism, transformation, volition

Within Blanqui's dualism human thought is, however, far from immaterial or absolutely free. Blanqui reasons that thought is 'ineluctably a product of nerve or brain tissue,'[22] which is itself a product of matter. Thought, as produced by the material organism of the brain, therefore cannot be disembodied or 'immaterial' in the spiritualist or religious sense; there is no form of divine intelligence or thought, no form of 'imaginary being, whatever it might be called, that is independent of the nerve or brain tissue'.[23] The brain is the 'centre and source of intelligence', Blanqui stresses.[24]

To this insistence on the basic materiality of thought and intelligence, Blanqui importantly adds that the brain can be developed and perfected through the practice of thinking.[25] As he explains,

> Thought varies in keeping with modifications of this tissue or substance, but these modifications in large part depend on us, and thereby they allow us to have a say in the matter. Man thus has the power to intervene in the course of his destiny, and ever since he first appeared on earth he has made use of this faculty with variable success, a success that corresponds to thought's capacity to react upon the cerebral organism.[26]

It is precisely this 'power to react on the organ so as to improve it'[27] that enables humans to fulfil themselves as individuals and humanity to advance as a collective. People, then, have the collective capacity to create and shape their own history by means of the political consciousness produced by individual intellectual development. The sociopolitical implications of this assumption are indeed decisive: materialism '[proves] that man is nobody's plaything, and that he depends solely on the conformation of the brain'.[28] And just as Blanqui defines humanity primarily by its capacity for thought, he equally maintains that this capacity to change, to improve, to be perfected, is humanity's 'essential quality', its 'special characteristic'.[29] Humanity, to be sure, 'can *only* develop and grow through the improvement of [the] brain itself',[30] through this collective process of individual cerebral transformation. All humans must therefore devote their lives to developing and expanding their intelligence and critical faculties.[31] We might note that, again unlike Marx, Blanqui assumes that class consciousness and the political subjectivity it engenders do not arise from the conditions inflicted upon the working class in the process of capitalist development – even an 'advanced' worker, he argues, can remain 'a blind dupe'[32] – but from enlightened instruction and intelligence alone. And again here we anticipate some of the basic ambiguities and tensions of Blanqui's project: How and when are these capacities exercised? To what extent is this a process of *self*-transformation and *self*-emancipation? To these questions we shall return.

For Blanqui, the inherent power of enlightened reason can only be realized in service of the oppressed multitude. As he already insisted in 1834, 'the intelligence that makes a mortal god of man only has real power on the condition that it be moral – that is, useful to the masses.' Human intelligence, 'in its highest form of expression, cannot be selfish, for the only salutary tendency it perceives is that which leads to equality'.[33] Enlightened thinking is bound first and foremost to egalitarianism and to the protection of the weak and vulnerable. 'Thought affirms above all the rights of weakness', he reasserted in the late 1860s, 'because thought is the common link among all men.'[34]

There are certainly echoes here of Rousseau's highly moralistic conception of politics. And like Rousseau, and Robespierre after him, there is certainly a moral tenor to Blanqui's writings more generally: he will often deride the rich, for example, for their greed, ambition, duplicity and wickedness. 'Our sphere of activity, our action,' Blanqui writes of enlightened thought and its advocates, by contrast, 'is of a moral nature.'[35] Rousseau, of course, insists not only on the transformative effects on humans of the passage from the state of nature to the civil state, a passage that '[replaces] instinct by justice in [their] behaviour' and '[confers] on [their] actions the moral quality that they had lacked before'. He also claims that, as well as 'the acquisition of moral status', the 'acquisition of moral liberty' that is gained through the social contract is 'the only thing that makes man truly the master of himself'.[36] According to this form of revolutionary moralism, which was equally central to the political theory of Che Guevara,[37] morality must underpin all cerebral activity and philosophy as it does all social arrangements. Just as Che stresses that 'the gigantic change in consciousness necessary to tackle the transition' to socialism 'must take place ... through education and socialist morality',[38] so Blanqui sees it is 'a disastrous error to think one can transform a country by purely material means'.[39] Only the realization of 'true morality' – that is, 'the more or less powerful expression of the humanitarian instinct that forbids people from mistreating one another and commands them to help one another,' a morality which is 'based on personal interest' but is 'inseparable from the general interest' and is thus 'the result of humanity solidarity'[40] – is capable of bringing about such a transformation.

What is the relationship between thought and volition? Do 'a man's actions depend upon his organism or upon his will', Blanqui asks, and is his will 'not equally a result of the organism'?[41] His response is clear: human volition is conditioned and produced by human thought. 'Will is a product of the nervous or neural substance, and it is determined by motives that emanate from other nervous elements,'[42] he insists; 'what we call will is the external manifestation of the encephalon in action.'[43] Blanqui rejects in the strongest terms the claim that 'the will is in no sense subject to the influence of the milieu it rules over', or that the will 'determines its own course of action, by itself, with absolute independence' from the human brain and its social environment. Such a metaphysical conception of absolute free will (*libre arbitre*), according to which 'everyone has an equal power of volition,' is, he writes, 'an absurd and senseless thesis.'[44] In the same way that every effect has a cause and every action has a 'motive', intelligence and thought precede and determine volition. Were things otherwise, then in any given situation all ways of 'feeling, understanding, judging and willing' would be identical for every person.[45] 'In all circumstances, from birth to death, you are never anything other than the echo of your organism,' Blanqui concludes. 'This organism, when all is said and done, is you.'[46]

Involuntary action or unconscious volition can certainly be exercised. A will can be 'unenlightened', just as an opinion can be 'unfounded'.[47] But not all actions and opinions are, for Blanqui, the product of conscious volition, strictly understood – any given will or opinion may not be 'the expression or result of a free choice but the product of constraint and fraud'[48] – and are not all of equal legitimacy as such.

The extent to which Rousseau anticipates many of Blanqui's concerns here is again worth noting. Freedom, according to Rousseau, consists in 'my being able to will only what is suitable to me, or what I deem to be such, without anything external to me determining me'.[49] Rousseau assumes that 'there is no true will without freedom', and that true freedom is the freedom to think and decide consciously for oneself as an enlightened and informed individual and then to act on that basis. This 'confluence of enlightenment and good will' must then be collectively exercised in order 'to achieve success'.[50] 'Every free act has two causes,' so the *Social Contract* summarizes, 'which cooperate in order to produce it. The one, which is moral, is the will that decides on the act, and the other, which is physical, is the force that carries it out.'[51] Only the truly enlightened consciousness of reasoned cognition can produce acts of genuine free will and, by extension, political legitimacy. Recall that for Rousseau 'no man has a natural authority over his fellow' and 'strength does not confer any right'. 'Let us agree then,' Rousseau suggests, 'that might is not right, and that we are obliged to obey only legitimate powers.'[52] Blanqui agrees. Existing powers, he too argues, are not legitimate by virtue of their mere existence. When it comes to the law – which, in the human realm, is only ever 'the expression of the will of the strongest' – it is 'possible', Blanqui states, that 'this will might, on occasion, conform to justice and right'; but by the same token it might well 'become the formula of iniquity and violence'.[53] The principle of justice, as developed through rational cognition, is thus the sole measure of truly free political action and of truly free sociopolitical arrangements in turn. Justice, in short, 'is the only true criterion that applies to human things'.[54]

Blanqui's writings can be read as a sustained reflection on what it means to be a conscious human being capable of reasoned thought and, therefore, of voluntary action. Just as Rousseau highlights the fundamental link between volition and freedom, such that 'if my will can be constrained I am no longer free,'[55] Blanqui sees this capacity for conscious volition as the primary characteristic of free human beings. His concept of 'stupefaction' (*abrutissement*) to denote the deliberate stultifying of people is crucial here. For those who remain the captive, unconscious agents of ignorance, who are deliberately prevented from exercising their capacity for thought – and, by extension, their capacity for conscious volition – are enslaved. Without the freedom to think freely 'man is no longer his own master'.[56] Elsewhere Blanqui goes even further, describing a process that reduces humans to the level of beasts. 'An ignorant person is barely even a man', he states, 'and can be led like a horse, with a bridle and spurs. Training such people to work and to obey is their master's sole concern.'[57] The 'ignorance and obedience of a horse' is, to be sure, 'the ideal that [the oppressor's] egoism dreams of for the worker.'[58] This is precisely why the Church wages 'an implacable war against devotion, against intelligence, against all that is great and good in man'. Its perennial concern has been to maintain popular 'servility, cretinism, degradation'.[59] This deliberate suppression of the human capacity for conscious volition is, in Blanqui's eyes, the most contemptible of acts. Any attempt to 'hinder education', and therefore the cultivation and development of the people's intelligence and cognitive faculties, is no less than 'a declaration of war against the human species'.[60]

If the workers' prescribed role or position of passive ignoramus deprives and denies them of their very humanity as conscious social beings, Blanqui's project seeks to create a social order that will enable the full realization of the self through the exercise of its natural capacity for voluntary self-determination. Since humankind is thought, as we have seen, it is only through the development of this unique cognitive capacity that humanity, individually and collectively, can truly realize itself, for 'the man of the community is he who is neither deceived nor led'.[61] While spiritualism 'treats people like mannequins, it stifles and mummifies them', materialism 'restores our dignity, activity, and autonomy'. It 'frees us ... from providentialist automatism' and 'restores us', in short, 'to full possession of ourselves'.[62] Intelligence and enlightened consciousness, otherwise uncultivated or stifled, are what make humans empowered and free.[63] Or as Rousseau puts it: 'To live is not to breathe; it is to act; it is to make use of our organs, our senses, our faculties, of all the parts of ourselves which give us the sentiment of our existence.'[64] Political struggle is therefore ultimately driven by a much more fundamental social struggle to develop and to realize humans, both individually and collectively.

The exercise of conscious volition, according to Blanqui, is what distinguishes an actor from an instrument, a human from an animal or automaton. Progress and change are only ever realized through the voluntary actions of humanity; humanity can only be truly realized through its own voluntary action for progress and change.

We can now see that this critique of free will and the insistence that 'acts are fatally determined by the nervous system'[65] have profound implications for Blanqui's entire political enterprise. Indeed, it is in these claims that we discover the primary movement from thought to practice, from knowledge to action, from consciousness to volition, that underpins his most basic political assumptions thereafter.

## The individual and the collective

The enlightened individual at the heart of Blanqui's theory forms the point of departure for his conception of collective interests and collective volition. Since the capacity for cerebral activity is shared by all humans, to be truly fulfilled it must be practically exercised precisely as a shared, collective capacity. 'It is through thought that [human beings] communicate,' Blanqui writes, 'through thought that they form one single being. It is through thought that universal solidarity is established, through thought that the interest of one becomes the interest of all.'[66] 'The brain,' in this sense, offers 'unity within multiplicity'.[67] To put it differently: collective thought and consciousness enable collective power.

This is entirely consistent with Blanqui's wider political tenets. As a matter of general principle, Blanqui affirms that 'a people is much more the master of its destiny than is an individual. Organic fatality weighs far more heavily upon an isolated individual than upon the collectivity.'[68] In the struggle against the rich and powerful, individual action, however determined and tenacious, will inevitably spell failure. In the face of oppression and domination, without collective unity the individual is doomed to isolation and impotence. The potentialities and capacities of the individual can therefore only be fulfilled, but also protected and defended, when individuals actively 'gather themselves together through association. ... Solidarity, progress, improvement [proceed] through association, not through the individual'.[69] Individual conscious volition, in other words, can only be politically actualized as collective conscious volition

But this prioritization of collective agency and interests is not at the expense of the individual as a conscious voluntary actor – far from it. Both in fact have to be thought simultaneously, such that many isolated individuals freely come together, as equals, to form one unified and organized collective body of enlightened individuals. 'If everything must be done in the interests of the collective,' Blanqui explains, 'nevertheless everything must be done by the individual.'[70] Or as Che would later write, making a similar argument: the masses make history 'as a conscious collective of individuals fighting for the same cause.'[71] In this sense everyone has a 'double life', that of the individual and that of the collective, from which emerges a 'double instinct', that of 'self-preservation' and that of 'social preservation' – the first being the more basic and constant, the second being weaker and more open to change and variation according to the wider level of enlightenment.[72] In every instance, however, without the conscious volition of the individual the conscious volition of the people as the association of these individuals is by its very nature impossible, their collective force non-existent, their political failure inevitable. The centrality of the enlightened individual to processes of social change is thus reaffirmed. 'With individual education, everything. Without it, nothing. Sunlight or darkness, life or death.'[73]

## The politics of (mis)education

The relation between human intelligence, popular education and collective progress is crucial to Blanqui's broader conception of society and politics. 'Education', he insists,

> is the only agent of liberation and social organisation. It is intelligence that governs the world, and it is education that produces intelligence. As the privilege of a small minority, it leads to monarchical or feudal oppression. As the prerogative of all, it alone will be able to create, through Equality, order, peace, freedom and happiness. It is thus the foremost necessity, the most important goal to pursue.[74]

Education – which is, as Blanqui never tires of repeating, 'the only instrument of salvation', 'the sole agent of human progress', 'the only true revolutionary agent'[75] – at both an individual level and a collective level can therefore be seen as a practical response to the problem posed by the privileging of thought and ideas as determinant of social relations and social change. By the same token, however, education in and of itself, regardless of its content, does not necessarily lead to enlightenment. 'Education is a matter of ideas alone,' Blanqui maintains. 'A reader nourished on foolishness will become a fool.'[76] Reason through enlightened education is the decisive weapon in the struggle for justice and equality, yet ignorance through reactionary mis-education is the key tool by which to cultivate and then maintain all forms of domination and submission. Let us pursue this point further, particularly in its practical political implications.

## Emancipatory education, reactionary manipulation

Here emancipation is the product of enlightenment, not vice versa; an enlightened society is the precondition of an emancipated society. The primacy ascribed to the idea in Blanqui's understanding of sociopolitical transformation thus leads to a causal chain between enlightenment, association and communism, as one unrevised note reveals:

> Communism is nothing but the (final) stage of association. ... Association grows, advances and spreads by enlightenment alone. Every step made along this path is the result of progress in popular education. Every victory of ignorance, on the other hand, is an attack on association. There is an intimate connection between these two realms of ideas – all facts attest to this. Communism will only be achieved through the absolute triumph of enlightenment. It will be its ineluctable consequence, its social and political expression.[77]

It follows that the foremost barriers to communism are on the one hand various social forces (work, impoverishment, hunger) that bind the masses into ignorance and prevent their enlightened instruction, and on the other hand institutions and organizations (schools, the press, the Catholic Church) that actively misinform and mislead the masses so as to maintain the power and privilege of the dominant classes. To be sure, for Blanqui ignorance is not simply caused by a 'lack of education'. It is 'caused above all by clerical teaching, which has as both its aim and its result the extinguishing of enlightenment and the stupefaction of the people through superstition'.[78] Ignorance, in other words, is principally caused not by *lack* of education but by *mis*-education – that is, by conscious and organized deception. (The distinction Blanqui makes in French between *éducation*, which generally connotes the clerical teaching that leads to deception and oppression, and *instruction*, which connotes the rational learning based on science that leads to enlightenment and emancipation – hence 'education creates slaves; instruction creates free men'[79] – is often lost in translation.) As the foremost institutional propagator of reactionary thinking, religion in particular, Blanqui reiterates in his numerous anticlerical polemics, comprises 'the cornerstone of oppression, the instrument par excellence of tyranny'.[80] Overall, then, just as Blanqui insists that education is the 'force' and 'the power that governs the world', as we have seen, he is also the first to recognize that this force and power 'can be used for vile ends. In the hands of a minority,' so he explains, 'it is a weapon of war, an instrument of oppression against the masses who have been disarmed by ignorance. This minority', he adds, 'is well aware of the value of the weapon they possess, and they seek to conserve their monopoly of it in order to ensure their continued domination.'[81]

How does this conflict manifest itself politically? Two examples are instructive here. Reflecting on the first *révolte des canuts* of November–December 1831 in Lyon, Blanqui describes how the uneducated masses' insufferable daily lives and their punishing work – upon which they are dependent in order simply to survive – provide no opportunities for intellectual emancipation. The brutal realities of starvation and the violent state repression of popular revolt can certainly reveal to these 'simple men' their 'true enemies' and bring to light the real cause of their suffering (in Lyon, Blanqui argues, the masses only rose up 'with such impressive unanimity' because the conflict between privilege and equality was so 'obvious' that it was impossible for even the most 'stupid of people not to see clearly that they were the victims of insatiable greed'). But such clear manifestations of the struggle between rich and poor are ephemeral, such revelations are extraordinary and often localized when compared to the masses as a whole. The basic problem therefore remains that the majority of the poor 'still misunderstand the source of their ills'.[82]

Blanqui's balance sheet of 1848 is informed by the very same concern. 'The fall of the red flag on 26 February 1848' – when the Provisional Government decided to retain the tricolour as the national flag – was 'the result of popular ignorance', he bluntly concludes. The people's 'political education was non-existent. The press had left the people in darkness. No fundamental ideas'. This abandonment of the red flag, Blanqui claims, was a backward step from the wave of struggles that followed July 1830. All the republican insurrections against Louis-Philippe (June 1832, April 1834, May 1839) were fought 'beneath the red flag' and 'against the tricolour flag', comprising as such the 'precursors' and the 'first acts' of February 1848. When considering the downward spiral of the popular movement from March 1848 to the plebiscite of November 1852 by which the Empire was re-established, however, Blanqui is clear as to its origins and consequences: 'The people are short-sighted, not to say blind. ... They watched their flag fall with the most perfect indifference, without understanding the first word of this drama.' That the masses were 'so impressionable' and 'so susceptible' to this betrayal could be explained by 'the absence of political education'.[83]

Recall Blanqui's assumption that thought conditions and determines volition. Unable to understand their plight and to identify their oppressor, the masses are passively complicit in the social order that is responsible for their own servitude. In other words, for Blanqui the masses' intellectual poverty reproduces their material poverty. Poverty certainly perpetuates ignorance, but ignorance is the primary cause of poverty. The people lack the enlightened political consciousness necessary to identify and to end their exploitation. 'To recognise one's own destitution is to be conscious of the need and to have the will to overcome it.'[84] In turn, and by an arrestingly simple inversion, Blanqui believes that to overcome ignorance is to overcome oppression and exploitation. Indeed, it seems logical to Blanqui that with the attainment of universal enlightenment and the reign of 'common sense' all economic problems will be resolved.[85]

The decisive conflict between enlightenment and ignorance, and its manifestation as a political struggle between emancipatory education and reactionary manipulation, becomes clear. After the revolutionary seizure of power, community and instruction must advance hand in hand so as to prevent the duplicitous manipulators of the people from re-emerging.

A free community of equals 'will be realised the day that no man, thanks to the universality of enlightenment, can ever again be the dupe of another. When that day comes, no one will be prepared to endure the inequality of wealth'.[86] Addressing the objection that equality of education would not lead to equality of intelligence, while conceding that perhaps 'there will always remain enough cerebral inequality to create an intellectual hierarchy, from genius to incompetence', Blanqui nonetheless maintains that 'thorough and general education will suffice to protect even the weakest of brains against deception, whatever its mask', through its cultivation of 'judgement', described as 'the most useful of all human faculties, the protective faculty par excellence, which defends us against both internal and external threats, against others and ourselves'. This universal faculty for critical 'judgement', then, will guard against the manipulation and deceit from which injustice and oppression arise; it will become 'the key weapon of the new society'.[87]

## A war of words

'It is regrettable that the philosophical idea does not penetrate the masses,' Blanqui confessed in 1866. 'They will only become seriously revolutionary through atheism.'[88] How might this problem be resolved? How might a vanguard group – a minority upholding and striving to realize a principle or goal – overcome its own isolated and embattled position within society as a whole, as it must? This brings us to a cornerstone of Blanqui's political practice: the popular press as a means to inform and educate the mass of the population so as to raise their political consciousness.

From his earliest writings Blanqui makes a clear link between the oppressed – whether in its successive historical incarnations as 'serfs', 'workers', 'artisans' or 'proletarians' – as forever 'the whipping boy of the aristocracy', and the imperative, on the part of the oppressor, to maintain common people in a state of 'eternal ignorance', as seen in the government's restriction of press freedom in the early 1830s.[89] Across the articles for *Le Libérateur* Blanqui mounts a sustained attack on the Orléanist regime's severe restrictions on press freedom as part of a wider attempt to 'destroy the press' and to suppress 'the freedom to think and write.'[90] The importance Blanqui continually places on newspapers and the public sphere throughout his life is indeed symptomatic of the more basic insistence on public enlightenment as the precondition for social emancipation. A writer has the capacity, he believes, to 'instruct and transform humanity'.[91] It is this understanding of the printed word as the vehicle for popular enlightenment and human development that explains his celebration of Gutenberg as a major figure in human history, as – along with Voltaire and other leading figures of the Enlightenment – 'far more useful to humanity than the most skilful artisan'.[92] 'The invention of the printing press has been the greatest benefit to humanity,' Blanqui claims.[93]

In the context of the nineteenth century, newspapers were therefore a key means by which the intellectual elite, carrying the 'weapon of thought',[94] could undertake the work of re-educating the mis-educated majority. In the context of Blanqui's life, the result was the series of newspapers – *Le Libérateur* (1834), *Candide* (1865), *La Patrie en Danger* (1870), *Ni Dieu, Ni Maître* (1880–1) – that he founded and edited. When repressive press laws outlaw such radical tracts, however, 'the people [are] no longer ... able to draw from them the principles of a pure morality'; 'they [are] shut off from this source of enlightenment and virtue.'[95] (One might note, parenthetically and anachronistically, that it is for these very reasons that Blanqui would have undoubtedly been wholly enthusiastic about the capacity of social media and the internet more generally to reach directly vast swathes of people, bypassing both the practical and political limitations of the print press.)

A notable corollary of this insistence on instruction as the sole force of human progress is an emphasis on communicability. 'The source of intellectual power resides in the capacity to communicate one's ideas,' Blanqui declares. 'The incommunicable idea is nothing; it does not exist.'[96] The writings of Auguste Comte, Blanqui's enemy number one in the late 1860s, are dismissed precisely because they are 'unreadable', their opaque and verbose prose merely serving to obfuscate intellectual inadequacy and political reaction.[97] Blanqui's own writings, by contrast, like Paine's *Common Sense* or Marx and Engels's *Communist Manifesto* or Che's *Guerrilla Warfare*, derive much of their political and literary force from the author's concern for their audience: they were written to be read and circulated, shared and quoted by ordinary people.[98] In this sense how we write is as important as what we write; a text's political power is ultimately determined by its communicative power. Political language must therefore be concise, lucid and inspiring. Blanqui's manuscripts attest to the authorial labour of constant revision and refinement, of removing tautologies, unnecessary qualifiers and any potential ambiguities so as to reduce the prose down to its core ideas and render them as clear and compelling as possible – hence the proclivity for aphorism and overstatement, hence the lack of caveats and qualifications.

Questions of style and form are thus fundamentally bound up with the political importance of popular consciousness. Since the people, if they are to be capable of decisive collective action, must be informed and have attained a certain level of political consciousness, political writings worth the name must serve this end. As Patrick Hutton notes, the Blanquists' emphasis on collective energy and enthusiasm led to a notable concern for 'aesthetic effect as the leaven of revolutionary agitation. Intellectual statement alone was insufficient', Hutton remarks. 'The need was to move men to a deeper awareness of the meaning of an idea.'[99] Political tracts, like political action, must be animated by vigour and confidence, by force and resolve.[100] Newspapers, like essays and pamphlets, were accordingly conceived as militant interventions, as weapons in the struggle against oppression.

## Enlightenment and revolution?

It will now be clear that, for Blanqui, social transformation hinges on popular education and mass enlightenment. Without the latter all revolutions will be socially unsustainable and politically vulnerable. 'There can be no lasting Revolution,' Blanqui proclaims, 'without enlightenment! There can be no emancipation without a basic level of intelligence! Freedom is education! Equality is education! Fraternity is education! Schools, books, the printed word – these are the real revolutionary agents! Harangues addressed to ignorant crowds have no impact.'[101] Failure to transform the individual and create an enlightened human being will inevitably translate into failure to transform the collective and create an enlightened society. It is for this reason that Blanqui became extremely critical of universal suffrage during and after 1848. Over the course of that year, the forces of reaction rolled back the revolution through successive victories at the ballot box – from the Constituent Assembly election of 23 April, which returned a large majority for the conservatives and moderates, to the presidential election of 20 December, which Louis-Napoleon Bonaparte won with 74 per cent of the popular vote.[102] Blanqui drew a fundamental conclusion from these events: an election in an unenlightened society, where the people are held in a state of ignorance by an oppressive church and state, will merely reflect this ignorance and reinforce the same structures of oppression. Universal suffrage in itself is by no means a force for progress. On the contrary, it can be employed in order to sanction counter-revolution and to consolidate the existing order. 'Recourse to the ballot the day after a revolution' – that is, prior to a campaign for popular education – 'can have only two equally reprehensible aims: to win the vote by constraint, or to restore the monarchy.'[103] Enfranchisement without enlightenment is meaningless at best, a dangerous political sham at worst.

At this point some structural tensions within Blanqui's project begin to arise. First, this conception of equality or communism as the product of universal enlightenment might seem to imply a form of evolutionary socialism or a moderate, reformist approach to social change. But Blanqui advocates no such thing. Only a revolutionary seizure of power can open the way to the complete transformation of social relations. Compare, for example, the passage noted above regarding communism emanating from enlightenment with the following extract, which states that 'the role of the revolution' is

> to smash, with a firm hand, the revolting inequalities that put opulence and education on one side, and poverty and ignorance on the other side, and that thereby turn universal suffrage into a dreadful lie, an instrument of tyranny and servitude; to destroy the oppressive influences on the body and the mind; to render, as quickly as possible, all members of the nation, both men and women, capable of judging and deciding things for themselves, based on their own understanding, and not under external influence or pressure, whatever it might be – this is the task that must be carried out. Only then, and no sooner, will France reconstitute itself and spontaneously decide on the form of its social order.[104]

The temporalities of revolutionary transformation clearly pose a problem here. It seems that one can neither skip nor accelerate the overthrow of all established political forms through which the French people will become capable of self-rule – the latter, we are told, will only be possible upon the completion of this preliminary task, 'and no sooner'. The no less ambiguous claim that collective self-determination will be realized 'as quickly as possible' – and the manner in which people are 'rendered' capable of exercising this capacity to judge and decide freely 'for themselves' rather than developing these capacities themselves and, in so doing, transforming themselves – likewise articulates an underlying tension between popular education and collective agency, and the sequencing of the two.

Blanqui himself is the first to recognize this problem. From his earliest writings he notes that 'profound ignorance' is the most 'deplorable' consequence of the masses' 'enslavement' precisely because it 'almost always makes them the docile instruments of the wicked passions of the privileged'. As a result of their systematic mis-education, the masses 'are ready to persecute at their master's signal the men of devotion who attempt to show them a better future'. Only in exceptional circumstances do they 'open their eyes to the truth and learn to distinguish between their friends and their oppressors'. At the heart of this article from 1834 lies a crucial and revealing question regarding the capacity of an oppressed and impoverished people to 'cultivate their intelligence, enlighten their reason, and reflect on social phenomena in which they play only a passive role'.[105] How and when, in other words, do an oppressed and impoverished people come to identify the sources of their oppression and impoverishment so that they might become capable of overcoming them?

Blanqui would later return to a similar question when accounting for the failure of 1848:

> After the February Revolution [of 1848], several years of intellectual preparation should have preceded and prepared the way for the popular vote. One must conquer a nation through ideas, never through force. But ideas must still be allowed to emerge, which is precisely what monarchy denies to the republican idea.[106]

Elsewhere he is explicit. 'Revolutions must take place in the mind before they can be carried out in the streets.'[107] Only intellectual emancipation can lead to social emancipation. 'Where is this initiation taking place today?', he accordingly asked in the wake of Louis-Napoleon Bonaparte's December 1851 coup d'état, before repeating, with urgency: 'A homicidal hand crushes the brain of the nation. Who will remove it?' And given his own outlook – the imminent rise of imperial grandeur that will captivate the masses, the confusion and fear that characterizes the revolutionary party, the impossibility of using the press, parliament or any democratic channels more generally – the conclusion is bleak: 'All is mournful and silent. ... Absolute submission.'[108] The practical steps that might change this situation seem to evade Blanqui; he seems unable to break the deadlock in his own theory, and the tone of this private letter as a whole is of uncharacteristic uncertainty, if not resignation. These passages certainly serve as a corrective to the image of a reckless insurrectionist forever calling for immediate insurgent action regardless of socio-economic or political conditions. 'Even to entertain the idea' of an insurrection, Blanqui tells his correspondent, 'would be madness'.[109]

In all of these examples the confluence of two seemingly contradictory sociopolitical processes appears to lead Blanqui to an impasse: popular education is the necessary precondition of genuinely revolutionary change, yet an unenlightened people is unable to act as the revolutionary force that is needed to seize power and initiate a programme of popular education.[110] How, then, does Blanqui square his 'revolutionary' socialism with his 'enlightened socialism'?[111] How can a new political order be established through which mass ignorance can be overcome and collective self-determination become possible? How, and when, do an intellectually stifled people become a conscious and autonomous political actor? The convergence of political and social forces, and Blanqui's proposed solutions to these problems, brings us to perhaps the single most controversial issue of his whole enterprise: leadership and organization.

## Leaders and popular forces

In February 1832 Blanqui presented a report to the Society of the Friends of the People on 'France's internal and external situation since the July revolution' of 1830. His analysis essentially turned on one basic issue. In July, Blanqui told the assembled audience, the people 'knew how to win, but not how to make use of their victory'; the people, he repeated, have 'shown themselves strong enough to win, but ... [they do] not know how to preserve their victory'.[112] How can an initial popular victory over an oppressive ruling power be consolidated? Who knows how to preserve and make of use of a victory? In Blanqui's mind these were the central questions posed by July 1830 and its aftermath. And they were questions to which he accordingly dedicated much of his report.

The knowledge of how – and how not – to proceed in a revolutionary situation in order to consolidate a popular victory, and the question of who possesses such knowledge and how it can be disseminated, were decisive in 1830, Blanqui argues. Following their triumph over Charles X and his loyal troops, the people unconsciously rallied around those who – unbeknown to them – were actively working against their interests. As a result they were lured into committing fatal tactical errors, particularly their withdrawal from 'the public squares' after the street fighting had ended. Lacking the necessary knowledge of the dynamics and requirements of revolutionary politics, the people were an easy target for the bourgeoisie to exploit for their own ends, as they duly did: on the back of the popular victory the Duc d'Orléans was offered the crown, a constitutional monarchy was established and a government of bankers and financiers took office. While Blanqui insists that naive miscalculation absolves the people of the lamentable consequences of July, it also presents itself as a major problem that must be resolved. His proposed solution is clear. The people, he claims, 'were not complicit in this shameful usurpation which would never have occurred with impunity if they had found men capable of guiding the blows inspired by their anger and vengeance'.[113] Blanqui certainly expresses his full confidence in the people's insurgent force. But for him this force alone is not enough. Insurgent force (the masses) requires knowledge (enlightened leaders) to guide it. A popular mobilization needs leadership and organization to ensure that any initial victories are consolidated and developed rather than weakened, manipulated and betrayed by the forces of reaction as they inevitably appear. Bourgeois revolutionaries indeed constitute, in Blanqui's eyes, the proletarian camp's 'principal – or at least its most persistent – force. They bring to it an enlightened contingent that the people are unfortunately not yet able to provide themselves', he would later write. 'It was members of the bourgeois class who first raised the flag of the proletariat, who formulated egalitarian doctrines, and who now spread them, and sustain them, and restore them after they fall. Everywhere it is the bourgeois who lead the people in their battles against the bourgeoisie.'[114]

A popular force requires intellectual and political leadership to anticipate its power, to initiate, encourage and then direct its empowerment, but also to prevent its demoralization and to uphold its essential principles when defeats and failures occur. This, according to Blanqui, is the essential condition of enduring victory; he never wavered from this conviction. Conceived in the wake of 1830, he repeated this basic insistence on principled leadership and effective organization during every subsequent revolutionary sequence of his lifetime.[115]

## Revolutionary vanguards

How, we should therefore ask, does Blanqui conceive the relationship between the revolutionary elite and the people? There are two possible answers to this question.

First, and perhaps most obviously, Blanqui proposes a small group of intellectually enlightened and politically committed revolutionaries. Emanating primarily from the educated bourgeoisie, unlike the ruling class and its supporters this group's knowledge of social relations and economic forces serves not the private interests of a privileged elite but acts in the name of the common interests of ordinary people. This group of *déclassés* understands both the existing structures of domination and is well versed in the strategic exigencies of revolutionary politics, from disciplined organization to the astute analysis of political conditions. The problem, however, is that systematic political repression renders conditions unfavourable, if not altogether impossible, for the mass propaganda through which popular education and the ensuing popular support could be achieved. Only through clandestine activity could this group ensure its own internal unity and conspire to launch a seizure of state power, after which the re-education of the masses could begin.

This is the conception of revolutionary organization for which Blanqui is best known, and for which he has been most consistently reproached ever since. The general contours of Blanqui's conspiratorial politics are largely familiar, from its origins (Philippe Buonarroti, the Carbonari) and organizations (Société des Familles, Société des Saisons) to the failed coup attempts (May 1839, August 1870) and its political derivations (Blanquists, Narodniks).[116] But rather than going over such issues, let us focus on how its central features relate to the more basic question of intelligence and consciousness.

A note from the 1860s provides a useful summary of Blanqui's general schema. 'An educated and devoted minority has all the qualities necessary to destroy a religion, without [the support] and even against the opinion or views of the majority,' Blanqui confidently states, and the same logic can be extended to all forms of unjust and oppressive rule, be it an absolute monarchy or conservative republic. 'This majority is incompetent as a result of its ignorance, which is the criminal and premeditated work of religion. The use of force precisely has as its goal and its result the liberation of the blind victims.'[117] Most of the salient features of Blanqui's conspiratorial politics are present here: an enlightened minority capable of overcoming its numerical inferiority through subjective dedication and determination; an ignorant and impotent majority requiring external assistance to free it from its unconscious servitude; the destruction of all forms of mis-education and manipulation. To this we should add a post-revolutionary transitional power based in the capital, a 'Parisian dictatorship', that represents the nation as a whole. With these components Blanqui's project becomes clear enough: an enlightened elite seize power in Paris, where all political and intellectual forces of the country are concentrated, and launch a dual process of popular education on the one hand and suppression of those actors who threaten to prevent, undermine or undo the work of enlightenment on the other. Following this transitional period, the general dissemination and development of enlightened thought and consciousness would give rise to the direct self-rule of the people. Blanqui's conception of post-revolutionary transition is thus properly dialectical: only through centralized, undemocratic rule could centralization end, power dissolve and true freedom, and a people capable of exercising that freedom, emerge; only the dictatorship of Paris could give way to democracy across France. Until that point, the effective organization of the group leading this project was essential. Failure to preserve organizational discipline and unity would fatally compromise the entire endeavour.

Such assumptions cannot but seem somewhat naive and, contrary to Blanqui's own insistence, practically unworkable, certainly in the seemingly straightforward and logical manner in which this process is often portrayed in his writings. As we shall consider the question of revolutionary transition at greater length in Chapter 4, our present concern is the particularly striking distance between the enlightened minority and the ignorant majority. The people here are not the active subject but the passive object of revolutionary politics. Perhaps more than anything else this is what inflects the classic image of Blanqui as the authoritarian elitist, the misguided 'putchist' completely divorced from and imposing an external will on the inert, unthinking masses. In this respect Engels's depiction, and dismissal, of 'revolutions carried through by small conscious minorities at the head of unconscious masses' is indeed quite accurate.[118] But is it entirely representative of Blanqui's politics as a whole?

To answer this question we should first consider the composition of the revolutionary vanguard that is organizing and driving this project, for this political force is not reducible to the clandestine group of bourgeois intellectuals noted above. In Blanqui's lexis *déclassé* denotes both the enlightened bourgeois intellectual and the enlightened Parisian worker.[119] As well as from the bourgeoisie, the revolutionary elite 'also recruits some of its members from those workers educated and trained in their broad school, and who become, in turn, leaders in their own right'.[120] So Blanqui's conception of leadership operates at two levels: revolutionary bourgeois and workers as the political vanguard of Paris, and Paris as the political vanguard of France (to which one might then add France as the political vanguard of Europe).

Although the vast majority of the middle class support 'the principle of legitimacy', fear popular power and are only concerned with their own material self-interest, as the political sequence inaugurated by July 1830 once again made clear, a 'minority of that class', Blanqui noted in 1832, 'composed of the intellectual professions and the small number of bourgeois who love the tricolour flag … will take the side of popular sovereignty'.[121] As the century passed and the political context changed, in Blanqui's writings the expression of this dichotomous antagonism would generally shift from republicanism against royalism to communism against capitalism. But as we shall see in Chapter 2, if the terms altered, the basic underlying political logic remained the same. In the necessary, unavoidable choice between two opposing groups and principles, Blanqui is clear where and with whom he stands. 'The principle of popular sovereignty rallies all men of the future, the masses who, tired of being exploited, seek to smash the framework that suffocates them.'[122] It is therefore the 'duty' of all 'men of heart and intelligence', whether bourgeois or proletarians, to 'summon the masses to smash the yoke of poverty and ignominy'.[123] One cannot find therein a form of conspiratorial substitutionism. The vanguard may do the calling, but the masses do the smashing themselves. Political action in this sense cannot be taken on behalf of the masses. The movement for equality is an 'invincible coalition, formed by the genius that conceives and the masses that execute'.[124] The function of a leadership, as Blanqui puts it, is akin to that of a 'fascine': 'When you have behind you a great people advancing to win their freedom and well-being' – that is, a people aware of the goals for which they are fighting and prepared to do what is necessary to realize them – 'you must be willing to throw yourself into the obstructing ditches in order to serve as a fascine and provide a way forward.'[125] The aim, in other words, is to create a platform for the people upon which they can work to realize their own freedom.

Bourgeois intellectuals and those oppressed workers conscious of their oppression unite in the name of *all* the oppressed and against *all* forms of oppression. The 'elite men' that comprise an insurgent force, so the *Instructions for an Armed Uprising* explains, are therefore simply those men from the 'popular ranks', be it through background or affiliation, who voluntarily and enthusiastically take up arms and 'fight for an idea' – the idea of social justice.[126]

## Insurgent Paris

A political project founded on the leading role of Paris and Parisians represents, in certain key respects, no major innovation on Blanqui's part. This was a model of revolution inherited from both the French Revolution (the insurrections of 10 August 1792 and 31 May 1793 in particular) and subsequent mass uprisings (27–9 July 1830 and 22–4 February 1848). Like Robespierre before him, for Blanqui Paris is 'the true representative, the concentrated essence of the country', 'the condensation of a great people'.[127] Paris plays the leading role in a national conflict; its streets are a 'bloody arena of civil war'.[128] This Paris-centred Jacobinism certainly distinguishes Blanqui from the 'utopianism' of Etienne Cabet and Charles Fourier, whose own projects for social transformation were based on the creation of autonomous, rural communes. But given the political history of the period in question, is it altogether surprising that Blanqui would insist on the political primacy of Paris? Parisians were a crucial revolutionary actor from 1789 to 1871; time and time again the French capital and its inhabitants played a decisive role in the struggles that would shape both country and continent. In this sense, Blanqui's privileging of Paris's insurgent force is nothing more than a 'concrete analysis of a concrete situation', to use Lenin's well-known phrase; his attempt to conceive from this idea of Paris a general practice of revolution, a revolutionary strategy rooted in a specific urban environment, a mere reflection of this political reality. Insofar as it concentrated and condensed a much wider social conflict, the capital city was and would remain the central battlefield of the national struggle between the people and the rich. One finds versions of this argument in other contexts. Trotsky, for instance, similarly recognizes that 'if the capital plays as dominating a role in a revolution as though it concentrated in itself the will of the nation' this was 'simply because the capital expresses most clearly and thoroughly the fundamental tendencies of the new society'. According to Trotsky, the 'role of the capital is determined not by the tradition of a bureaucratic centralism, but by the situation of the leading revolutionary class, whose vanguard is naturally concentrated in the chief city; this is equally true for the bourgeoisie and the proletariat'.[129]

Although Blanqui, after Robespierre, no doubt shares Trotsky's insistence on 'the initiatory role of the centres',[130] it is nonetheless important to note a fundamental and distinctive feature of Blanqui's analysis: Paris's political primacy is ultimately the result of its *intellectual* primacy. 'Paris, the national representative,' he writes, 'gives France its strength by concentrating all its intellectual forces in one point.'[131] As 'the centre of thought, the volcano from which ideas arise like bursts of flame', Paris is 'the liberating saviour of the countryside'.[132] Elsewhere the French capital's intellectual primacy is qualified in a more precise sense: 'If Paris is the head of the world, it is because Paris is atheist.'[133] The enlightened consciousness that is incompatible with religious belief grants a leading role to those who have attained it.

Blanqui maintains that in nineteenth-century France, as in 1789–94, the struggles in Paris, and the struggles for Paris, determine the destiny of the country as a whole. This is why the brutal repression of the popular movement during the Parisian June Days of 1848 is seen as 'fatal' for the entire country: without its 'brain' France will be reduced to 'a corpse'.[134] 'The counter-revolution wants to halt [the nation's] forward march by suppressing its brain', Blanqui warned in September 1848, enjoining Parisians 'to stop France from being decapitated.'[135] These same counter-revolutionary forces, he noted two years later in June 1850, were undertaking 'the destruction of Paris so as to bring about the enslavement of the nation', for 'tyranny' could only be established 'on the ruins of the city of light'.[136] Such strategic preoccupations were also at work during the Second Empire, when Napoléon III's government set about pacifying the imminent threat posed by the revolutionary city through Baron Haussmann's *grands travaux*.[137] In all these instances Blanqui's underlying assumption is clear: Parisians, unlike the majority of the French population, are enlightened and as such politically conscious, capable of the purposeful, determined action that revolutionary politics demands. Paris provides the majority of 'the workers who are devoted to the emancipation of the masses'.[138] Parisians think for, act for and stand for the French people as a whole.

It is this strict insistence on enlightened consciousness as determinant of decisive political action, on *conscious* popular force, that should be added to Peter Hallward's 'three basic principles' of Blanqui's politics. Blanqui certainly believes that 'when concentrated in a large city like Paris people already have all the power they need, if they choose to exercise it, to challenge an unjust government and overcome its forces of repression', as Hallward notes.[139] But the latent power of the people of Paris fundamentally derives from their consciousness of their oppression, their understanding that together they have the capacity to end it through their own collective action and their knowledge of what this successful action will involve. In other words, the choice to exercise collective power presupposes consciousness of the choice itself. The established order, to be sure, 'is only really maintained because the people do not think to destroy it'.[140] At stake, then, when assessing the balance of social and political forces is a more basic and decisive question: do a people *think* and *know* that they have the capacity to exercise their own power? The capacity to choose a certain course of action and to pursue, actively and purposefully, a certain end, depends on and varies according to the level of consciousness. If 'a people in chains is degraded by servitude to the point that they are no longer conscious of their abjection',[141] then the people of Paris, conscious of its present oppression and prepared to take up arms in the cause of the entire people's emancipation, are 'the precursors of the future, the pioneers of humanity', a 'prophetic and martyred people'.[142]

Blanqui's stated point of departure here is the 'Mountain', the most radical group of deputies in the National Convention of 1792-4. The Mountain's 'salient trait', Blanqui suggests, is 'its close alliance with the Parisian proletariat – not because it had a sense of profound affection for only one city, but because, among so many populations equally laid low by suffering, it found at hand and ready to fight this energetic group, impassioned by consciousness of its sufferings. The Mountain therefore made it the liberating army of humankind'.[143] Blanqui's aim is to revive this alliance of dedicated, principled leaders and a mobilized, combative Paris to act not only in the name of all but potentially *in spite of* all, since it may be necessary to confront and overcome 'a reactionary majority' that is unconsciously acting against its own interests.[144] Such a concentrated, organized, conscious and committed popular force has the collective capacity to initiate and then to drive forward, in the face of mass resistance, the political process through which public enlightenment and social change will become possible.

So if the people of Paris, conscious of the structures of domination and capable of exercising the collective action necessary to overcome them, is the key political actor of Blanqui's project, what about the 'non-elite' sections of the people? How do they figure in this project?

Across his writings, Blanqui often appears to suggest that the unenlightened ignorance of the masses and their susceptibility to material seduction should not obscure their fundamental and incorruptible inner goodness or integrity. 'The people are not ungrateful; they are only forgetful. Forgetfulness is due to a weak intelligence; ungratefulness is due to a weakness of the heart [*vice du cœur*]. Far from ungrateful, the people on the contrary push gratitude to the point of blindness and unreason.'[145] The people, he reaffirms elsewhere, 'do not have any ulterior motives';[146] 'the people, simple and loyal, have no defence against trickery, and their good faith makes them easily duped'.[147] Blanqui appears to rehearse Robespierre's argument, building on Rousseau, that the people's 'natural goodness predisposes it to being duped by political charlatans. These men are well aware of this and take advantage of it'.[148] But in spite of this externally produced ignorance and deception, the people always retain their internal goodness. 'Whether in their ignorance and ablaze with religious fanaticism, or more enlightened and inspired by enthusiasm for liberty', for Blanqui the people 'are always great and generous'.[149] Evoking the example of the eighteenth-century *philosophes* – the 'nobles geniuses' who successfully fought for equality against the aristocracy and clergy 'and were followed by a whole people attuned to their voice and deaf to the anathemas of selfish priests who grew angry when they were no longer listened to'[150] – the task, as Blanqui conceives it, is to renew this paradigm of intellectual emancipation.

By way of conclusion let us return to Rousseau, who might help to shed some light on these issues of enlightened thought, consciousness, leadership and popular goodness in Blanqui's politics. As I shall explore this comparison further in Chapter 4, I shall simply offer some preliminary remarks here.

We have seen that Blanqui's project begins with the cognitive capacities of humanity as the site and source of sociopolitical struggles; politics is determined, in the last instance, by human intelligence and ideas. Education is therefore imperative for the necessary cultivation of the people's critical faculties and the raising of popular consciousness. Blanqui places great emphasis on the practical means, particularly the popular press, that must be harnessed in order to disseminate enlightened thought and, ultimately, to transform the mass of the people into thinking social beings, without which the transformation of the social order will prove impossible. By the same token, Blanqui is equally insistent on the extent to which enlightened thought is repressed, and popular enlightenment stifled, by clerical teaching. The church, with the support of the state, deliberately deceives the people so as to stupefy and dominate them. Education and enlightenment emancipate, miseducation and ignorance enslave.

Blanqui evidently shares Rousseau's fundamental insistence on the people being 'properly informed' as a prerequisite for the exercise of the general will.[151] Blanqui similarly often appears to reason, like Robespierre, that, to quote the *Social Contract*, 'the people can never be corrupted, but it can often be led into error, and it is only in this case that it seems to desire the bad'.[152] Could Blanqui's preoccupation with enlightened leadership therefore not be seen to follow Rousseau's attempts to solve the problem of how to empower and enlighten a 'blind multitude' – a term Blanqui himself employs[153] – 'often ignorant of what it wants, because it seldom knows what is good for it'? Rousseau outlines what is at stake:

> The people, of itself, always wants the good, but does not, of itself, always see it. The general will is always in the right, but the judgment guiding it is

not always enlightened. The general will needs to be shown things as they are, and sometimes as they ought to appear, to be taught which path is the right one for it to follow, to be preserved from the seductiveness of particular wills, to have comparisons of times and places made for it, and be told of those remote and hidden dangers which counterbalance the attractions of visible, present advantages.[154]

To realize the people's passage from not simply uninformed but *mis*informed passivity and powerlessness to sovereign authority, Rousseau introduces the figure of 'the legislator', as we shall see in Chapter 4. A few initial points are worth noting here. At times Blanqui goes beyond Rousseau's prescription of the relation between a general will and its guides, advocating and undertaking isolated political action that could only impose an external will upon a passive people rather than encouraging the active mobilization of the people and the direct exercise of their own collective will. The primacy accorded to the subjective engagement of a vanguard group would seem to deny or delay the conscious agency of the seemingly unconscious, inert masses; they become simply an object to be shaped by an external subject. On other occasions, Blanqui seems broadly to follow Rousseau, as is perhaps most clearly seen in his claims that the people must follow the bearers of enlightened thought on the one hand, and the enlightened guides must be devoted to equality and to the people on the other hand. With the coalescence of these two mutually dependent forces, it becomes possible to seize (and then retain) political power and initiate a process of radical social transformation. Arguably, however, both Rousseau and Blanqui could be accused of creating too great a distance between the supposedly 'superior intelligence'[155] of the leaders and the 'credulous ignorance' of the led, a position that has the potential to undermine any egalitarian political project from the outset. At the heart of Blanqui's thought lies the strict insistence that intellectual consciousness, produced through enlightened instruction alone, is the prerequisite to decisive political action. Such an insistence will, at times, no doubt lead him to an unduly elitist conception of politics. With this an ambiguity regarding the possibility of popular self-emancipation also emerges, with Blanqui seeming to suggest the necessity of an external, hegemonic power in the development of the masses' intellectual and political consciousness. When he translates these assumptions into the question of post-revolutionary social transformation, as we shall see in Chapter 4, it would appear that this view of the mass of the people's inability to develop their own consciousness themselves will ultimately limit his ability to conceive a politics of *self*-emancipatory practice. The result is a structurally flawed conception of sociopolitical change in which a gap between intelligence and ignorance – a gap rooted in some of Blanqui's primary philosophical assumptions outlined above – will fail to be convincingly overcome.

Blanqui's evocation of the 'weapon of thought' is therefore neither throwaway hyperbole nor rhetorical flourish. Thought is a revolutionary force, a weapon that must be wielded in service of equality and the oppressed through uncompromising, unyielding intellectual devotion. And it is to the importance of first principles and commitment that we shall now turn in Chapter 2.

2

# Conflict

*The contempt for or the absence of ideas, the substitution of the politics of expedients for the politics of principles – this is what led to our downfall.*[1]

Blanqui's politics is conflictual to the core. Politics, Blanqui maintains, is divisive; it is dispute and disagreement, confrontation and combat. This assumption emanates from two sources, what we might call the real (an analysis of history and social relations) and the ideal (the realm of political/moral principles), both of which inform and reinforce the other.

'We should not conceal from ourselves the fact that there is a war to the death between the classes that compose the nation', Blanqui declared in early 1832. Such a diagnosis is not speculation or conjecture but an actual sociopolitical 'truth'.[2] Society, Blanqui repeats, comprises not 'a community, but rather a conflict of interests', in which 'there is no other relation between the two unequal halves of society than that of struggle'. 'Contrived words of concord and fraternity that mask an insatiable thirst for exploitation may fool some dupes,' Blanqui continues. But facts and events 'are also eloquent, and they are ultimately far more persuasive and far more consequential'. And the facts show that 'there is a struggle, and that in this struggle one of the parties must succumb'.[3] Blanqui's insistence on conflict is, then, in the first instance, a reflection of existing social dynamics. To change society one has to understand and reflect its own internal logic. This has a crucial practical implication: for any movement for radical social change the question of political power in general, and state power in particular, is decisive.

But Blanqui's insistence on conflict also derives from the principled commitment to an ideal. Politics, according to Blanqui, is a struggle of opposing, irreconcilable ideals and interests. He thus presents an alternative and compels a choice: equality or inequality, freedom or servitude. That Blanqui imposes an either/or between groups and interests is precisely to allow no room for compromise or compliance. It implies, indeed demands one take a principled, profoundly moral stand for one side or the other. Either you are for the exploited or for the exploiter, an agent of justice or an agent of injustice. Between enlightenment and ignorance, progress and reaction, a choice must be made, a side must be taken. Purported neutrality is the greatest enemy, opportunism the greatest disgrace. One must make a choice and fully assume one's choice to the end. Invoking Saint-Just's motto, 'the wretched are the powerful of the earth', Blanqui arrives at the guiding maxim of his entire project: 'We are always and everywhere with the oppressed against the oppressors.'[4] Politics ultimately comes down to a simple moral choice and conviction. Emancipatory political practice therefore presupposes principled commitment; it is informed by subjective passion, confidence and a determination to prevail, not to concede or compromise, whatever the consequences. Blanqui extends this logic to all facets of his project. To become all or to remain nothing, to take power or to languish in impotence, to achieve victory or to admit defeat – for Blanqui there is no third way, no middle ground, no partial success. Either one commits oneself to the ideal, or one does not. Either equality and justice triumph, or they do not.

In order to understand Blanqui's theory, it is necessary to accord greater significance to this divisive political logic than has previously been the case. Without piecing together and foregrounding this issue we cannot fully grasp many of the notions – power, struggle, the people, duty … – that define and animate Blanqui's politics.

This chapter will begin by examining Blanqui's concept of civil war and the manner in which it is grounded in an analysis of property, the state, history and contemporary politics. It will then turn to Blanqui's 'politics of principles', to adopt his own term, and consider its implications for some key aspects of his project. My central concern is to consider *why* making a choice and taking a side is necessary in the first instance. Questions of *how* practically to exercise this choice and actually realize these first principles, of the subjective resources through which one remains committed to the initial choice, will be examined at greater length in the following chapters.

# Civil war

## Property

In the early 1830s Blanqui used the pages of *Le Libérateur* to outline the fundamental structure of the existing order as he saw it. Following Rousseau's critique of property as described in the *Discourse on the Origin of Inequality* (1755), Blanqui argues that, usurping the natural order, individuals seized common land through 'deceit and violence', declared themselves to be 'the exclusive owners of this land' and established, by law, their right to this property as 'the basis of the social order'. Their right to property, they declared, 'shall dominate all the rights of humanity' to the extent that 'if need be, it may absorb them all'. Indeed 'it may infringe upon the right to life that every man acquires at birth, if this right, which is the right of all men, in any way conflicts with the right to property of a privileged few'.[5] 'After the land,' Blanqui goes on, 'this right to property was then applied to other instruments of labour linked to the land without being an integral part of it, to which we can give the generic name of capital.' But since land and capital are sterile in themselves, requiring labour to fructify and acquire value, the majority of the population – dispossessed of the instruments of labour and excluded from the possession of the land – was duly transformed into 'vile cattle destined solely to work and manure the land of these monsters'.[6] The people are therefore all those who are forced to provide for – and all those who are thus exploited by – these wealthy, parasitic usurpers; they are 'the immense majority of citizens' who are 'forced to toil on land whose produce they do not reap'. Blanqui depicts an order in which 'neither the instruments nor the fruits of labour belong to the working masses but to a usurping aristocracy that consumes and does not produce. ... The honey produced by the bees is devoured by hornets'.[7] This dichotomy between industrious workers and idle consumers, producers and non-producers, comes straight from Saint-Simonian doctrine (Saint-Simon himself had employed the metaphor of bees and drones in 1819 to illustrate his conception of social relations).[8] Beyond Rousseau and Saint-Simon, Blanqui's analysis is also close to Marx's later theory of primitive accumulation.[9] Like Marx, who writes that 'the expropriation of the great mass of the people from the soil, from the means of subsistence and from the instruments of labour ...

forms the pre-history of capital',[10] Blanqui describes a social order 'founded on conquest and which divided the population into two categories, the victors and the vanquished',[11] in which the exploitation of the latter is a product of – and thereafter maintained by and reproduced through – the former's hereditary and oligarchic control of land, capital and production.

Moreover, 'since land only derives its value from labour', the 'logical consequence', Blanqui suggests, is to own the people who 'make it fertile'.[12] Wherever private property is established, enslavement follows.[13] This is true of France as it is its colonies, where the 'barbarism' of slavery represents a 'permanent affront to humanity'.[14] While acknowledging that the slavery of nineteenth-century France certainly is not and could not be slavery 'in all its naked brutality', Blanqui nonetheless reasons that between Paris, Martinique and ancient Rome, 'the right to property' – the common origin of all social orders – 'is neither less insolent nor less aggressive'.[15] One must identify the 'serfs' of contemporary French society, Blanqui reaffirms in 1852, 'who have all the appearances of freedom amid all the pains of servitude'. One must recognize that 'hunger is slavery'.[16] One must understand that 'if [slavery] does not exist in name, it exists in fact'.[17]

Servitude, then, for Blanqui is not the mere fact of being owned by another human, as in the ancient world or in colonialized countries; it is not a contingent political issue, nor is it the consequence of a certain form of government. Servitude is structural in origin. Across human history all social bodies have been founded 'on the principle of property – or in other words, on the servitude of labour. The majority works and must work for the minority'.[18] Servitude means being 'completely dispossessed of the instruments of labour, and then being put at the mercy of those who usurped them, and who retain through violence their exclusive ownership of these instruments that are indispensable to the workers'.[19] 'For from the moment a privileged caste passes on land and capital through inheritance,' Blanqui insists, 'all other citizens, though not condemned to remain slaves of any given individual, nevertheless become absolutely dependent on that caste, since their only remaining freedom is the choice of which master will rule over them.'[20] In other words, and indeed Blanqui does not use the term himself, servitude in its modern sense means wage slavery. 'The worker and the peasant that poverty delivers as beasts of burden to the manufacturer and the owner,' he asks rhetorically, 'are they free?'[21] The masses' servitude is inherent to a social and legal order built on the usurpation of land, production and capital by a privileged few. Private property, understood as an enduring, fundamental social structure responsible for an equally enduring, fundamental form of social relation, is thus 'a permanent despoilment' for the masses.[22]

After Rousseau, who, in accounting for the ills of society – servitude, domination, deceit, egoism ... – held that 'these evils are the first effects of property and the inseparable escort of nascent inequality',[23] Blanqui also sees inequality and exploitation as products of the individual usurpation of common property. He too depicts a social order that is preserved through hereditary privilege and oligarchic power, the law and the constitution, duplicity and violence – all of which ensure the continued servitude and suffering, generation after generation, of those who work the land, those who are deprived of the instruments and fruits of their labour. Blanqui's critique of property essentially restates Rousseau's belief that the origin of society and of laws 'put new shackles on the weak and gave new powers to the rich ... destroyed natural freedom irretrievably, laid down for all time the law of property and inequality, made clever usurpation into irrevocable right, and henceforth subjected, for the benefit of a few ambitious men, the human race to labour, servitude, and misery'.[24] By the same token, Blanqui's assumption that the instruments of labour 'should belong only to those who use them to work', just as the fruits of labour should belong only to those who produce them,[25] anticipates Marx's reflections on 'the transformation of capitalist private property, which in fact already rests on the carrying on of production by society, into social property. In the former case,' Marx explains, 'it was a matter of the expropriation of the mass of the people by a few usurpers; but in this case, we have the expropriation of a few usurpers by the mass of the people.'[26] Since land should be an 'instrument ... to sustain the life of society', Blanqui similarly argues that 'the lands should belong to all members of society equally, who, through their combined efforts, would be able to exploit the wealth it holds in its depths'.[27] Given that Blanqui would maintain throughout his life that the revolution must bring about, as he explained in 1852, 'the destruction of the existing order, founded on inequality and exploitation, the ruin of the oppressors, and deliverance of the people from the yoke of the rich',[28] we can see how this early critique of property and wage slavery was fundamental to his revolutionary project. As Marx would later insist, communist revolution, the movement to abolish private property, would bring about 'the expropriation of the expropriators'.[29]

This analysis of the inequality and injustice of property, of a socio-economic arrangement that is inherently and invariably opposed to the interests of the working masses, forms the basic framework upon which Blanqui builds his concept of conflict. Before proceeding with how Blanqui undertakes this task, let us pause momentarily to address one point.

It will have become apparent that Blanqui's theoretical approach, here as elsewhere, is more concerned with broad overviews and general assumptions than exhaustive analyses based on sociological enquiry or empirical investigation. These writings were not the starting point for an extensive research programme. Indeed, having established in 1834 his conception of property as outlined above, at no point did he return to these issues with a view to reworking, developing or refining the basic maxims. Not only did the maxims therefore remain unaltered during his lifetime, they also remained just that, maxims, never to be afforded systematic exposition – a tendency that applies to Blanqui's thought more generally.

What might we conclude from this? First, it demonstrates not only the intellectual importance of the early 1830s as the period in which Blanqui formulated the foundations of his political project but also the general consistency of his thinking thereafter. In both theory and practice, Blanqui remained faithful to his early account of the origin of inequality and what was at stake in overcoming structural domination. Second, as noted in Chapter 1, we see here, as we shall see elsewhere, the limits of Blanqui's ability to understand and explain real, existing social conditions and the manner in which they influence and inform collective political action. Although right to assume that politics must insert itself within the social field, his inability or unwillingness to fully comprehend the latter – not to mention his insistence on intelligence and ideas as the fundamental basis of social relations – limits the scope of his insights in this regard. Finally, and linking the two previous points, it shows that the critique would therefore remain analytically unsubstantiated, thereby detracting from its potential intellectual incisiveness. The sociopolitical logic and consequences of private property on the whole remain unexplored, then, and one would need to look elsewhere for more detailed and developed treatments. Yet it could be said that Blanqui's aim was in fact to conceive a concise and generally intuitive account so as to guide political engagements – and by this criteria arguably he could claim a certain success. Blanqui recognizes that any form of militant political struggle requires establishing clear principles so as to direct determined action; only through declaring and disseminating its basic assumptions and goals can a political movement work, collectively and decisively, towards their realization.[30] So while the reasoning has flaws, as is at times, though not always, the case with Blanqui's project, the political ends remain astute.

## The state

If 'the usurpation of property' is 'the fundamental basis of the existing social order',[31] then the state, according to Blanqui, represents and defends the interests of private property. This assumption, which predates the writings on property from 1834, is best seen in Blanqui's defence speech at the 'Trial of the Fifteen' of January 1832, a public platform he used to launch an all-out assault on the July Monarchy, exposing its benign, democratic pretentions as the façade behind which a war between rich and poor was being waged.[32]

Addressing the prosecuting lawyer's accusation that the poor were waging war against the rich, Blanqui agrees with the diagnosis of war, only to propose an alternative account of its origins and primary aggressor. Echoing Babeuf's belief in a pre-existing civil war between rich and poor, between patricians and plebeians,[33] Blanqui rejoins: 'Yes, gentlemen, this is indeed the war between rich and poor: the rich wanted it so, for they are the aggressors.'[34] The war Blanqui speaks of is the daily assault on the poor by the rich through the various forms of sociopolitical inequality and injustice that he outlines during the course of his speech. He attacks the nascent Orléanist sociopolitical order and its supporters, apologists and profiteers – the rich, in a word – and seeks to hold them to account on behalf of the oppressed. He seeks to show the manner in which this war of rich on poor is waged institutionally by the government, primarily through the law and the tax system. 'Thirty million French people', Blanqui notes, 'pay a billion and a half to the tax office and about an equal amount to the privileged few. Meanwhile the proprietors, whose power must be protected by the whole of society, comprise two or three hundred thousand idlers who calmly devour the billions paid them' by the 'greedy rabble'. The present government, Blanqui summarizes, 'has no base other than this iniquitous distribution of benefits and burdens' that brings greater riches to the few and greater ruin to the many.[35] While the force and lucidity of such statements were Blanqui's alone, many of the basic ideas that informed them were not. As Jill Harsin notes, many radical republicans during this period believed that 'in order to understand society, one had to comprehend the economic and social relations between classes and the manifestation of these relationships in the government'. It followed that these 'republicans did not see the government as a neutral force, but rather as the repressive arm of the financial and commercial bourgeoisie who ruled'.[36]

Such a view underpinned the 'Defence Speech' and its scathing polemic against oligarchic and plutocratic rule. Blanqui states that the government 'has been established to serve only the exploitation of the poor by the rich' and 'has sought no other basis than an ignoble and brutal materialism'.[37] His central aim is to expose and denounce this corrupt and illegitimate sociopolitical structure as the primary cause of the injustice suffered in its name – the injustice present in the gap between the idle, wealthy elites and the impoverished, toiling multitude; the injustice of a tax system that is not simply unfair or unequal, but deadly: 'Workers are dying everywhere, crushed by taxes.'[38] The speech employs arrestingly violent metaphors to reinforce the idea that an order rooted in inequality, exploitation and oppression amounts to a systematic attack against the French people. Painting a somewhat different picture of the new order to the 'best of republics' lauded by contemporaries,[39] Blanqui, after Paul-Louis Courier, describes the Orléanist government as 'a suction pump that crashes the matter called the people, so as to suck the billions out of them and then pour them continuously into the coffers of a few idlers – a pitiless machine that grinds down twenty-five million peasants and five million workers, one by one, in order to extract their purest blood and transfuse it into the veins of the privileged'.[40] This is the political violence of everyday life for ordinary people, the social consequences of a political regime that serves only the aims and interests of the privileged few, that actively wages war on the poor. 'The workings of this machine, whose cogs are assembled with amazing artistry,' Blanqui declares, 'affect the poor every minute of the day, pursuing them in the most basic necessities of their humble lives, taking half of the most meagre of their earnings and the most miserable of their pleasures.'[41] As Maurice Dommanget points out, this marvellously built machine exploiting and oppressing the mass of the population on behalf of the privileged class is of course the state. In this respect Blanqui's analysis is highly innovative, Dommanget goes on to argue; its basic insights paved the way for the theory of the state later taken up by Marx and developed in turn by Lenin.[42]

Does Dommanget have a case for such claims? One can undoubtedly discover echoes of Blanqui's words in certain passages of the *Communist Manifesto*, for example, be it in the description of proletarians as 'slaves of the bourgeois class and of the bourgeois state', or in the claim that 'the executive of the modern state is but a committee for managing the common affairs of the whole bourgeoisie'.[43] Later, in *The Civil War in France*, Marx would note how 'at the same pace at which the progress of modern industry developed, widened, intensified the class antagonism between capital and labour, the State power assumed more and more the character of the national power of capital over labour, of a public force organized for social enslavement, of a machine of class despotism'.[44] Blanqui is likewise close to Lenin's observation, among the repeated exhortations to 'smash the bourgeois state machine', that 'under the rule of the bourgeoisie ... working people are enslaved' and 'democracy is restricted, cramped, curtailed, mutilated by all the conditions of wage slavery, and the poverty and misery of the people'.[45] However, given the obvious lacunae of Blanqui's analysis – questions such as the state's historical origins and development, the institutional and ideological apparatuses of state power or how France compares to other countries on this score remain largely unexplored or altogether absent – one should be wary not to overstate his overall theoretical contribution to this issue.

Analytical limitations aside, Dommanget is certainly correct to highlight the basic political significance of Blanqui's recognition of and insistence on the inherent link between burgeoning forms of capitalist production, the intensification of exploitation and the political forms and forces at work in such processes. Blanqui's depiction of the state as a machine is particularly perceptive in this respect. It makes clear that the capitalist state is not a natural and inevitable development or a neutral mediator of social affairs but a consciously constructed and purposefully wielded instrument, deliberately directed towards specific ends in order to satisfy specific interests. The state, in other words, acts on behalf of the dominant classes: it maintains their rule, it protects their power and privilege, it advances their interests – in short, it wages their struggle against the subordinate classes.

Structural oppression and mass impoverishment are as such neither natural nor unavoidable, Blanqui shows, but the necessary conditions of a sociopolitical order in which the few maintain their wealth and privilege on the back of the exploitation of the many. The rich, he writes, like all slave-owners – again one finds here the concept of wage slavery in all but name – employ workers 'so as to nourish their all-consuming idleness from the sweat of these workers. Even if they agree to leave their victims just enough bread to spare them from death, they do so only out of self-interest, just as one might add a few drops of oil onto the cogs of a mechanism to prevent rust from causing it to break down.'[46] Note the description of the workers as 'victims'; the term reinforces the view of the existing economic order as a 'permanent social war', to use a phrase from 'Communism, the Future of Society' (1869),[47] in which the poor were not only the prime or unavoidable but the necessary casualty, the forever vanquished. Indeed, Blanqui acknowledges how the fear of starvation binds the masses into this order and this social conflict in which the privileged invariably have the upper hand. For with the possession of the instruments of labour, the idle aristocracy or the capitalists[48] also possess the power to starve the population.[49]

It would be wrong to suggest, however, that Blanqui conceives power solely in terms of coercive force. He recognizes that, when it does occur, the amelioration of the masses' material conditions in particular can serve to generate popular support for a despotic regime, as witnessed under the Second Empire. Similarly, popular mis-education, though depicted as nothing less than a form of violence such is the injustice it represents, is nevertheless reproduced on an everyday basis, Blanqui insists, by institutions like the Church, schools and the press. But whether coercive or seemingly consensual, whether imposed through direct force or ideological mystification, all these forms of class power are different fronts of the same civil war.

Overall, then, the suffering of the people is not an unfortunate, disagreeable yet on the whole negligible or contingent consequence of an otherwise humane, largely free and equal society. Suffering is at once a product and a component of the sociopolitical order; it is, as Blanqui's metaphor strikingly conveys, the essential lubricant that enables the machine to function. 'It is in the interest of the wealthy,' Blanqui writes, 'that the workers are able to perpetuate their miserable flesh so as to bring into the world the children of the slaves who are destined one day to serve the children of the oppressors, and thereby continue from one generation to the next this dual, parallel inheritance of opulence and poverty, of pleasure and pain, that constitutes our social order.'[50] The humanism of Blanqui's project will now also be clear. All of his reflections on injustice and inequality turn on their human impact, on the manner in which the everyday degradation and dehumanization of ordinary people are intrinsic to a social order that is organized solely to serve the interests of wealth, property and privilege. It is the misery, pain, harm and destruction caused by exploitation and domination that leads Blanqui to assert the invariably conflictual nature of the order that produces them.

## Revolution and repression in perspective

Blanqui's concept of civil war is informed by two principal concerns. On the one hand, he explores struggle and conflict at a structural level. As we have seen, great emphasis is placed on the unseen or unrecognized cruelty and suffering of everyday life for ordinary people, what Johan Galtung has since called structural violence.[51] To depict a latent social war is to foreground the conflict of interests that lies at the heart of the established order and that underpins its entire functioning. On the other hand, Blanqui conceives civil war as the actual, and often extremely violent, outburst of these opposing sociopolitical interests in the form of revolutions, riots and uprisings. It was in these episodic moments of sociopolitical upheaval, of popular revolt and state repression alike, that for Blanqui the true nature of politics and society could be clearly seen, understood and learned from.

A persistent concern in Blanqui's writings is the status quo's recourse to violence. Considering the period in question it is easy to see why. From witnessing the White Terror during the Restoration[52] to hearing of the mass bloodshed in Paris in 1871, the series of state repressions that punctuated the nineteenth century had a profound effect on Blanqui, providing grounds for critical reflection as both actor and onlooker. All informed, challenged or reinforced his political practice. All provided evidence, he concluded, of the war of rich against poor, of a conflict in which 'the blood of the workers' was forever on the hands of the reactionaries.[53]

Here as elsewhere the French Revolution is central to Blanqui's thinking. The struggle of the masses against the bourgeoisie 'has been relentlessly waged' since 1789, he writes. The conflict between these two social groups is indeed 'forever the same yet forever new'.[54] The events of 1848 in particular reconfirmed this. As Blanqui declared in November of that year, 'the struggle of 1793 has just begun to start up again', pitting the same forces against each other as half-a-century earlier.[55] This struggle had already been apparent seven months earlier in Rouen, which witnessed major clashes following the 23 April elections. It was therefore necessary to place 'The Massacre in Rouen', as a text produced by the Société Républicaine Centrale (which Blanqui led) is titled, within a much longer history. For this new 'royalist terror' of 1848 brought certain eternal truths to light: not only is the counter-revolution reliant on violence to maintain its power – it relishes bloodshed. The 'hired assassins of a fallen dynasty' were 'thirsty for a bloody revenge'. Hence these 'cowardly admirers of force', whose repression in Rouen, as the text declares, surpassed the notorious April 1834 rue Transnonain massacre in Paris, embodied the bloody spectre of counter-revolution that haunted all popular uprisings. Events in Rouen thereby merely marked the latest episode in a long-standing conflict: 'These are exactly the same executioners and the same victims! On one side are the frenzied bourgeois, inciting to carnage stupid soldiers whom they have gorged on wine and hatred. On the other side, poor and defenceless workers falling under the bullets and bayonets of the assassins!'[56] And yet, despite the counter-revolution's continual and consistent recourse to violence, it is still the Terror of 1793 that is only ever mentioned. Blanqui offers a different version of events. 'Who spilled the first blood of the Revolution?', he asks. 'You! Who spilled the last? You!'[57] Both this political sequence itself and the history that recounts it attest to the age-old struggle between the oppressor and the oppressed for supremacy. Both also attest that the oppressor will stop at nothing when faced with any threat to its power and privilege.

What is particularly striking in Blanqui's thought is the manner in which both these forms of state and insurrectionary violence are explicitly linked to the social order they respectively seek to enforce or overthrow. 'Reaction simply followed its vocation when it slit democracy's throat'[58] in 1848, he remarks, indeed it always pursues its interests and achieves its goals by the same means – 'brutality, violence'[59] – whatever the political climate. It is in this sense that the war between rich and poor depicted in the 1832 'Defence Speech' should be read: Blanqui turns the prevailing conception of (active) aggressor and (passive) victim on its head. Like other contemporaries on the republican left, he seeks to 'redefine the nature of violence', recasting the roles of victims and aggressors in order to show that 'a government that allowed its citizens to starve was itself committing a violent act'.[60] It is, then, not the insurgent poor but the orderly rich who are the real aggressors in this social war. Yet the rich have the audacity to blame their victims.[61] 'How strange,' Blanqui noted again in 1836, 'that those who cause suffering accuse those who suffer of barbarism!'[62] The task, not to say the duty, as Blanqui sees it, is to expose the fundamental order of things, the background of starvation and suffering which pushes people to choose death in a revolt for justice over a life of enduring injustice.[63]

It would certainly seem that Blanqui has some notion of personal–direct violence on the one hand and structural–impersonal violence on the other, to employ Galtung's terms, often seeking to bring into relief the relationship between the two.[64] Again, perhaps nowhere is this clearer than in his reflections on the French Revolution. Before 1789 popular suffering was socially prescribed, Blanqui claims. 'History up until that point is nothing but the eternal tale of your ferocity and of the brutality of the punishments you inflicted. You reigned by the sword for 1,400 years.'[65] Therein lies the historico-political function of the Terror of 1793: it breaks the cycle of social violence; it is the moment 'when the people, having broken their chains, turned fear and dread back on their tyrants'; a 'deliverance', its aim was 'to fight, with its own weapons, the eternal terror that weighed upon humanity'.[66] Blanqui challenges those who, in the face of the explosive upheaval of the Revolution, are blinded to the far greater 'eternal' violence of society under the *ancien régime*, as if the Terror were a violent aberration on an otherwise peaceful historical plane.

Civil war is thus latent and explosive, ongoing and momentary, structure and event. But whether 'oppression takes the form of military or commercial aristocracy' or 'the people are exploited by the sabre or the coin', whether seen in 'the sufferings of the peasant trampled by his master's steed' or heard in 'agony of the worker whose blood serves to oil the gears of the industrial overlord', all these forms of violence are products of a sociopolitical order based on private property.[67] All the violence and suffering of French society – including the masses' unenlightened ignorance – are fundamentally rooted in the 'monopoly of property'.[68] These are the 'disastrous consequences of a social law that concentrates all wealth in the hands of a few and that confers on a privileged caste the vast majority of the population's right to life or death'.[69] It is property that has brought about the 'horrific degradation of a great people'.[70] As Blanqui summarizes in one particularly instructive note:

> Oppression has certainly triumphed everywhere and always, up to the present day, but not without a fight. History is nothing but a long account of this fierce battle. It has chronicled the bloody victories of property, its dreadful laws, its merciless rule. Property has only been able to protect itself through the torture and suffering it has meted out in response to the instinctive and unconscious demands of labour. What we are beginning to see clearly in the annals of every people is the ferocity of the methods employed to maintain the enslavement of the worker and the domination of the property owner.[71]

Property is inequality is violence – whether witnessed in the social order itself or during an uprising against it. Such is one of the essential lessons of the Lyon *canuts* (silk weavers) revolt of November 1831: those workers who do rise up against a social order in which they each figure as a mere 'machine man' will face an uncompromising military repression; they will be exterminated 'to the last man' and dealt with like an 'invasion of locusts', dehumanized in revolt as in daily life.[72] Workers indeed face a stark choice:

> Extermination or humble acceptance of their duty – this is the only alternative offered to the workers. The duty of the workers is to consider themselves as machines that operate in order to create pleasures enjoyed by the privileged. The duty of the workers is to die of poverty upon the silk fabrics they weave for the rich; the duty of the workers is to … see their wives and children slowly perish, consumed by famine, and then to expire themselves.[73]

Or as Blanqui states more concisely in 1850: 'Servitude or death – this is the motto of extermination adopted by the rich.'[74]

For Blanqui and his followers, popular revolt 'helped to clarify the terms of the struggle, ever-present but often obscured'.[75] After the *canuts* revolts of the early 1830s, the June Days of 1848 illuminated things; after Lyon, Paris set the record straight once again. Where the *Réveil* newspaper evoked 'the misunderstanding of June [1848]', for Blanqui the exact opposite was true. 'Never have we understood each other so clearly as on that day'.[76] Gustave Tridon, one of Blanqui's closest followers and a leading intellectual figure of the Blanquist movement that emerged during the Second Empire, would make a similar point in September 1870 just as the Prussian siege of Paris began. It is all too easy, Tridon argues, for the well-fed bourgeoisie to preach class cooperation. For the poor, hunger dispels this fantasy. Conditions in Paris during the Franco-Prussian War are not an exception, Tridon writes, but the manifest extension and intensification of everyday injustice. The rich gorge themselves on the boulevards while the people of Belleville are dying from starvation. That this situation is avoidable through rationing renders it even more disgraceful. The need of the many must be placed above the greed of the few. Reprising the line of thinking developed by his master, Tridon infers from the hunger and starvation devastating the poor neighbourhoods of the French capital a vital political lesson: 'There is no fraternity between the tiger and its prey, between the oppressor and its victim'.[77] Little time was required before Tridon received further confirmation of his hypothesis, for just eight months later the *semaine sanglante* destroyed any remaining illusions of 'republican fraternity'.[78]

For Blanqui, it was with these momentary outbursts of an ongoing civil war that many fundamental social illusions were exposed, many political realities revealed. Such moments of open political conflict have the potential to sharpen latent social antagonisms, Blanqui believes. But the extent to which the people as a whole could grasp these realities and act upon them is no less of a problem, he equally believes, and it is this view that will lead him to assume the need for an enlightened leadership that is capable of revealing to the people the real state of things. If we put that issue to one side, however, the underlying political point no doubt still retains its force of insight. Eric Hazan speaks of the 'immense truth effect' produced by the recurring defeats of the nineteenth century. 'Defeat suddenly reveals the true nature of the enemy,' Hazan writes, 'it dissolves the consensus, dismantles the ideological mystifications of domination. No political analysis, no press campaign, no electoral struggle, so clearly bears a message as the spectacle of people being shot in the street.'[79] And yet if the violence upholding the status quo was clear for all to see in 1830–4, 1848 and 1870–1, these were only the localized explosions of a much wider and more sustained social struggle rooted in the injustices and inequalities of private property, and waged through the policies and practices of the state. Behind seeming political tranquillity and social harmony, for Blanqui as for Hazan, the civil war continues 'by other means'.[80] Where destitution and oppression abound, a political conflict is being fought. Starvation and the everyday suffering of ordinary people are fully within the domain of politics; as such, they require political solutions.

## No half measures

So far we have seen that as long as private property exists, no matter when or what its form, a privileged few will maintain control of production and reap its fruits, the state will act on behalf of this group, enforcing its rule and defending its interests, and, in all such respects, a war will be waged against the mass of the people. Blanqui's first move is to go from the recognition of conflict in material, human experience to the naming of it in thought.

How, then, are these observations translated into first principles and concrete practice? Blanqui's response is simple: a diagnosis of politics as conflict calls for a full engagement in that very conflict. So follows the necessity of taking sides, of completely rejecting any appeals to consensus or cooperation in the resolute waging of this struggle.

### Two irreconcilable principles

Across Blanqui's life there is clear continuity between the analysis of contemporary political struggles on the one hand and the affirmation of an intensely principled political theory on the other. The intellectual origins of this battle of first principles can be traced to his reflections on the politics of the July Monarchy.

Tautological manoeuvres – Louis-Philippe was crowned 'King of the French' (a title taken from the 1791 constitution) rather than 'King of France and Navarre', as the Restoration monarchs had styled themselves – could not conceal the fact that a monarchical order, a so-called political 'compromise', had been illegitimately imposed on the people. Against the claims to have created with the new Orléanist regime 'a popular throne surrounded by republican institutions', a 'republican monarchy' led by a 'citizen king',[81] for Blanqui there was only 'the monarchical monarchy and the republican republic'. 'In France there are and can only be royalists and republicans,' he states, unambiguously.[82] Between the principle of legitimacy and the principle of popular sovereignty 'there is no third flag, no middle term'.[83]

Blanqui appealed to the same logic when faced with a similar political conjuncture twenty years later. President Louis-Napoleon, Blanqui argues, only receives lukewarm support. By the same token, however, 'he has against him only muted hostility from the various parties. No love, but no hatred either. He is no one's total enemy.' Just as the soon-to-be-crowned Napoleon III – a 'counter-revolutionary dictator protected by the mask of a parvenu'[84] – revealed the threat of supposed consensus, so too had the Orléanist '*juste milieu*' been a cunning façade that enabled inequality and oppression to continue as before.[85] Early and late, Blanqui recognizes that the war against the poor is often waged through deceit and manipulation more than actual physical violence.[86] The idea peddled by the press of the rich – and shared, we should note, by all of the most notable pre-1848 French socialist thinkers in their various appeals to bourgeoisie and proletariat alike[87] – that unity is possible between the people and the privileged few, that equality and emancipation can be achieved through class cooperation, must therefore be fully rejected. Attempts to portray social cohesion and harmony, in which the mutual necessity of working together seemingly reveals a common interest between capitalist and worker, are tantamount to reconciling Cain and Abel, the lion and the lamb. Class conflict, not class cooperation, is for Blanqui a sociopolitical reality. 'The classes only subsist on condition of boundless tyranny on the one hand and absolute submission on the other.'[88]

Neutrality is not an option. To renounce any form of conviction or passion, to claim impartiality 'between those who suffer and those who cause suffering' is, as the 'But du journal' of *Le Libérateur* unequivocally states, a cowardly, dishonest illusion – hence the newspaper, subtitled the 'Newspaper of the Oppressed', is explicit and unashamed about its allegiance and aims.[89] Blanqui is himself emphatic that his writings in the newspaper express his 'profound convictions', convictions that are 'mortally hostile to the social order in which we live'.[90] For an 'honest man' must 'avow loudly and clearly his loves and his hates. Those who pride themselves on neither loving nor hating anyone should be pitied'.[91] Any talk of a so-called *juste milieu* is an 'absurdity' that only serves to delay the necessary moment at which people will take sides and choose, 'according to their passion and their interest', between two opposing principles.[92]

Blanqui knows that he is not alone in seeing past the obfuscatory conflation of first principles. While one part of the aristocracy – 'the most rotten part, which wants gold and pleasure above all else' – may temporarily welcome Louis-Philippe's advances and support the July Monarchy out of its own opportunistic self-interest, 'the other part,' he notes, 'the one I shall call the least gangrenous or corrupted (so as not to use the use the word *honourable*), the part that has some self-respect and faith in its opinions, which worships its flag and its pious memories – that part disgustedly rejects the cajolery of the *juste milieu*'.[93] One discovers in this passage from the early 1830s an important insight into Blanqui's thought. A certain degree of respect – albeit very minor – is professed for an outright adversary precisely because they too, through their principled integrity, dismiss the idea of a middle ground or middle course as a nonsense. In this conflict of morals, passions and interests, the fundamental choice at stake could not be clearer. In the 'war of ideas', so Blanqui insists, 'neither peace nor truce' was possible, and 'the combat must always end with the destruction of one of the parties'.[94] The relationship between equality and privilege and the social groups that represent these principles – however much they may deny or obfuscate this fact – is but one of irreconcilable enemies. One side will be overpowered. Which will prevail?[95]

Formulated in response to the consensual pretences of the Orléanist order, this politics of clear and principled conviction was conceptually extended to underpin Blanqui's entire project thereafter. As the century progressed and even republicanism had become appropriated by reactionary forces, it seems that Blanqui indeed felt compelled to restate the essence of his doctrine in the late 1860s. Citing Jules Ferry's claim to be a 'Republican, but a conservative

Republican', Blanqui retorts that 'a conservative Republican' is no different to 'a conservative Royalist'. True politics is rooted in the assumption that 'there are only two parties: those who want to conserve the current social order, and those who do not want to conserve it. Everything else is nothing but a sham, a mask'.[96] All interests, choices and actions are reducible to this basic social conflict. The task of politics, therefore, is to clarify the terms of the conflict. In the face of opportunistic appropriation and deceitful equivocation, Blanqui seeks to return politics to an either/or, to its essential alternatives: equality or privilege, freedom or servitude, revolution or reaction.

## Practical implications

Political practice must therefore cut through the veil of illusory rhetoric and deceptive manoeuvring and act according to the actual state of things.

In the first instance, this means rejecting any form of tepid reformism as a matter of course. Certain texts may appear to suggest that Blanqui's programme is based around a set of fairly moderate reforms (some readers have noted that the proposals outlined in the 'Defence Speech', for example – which calls for universal suffrage so as to allow the French people to choose their government and legislators; for an equitable, progressive tax and credit system; and for the Stock Exchange, and its 'disastrous swindling', to be replaced with a system of national banks[97] – are not particularly radical in themselves, even by contemporary standards).[98] But to think of Blanqui's proposals within our own understanding of 'reform' is misleading. As Dominique Le Nuz points out, 'social reforms' and 'social revolution' are broadly synonymous terms for Blanqui.[99] His seemingly modest reforms will not and cannot be realized within the existing order, for they are incompatible with it. Their condition of possibility is the fundamental redistribution of wealth and power – that is, the fundamental reorganization of society. 'Let the people choose', Blanqui repeated in the wake of the revolutionary movement's failure to implement a clear and uncompromising socialist programme in 1848: 'Either slavery or the complete transformation of society! Half-measures are their ruin.'[100] Only structural change can end structural servitude. And structural change is first and foremost a matter of direct popular empowerment. 'The people do not need alms,' so the 'Defence Speech' explains, 'they aim to secure their own well-being themselves.' Collective self-determination means that 'the people want to make the laws that should govern them, and they will make them. Laws will then no longer be made against them; they will be made for them because they will be made by them.'[101]

Acts of charity or any minor concessions conceded to the people must be dismissed, then, just as an exclusively legal path to social justice must be rejected. Indeed, as we saw in Chapter 1, in Blanqui's eyes the mere existence of a law did not mean that it was not 'ridiculous', 'odious' or 'immoral'. The rich, to be sure, hide behind the 'abstract word' of the law so as not to confront the suffering produced and reproduced by or in the name of that very law.[102] 'When powerful men abuse it,' Rousseau had declared, 'the law becomes an offensive weapon for them and a shield against the weak, and the pretext of public security is always the most dangerous scourge of the people.'[103] Like Rousseau, Blanqui seeks to expose legally sanctioned injustice, particularly when justified in the name of public order. Against the belief that 'the law should be respected because it is the law', for Blanqui the law 'should only be respected if it is rooted in public conscience or consciousness and in justice. Anything outside of this is nothing but brute force.'[104] The struggle for justice does not recognize and will not yield to illegitimate forces.

Like Machiavelli, who claims that to change society one must first take and then retain political power, Blanqui assumes that social emancipation can only be realized through political struggle. Universal freedom and happiness, in other words, are a matter of mass mobilization, popular force and militant organization. This marks the clearest difference between Blanqui and the 'utopian' socialists. What linked the various utopian-inspired projects of the nineteenth century, from the *phalanstères* of Fourier to the Icarian communities of Cabet, overall was the attempt to change society through forms of social withdrawal and localized association. Equality would (and could only) be created in the confined isolation of rural France or the United States, not here. In direct contrast, Blanqui's project to seize centralized state power in Paris in order to institute popular rule across France affirms the transformative potential of collective political action here and now. Socialism, for Blanqui, is not about theorists 'inventing the future' in the abstract;[105] it is only through collectively working to realize the principle of equality that its actual form will become clear, as we shall see in Chapter 4.

One must not deny or retreat from the social conflict, Blanqui accordingly maintained across the course of his life, but recognize and confront it head on, directly and immediately, through organized revolutionary struggle. This is one of central messages of the 'Letter to Maillard': to be a socialist is to be a revolutionary, and vice versa. Not all socialists were so, of course, Blanqui is keen to remind his interlocutor. The likes of Louis Blanc, Alexandre Ledru-Rollin and other prominent figures in the Provisional Government of 1848, not to mention the 'utopian' socialists, were, in Blanqui's eyes, *'peaceable socialists*, desk-bound men of a quiet and peaceful character, who are not at home in the midst of tumult and weapons'. Evading the question of how actually to overthrow the old order and make revolution – and in some cases wary of doing so at all – they were 'revolutionaries in ideas alone'. Blanqui's revolutionary socialism, by contrast, unifies revolutionary thought with revolutionary action; it is in every respect a 'practical socialism', as he terms it, a politics rooted in the exigencies of the practical so as to realize the possible.[106] How, Blanqui asks, will equality and justice be achieved? What will this take? Any deviation from the practical imperatives of popular empowerment – any failure to recognize the necessity of an organized and determined insurgent force, of the seizure of power and of the overpowering of the enemy in the realization of this egalitarian principle – would forever hold the same outcome, defeat, in all its consequences: 'holy water, then insults, and, finally, grapeshot – and destitution forever!' The choice, Blanqui insists, is the people's to make.[107]

The role of the republic within this schema is that of a vehicle for the principle. Blanqui sees the republic as but a (political) means or form to realize the (social) end; it is not the definitive means, still less the end in and of itself: 'The republic is not a goal; it is only a means. Equality – that is our goal.'[108] Revolutionaries are, to be sure, 'profoundly indifferent to the form of society and go right to its basis instead' – to the struggle of equality against privilege.[109] They self-identify as republicans only because they 'hope the republic will succeed in implementing the social transformation that France so urgently calls for and which is its destiny'. But a caveat must be added: 'If the republic were to fail to fulfil this hope we would cease to be republicans, for in our eyes a form a government is not an end but a means, and we only want political reform as a step along the road to social reform.'[110] 'The Republic would be a lie if it were to be nothing more than the substitution of one form of government for another,' Blanqui's Société Républicaine Centrale later insisted in March 1848, when the struggle to determine the actual content of the new republic was still raging. 'Changing words is not enough; we must change things.' Therein lies the relationship between social transformation and the political form delivering it: 'The Republic means the emancipation of the workers; it means the end of the reign of exploitation; it means the advent of a new order that will free labour from the tyranny of capital.'[111] Any form of government, republican or otherwise, that failed to achieve such ends must be rejected and opposed. The social republic of nineteenth-century France is, then, it would seem, but another stage in the historical struggle to achieve real equality.[112]

## First principles

Blanqui's is a politics of principled conviction over opportunistic calculation. Alongside the rejection of any *juste milieu* on the grounds that the rhetoric of neutrality, the denial of passion or self-interest, are the mask that conceals the face of the continued material impoverishment and political disempowerment of the poor, Blanqui also rejects 'the politics of expedients' for 'the politics of principles'. So what is the content of these principles, and how does this link to the (more formal) concerns discussed above?

### Equality and justice

In his articles for *Le Libérateur* Blanqui traces a centuries-long conflict between privilege and equality – 'the two principles which have struggled over France since its infancy' – highlighting equality's successive struggles against various forms of exploitation, ignorance and oppression, struggles which have adopted different guises over time and across the world.[113] These writings certainly do not lack breadth and ambition. Blanqui's perennial concern with political practice in the present is always understood in relation to a much wider historical struggle over the basic structure and organization of society – over the ownership of property, the distribution of wealth and the exercise of power. In many ways Blanqui sees himself as the contemporary agent of a historical, if not eternal, struggle that transcends the temporal and geographical boundaries to which his thought is often reduced and confined.

'Equality Is Our Flag'. This declaration – the title of an article from *Le Libérateur* – heralds the arrival of the core, animating principle, alongside justice, of Blanqui's project. Against mere equality before the law or equality of opportunity, Blanqui seeks, as he later explained in 1852, 'real equality between citizens and the overthrow of all castes and all tyrannies'.[114] Equality means the abolition of 'all forms of exploitation of man by man' – that is, in the first instance, the abolition of private property, understood as the origin of all other forms of exploitation.[115] Equality means the end of egoism, suffering, the usurpation of natural rights and the enforcement of autocratic rule – all of which are not only profoundly harmful and destructive but also utterly irrational, hence equality is not only 'possible' but 'necessary'.[116] Based on the 'equal sharing of the burdens and the benefits of society', the reign of equality 'imposes on everyone equal duties' and 'grants the same rights'; it guarantees the 'dignity' of all.[117] As 'the principle of order and eternal justice', equality seeks 'to heal the hideous wounds inflicted by privilege'.[118] The highest expression of enlightened thought, equality seeks to establish unity, fraternity and 'the well-being of all' on earth; it will bring an end to 'the distinction between the privileged and the proletarians', which 'will be its greatest service to humanity'. Put simply: 'Equality, common law – these two words sum up all of our projects for [material] amelioration and for social reform.'[119] Where egoism and competition, hatred and isolation, war and destruction, servitude and misery, ignorance and deceit once reigned, unity and fraternity, association and collective well-being, peace and dignity, freedom and happiness, enlightenment and probity would emerge.

Blanqui does not appear to have strict definitions of equality and justice; neither seems to have any single, precise meaning. Indeed he tends to employ the notions almost interchangeably. At times justice is described (using the same terms as when explaining the meaning of equality) as the universal 'unity of rights and duties', or equality and solidarity are said to be the meaning of justice.[120] 'Justice is,' he claims, as we saw in the previous chapter, 'the only true criterion that applies to human things.'[121] Elsewhere, however, as we have seen above and will see again below, equality is understood as the overarching principle through which justice derives its essential meaning.

In more concrete terms, equality and justice could not be achieved through 'the equal distribution of the land among all members of society', Blanqui insists, for this would merely recreate individual property ownership and private possession of the instruments of labour. 'It would lead only to an extreme division of property that would, at bottom, change nothing of the right to property itself'. The 'spirit of individualism' would have 'all its force ... left intact'. Large-scale properties would be gradually reconstructed and social inequality would promptly return. Individualism and 'the reign of individual property' can only be overcome by collective ownership of the land and of the instruments of labour – that is, through 'a regime of association'.[122] And indeed communism, as Blanqui understands it, is 'nothing but the (final) stage of association'.[123] But beyond holding up the ideal of association or communism, Blanqui offers no further insights into the functioning of such a system – again, an intentional omission on his part, for he renounces any capacity to prescribe in advance the ends of an emancipatory process. A passage from 'Communism, the Future of Society' provides a useful insight into this relationship between first principles and prospective sociopolitical arrangements. 'Under the communitarian regime,' Blanqui writes, 'what is good profits everyone and what is bad profits no one. Good harvests are a blessing, poor ones a calamity. No one benefits from that which causes harm to others; no one suffers from that which is advantageous to others. Everything is organised according to justice and reason.'[124] Just as we saw with Blanqui's critique of property, the point is not to provide a detailed outline of what equality and justice might look like in practice so much as to maintain them as guiding principles in the collective realization and eventual organization of social arrangements. The revolution, Blanqui accordingly notes in deliberately broad terms, 'must be carried out for the benefit of labour against the tyranny of capital, and must reconstitute society on the basis of justice'.[125]

## The struggle over words

The relationship between equality and freedom is a problematic yet politically significant issue worth considering. In the first instance Blanqui is more or less clear: 'Democracy with the principle of authority means the Asian system of government, the equality of slaves. Democracy with freedom means the modern idea, the equality of citizens.'[126] Until 1848 – and sometimes after[127] – the evocation of such terms or indeed of the tripartite republican motto often remain unqualified in Blanqui's writings. But in the wake of 1848 and during the Second Empire the extent to which words like 'democracy' and particularly 'freedom' had been or were being appropriated by reactionary forces increasingly drew Blanqui's attention. He noted how a certain notion of freedom, conceived broadly in the liberal sense as the absence of interference, is ultimately invoked in order to legitimize the domination and exploitation of one individual or group by another (freedom in this sense amounts to 'the freedom to enslave, the freedom to exploit at will, the freedom of the great and the good') and is accompanied by a belief in equality before the law as the only possible form of equality.[128] Blanqui himself, however, not only conceives freedom in terms of emancipation from domination and exploitation – dispossessed of the instruments of labour and at the mercy of those who own them, the working masses are not free, as we have seen – but also insists that freedom and equality are indivisible. 'There cannot be, there is no equality without freedom. Only equality can establish and preserve freedom.'[129] The end of exploitation alone is capable of bringing about the end of domination, and vice versa. But under no circumstances could freedom be separated from equality as its sine qua non condition, for 'without equality, there is no other freedom than the freedom to oppress'.[130] Appeals to freedom in the name of cupidity and egoism strip the word of its real meaning and mislead the people, Blanqui argues. Those, like himself, who uphold the true sense of freedom – and in so doing demarcate the parameters of their specific political space and its distance from the nefarious forces of opportunistic manipulation – are therefore left with no choice: 'Let us remove this word from our dictionary. It has been dishonoured and disgraced, for it has been uttered by the enemy. Equality, that is our watchword. It encompasses everything.'[131]

Blanqui's concern for the reactionary appropriation of once progressive notions no doubt resonates today. Take recent debates on the continued relevance of the word 'democracy'. If at times Alain Badiou voices scepticism as to whether the word can be salvaged from its contemporary usage,[132] on other occasions he is unequivocal: 'The enemy today is not called Empire or Capital. It is called Democracy.'[133] Blanqui explores a similar point. 'For thousands of years', he writes, individualism has continuously killed both freedom and the individual. How many individual members of the human race have managed to avoid becoming either its slaves or victims? One in every ten thousand, perhaps. Ten thousand martyrs for one executioner! Ten thousand slaves for one tyrant! And still they plead [against communism] in the name of freedom! I see what they are up to! What a sinister subterfuge, concealed behind a definition. Does not oligarchy call itself democracy, falsity honesty, slaughter moderation?[134]

The enemy has successfully hijacked certain words, once proclaimed beneath the 'popular flag', and redefined them as the 'diametrical opposite' of their original meaning: 'freedom' is now synonymous with 'slavery', 'duty' with 'egoism'.[135] 'Let us leave this word behind us', Blanqui therefore concludes with regard to 'democracy'. 'It has been dishonoured and disgraced ever since the henchmen of servitude ... took it up as their banner. Their tactic is to deceive the people by dressing themselves in our livery. An enemy ruse that puts on the uniform of the besieged in order to take their place.'[136] The aim behind this use of 'obscure words', Blanqui likewise told Maillard in 1852, is 'to prevent the two opposing flags from confronting each other directly, so as to cheat the victorious flag of the fruits of victory, and to allow the vanquished to join the victors gradually and smoothly once the fighting has ended'.[137] Here again we can appreciate the central importance Blanqui places on political clarity, on the imperative – which is as much a matter of practical necessity as it is of moral principle – of the unambiguous and explicit taking of sides. And so just as the word 'freedom' 'has been stolen by the oppressors in order to disguise tyranny', it follows that any word, however cherished, whose meaning has been changed or 'distorted' by the enemy so as to become an '[instrument] of iniquity' must be abandoned.[138]

No less than one hundred and fifty years apart, in both cases the same question nonetheless arises: when oligarchy operates under the banner of democracy and egoist greed is celebrated in the name of freedom, should we follow Blanqui and Badiou in discarding these terms? Just as both Blanqui and Badiou alike insist on retaining the true meaning of an equally contested and contentious notion like communism,[139] do democracy as the rule of the people and freedom as the collective transcendence of domination not also have enduring meanings worth salvaging? Commenting on this problem of 'central concepts of our political vocabulary' having been 'so corrupted that they are almost unusable', Michael Hardt offers a perceptive response. 'We could abandon these terms and invent new ones,' writes Hardt, 'but we would leave behind the long history of struggles, dreams and aspirations that are tied to them. I think it is better to fight over the concepts themselves in order to restore or renew their meaning.'[140] Commitment to first principles must surely extend to this task. To disavow such concepts for the sake of maintaining at all costs their original meaning or their divisive function is to concede victory to the usurpers, surrendering to their hegemonic triumphs; it is to abandon the terrain on which the struggle for principles that help to define and shape what is politically possible is won or lost. 'Liberty! Equality! Fraternity! This motto that adorns the pediments of our buildings must not become a hollow architectural embellishment', Blanqui's own club wrote in 1848. A politics of principles is undoubtedly at its most forceful when engaging in this struggle over words and thereby opening up space for the division, choice and commitment it itself prescribes. As the club's proclamation continues: 'There is no freedom where there is a shortage of bread. There is no equality where opulence causes outrage in the midst of poverty. There is no fraternity where workers and their famished children grovel at palace gates.'[141] Blanqui fails to follow the logic of his own position to the end, seemingly abandoning a crucial question he himself once appeared to pose: what do we mean by genuine freedom, equality and fraternity?

Writing in the wake of the *semaine sanglante* of 21–8 May 1871, Marx concluded that 'there can be neither peace nor truce possible between the working men of France and the appropriators of their produce'.[142] Perhaps taking his lead from Marx, Walter Benjamin suggests that 'the Commune puts an end to the phantasmagoria holding sway over the early years of the proletariat. It dispels the illusion that the task of the proletarian revolution is to complete the work of 1789 hand in hand with the bourgeoisie. This illusion dominates the period 1831–71, from the Lyons uprising to the Commune'.[143] Reworking Benjamin's formulation, Eric Hazan pushes back the shattering of this 'illusion' to the June Days of 1848, adding that 'this is why, unlike July 1830 and February 1848, the June Days are absent from the annals of republican history'.[144] If, however, as Benjamin goes on to say, the 'bourgeoisie never shared in this error', for its 'battle against the social rights of the proletariat dates back to the great

Revolution', then before May 1871, before June 1848, Blanqui certainly never shared in this error either.

Blanqui's battle *for* the social rights of the proletariat dates back to his great revolution, July 1830. The experience of July and its aftermath dispelled any illusion of cooperation or neutrality to the point that their continued propagation was a dangerous, deceitful instrument wielded by the forces of reaction. Conflict in theory, conflict in practice, is the only maxim to which a revolutionary should subscribe. From this basic assumption Blanqui lays the groundwork for an understanding of the insurgent force popular power will necessarily demand, the obstacles it will necessarily face, the subjective resources it will necessarily require. In other words, it underpins his entire political project. The manner in which this also informs his conception of the people and the proletariat is explored in Chapter 3.

3

# Actors

*Society comprises rich and poor, powerful and weak, exploiters and exploited. One must choose between these two categories. Who could hesitate? Doing away with both of them is the true form of progress that we should pursue.*[1]

For a political project built on the basic assumption that social change only occurs through conscious and deliberate human action, that humans are capable of shaping their own destiny through what they know and do, the question of political agency logically follows.

We have seen that Blanqui conceives politics as an irreconcilable struggle of interests and ideals. The resulting understanding of society as divided into exploiters and exploited paves the way for a conception of the proletariat as a means of identifying and identifying with the exploited and their exploitation. So who or what exactly is this group with whose interests and ideals Blanqui so emphatically aligns himself? Is there, for Blanqui, a universal subject of history? How and when is this subject constituted? Does an oppressed class bring about the dissolution of class? Does one actor's own emancipation herald the emancipation of all? And how and when can or will this occur?

I begin this chapter by outlining the central features of Blanqui's proletariat before engaging with its critical interpretation, showing how and why many previous accounts are, in my opinion, flawed and misleading. Together with Rousseau, I suggest that reading Blanqui, the 'pre-Marxist', alongside two of the foremost 'post-Marxist' political theorists, Ernesto Laclau and Jacques Rancière, can, in certain ways, help us to appreciate the properly political dimensions of his proletariat. That is not to say, however, that Blanqui's proletariat is not a social group or sociological category, broadly speaking, or that Marx is a redundant point of reference here. Instead, we are dealing with a notion of the proletariat and the people that is at once a subjective political position (principled commitment to universal equality and freedom) and an objective social category (a group of people that is exploited and impoverished as a result of their socio-economic role, position and background), but that ultimately places primacy on the former.

# A political actor

## Two classes

Who are 'the people'? As we saw in Chapter 2, Blanqui sees the people as the majority of the population who are forced to work for – and are exploited by – a wealthy minority of idle, parasitic usurpers. This privileged few do not work, yet it is they, and not the workers, who own the instruments and enjoy the fruits of labour. In the first instance, then, Blanqui is clear: 'The people are all the citizens who work'; the people are 'the poor and labouring class', those who 'live by the sweat of their brow'.[2]

These exploited and impoverished workers have no representatives in power to defend their rights and interests.[3] Non-representation and non-recognition at the level of state and government have obvious consequences. 'Our current laws are all in favour of the rich,' Blanqui argues, 'and with our existing political organisation, things cannot be otherwise; our legislators have their own interests in mind, and our legislators are rich; they have the interests of their principals in mind, and their principals are rich.'[4] Designating the thirty million French people who live solely off their labour and are 'deprived of all the rights of the city',[5] as Blanqui famously declared in his 1832 'Defence Speech', the proletariat are defined by their exclusion. In a system that 'concentrates the three powers [legislative, judicial and executive] in the hands of a small number of privileged people who are united by the same interests', a system that thereby constitutes 'the most monstrous of tyrannies', 'the proletarian remains on the outside'.[6] The proletarians are all those who have no right to education, whose voice and interests are simply unrecognized by the government, the legal system and the press.[7] As Blanqui reaffirmed in 1869, the established order is comprised of 'two categories': 'the privileged and the pariahs'.[8]

Immediately we are struck by two points. First, we see that Blanqui's subject is an extremely wide and inclusive, not to say imprecise, construction, employing catch-all terms to designate, in the broadest possible sense, the unprivileged many as distinct from the privileged few. 'Class', where it appears in relation to the former group, denotes an approximate set of common sociopolitical properties or attributes: labour, exploitation, impoverishment, powerlessness. Second, and directly following the first point, 'the proletariat' and 'the people', along with 'the multitude', 'the poor', 'the masses', 'the plebs' and 'the oppressed', are employed as interchangeable synonyms, to the extent that Blanqui will switch between the terms in the course of a few lines.[9] Hereafter I will therefore do likewise. (We shall return to the import and implications of these two characteristics below.)

Contemporary struggles, and the reactions they provoked, informed Blanqui's outlook on this issue. After July 1830, the *canuts* (silk workers) revolt in Lyon of 21 November–3 December 1831 was a formative event in this respect. A few days after the government had sent in thousands of troops to regain control of the city, an article from the *Journal des Débats* gained notoriety for suggesting that the uprising had revealed 'a grave secret, that of society's internal struggle between the class that owns [property] and that which does not own [property]'. The author, Saint-Marc Girardin, continues: 'The barbarians who threaten society are neither in the Caucasus nor in the steppes of Tartary; they are in the *faubourgs* of our industrial cities. ... It is there that one finds the danger to modern society; it is from there that the barbarians who will destroy it will come.'[10] The article seemed to articulate what many across the political spectrum were thinking: not only the existence of a society split into two groups – the proletariat and the privileged[11] – but that the former were debased and depraved feral animals with the 'appetites of beasts', and who were indeed 'doomed to a bestial existence', as Blanqui subsequently declared.[12] It is in this sense that the struggle of the proletariat is for Blanqui the struggle of the 'rabble' – the anonymous masses who provoke fear and revulsion, who are said to pose a threat to social peace and public order, who are vehemently despised by and deliberately excluded from the established regime.

Another significant point of reference in Blanqui's thinking here is Roman history. The people, according to Blanqui, are the modern-day plebe. The 1832 'Defence Speech', to be sure, speaks of 'the plebeian flag of 1830'.[13]

Elsewhere, a text thought to be written just prior to the first edition of *Le Libérateur* in 1834 explores the lineage between the proletariat of ancient Rome and the nineteenth-century usage of the term to designate 'the immense majority of French people'.[14] Responding to the reproach that allusion to the Roman proletariat is an anachronistic misnomer under a regime in which all are equal before the law, the text notes that the condition of the proletariat in Rome – whose triumphs on the battlefield were only for the benefit of the patricians; who in return for completing the most gruelling public works received nothing but hatred and ill treatment from the aristocracy; who were granted no political rights in return for their service to the country; who were quite simply 'crossed off the list of men, and reduced to the level of beasts' – is precisely the condition of the workers and peasants in Orléanist France. The proletariat of both ancient Rome and nineteenth-century France, the text states, in terms used almost verbatim by Marx and Engels in *The German Ideology*, 'bear all of the burdens of society, without enjoying any of its advantages'.[15] It is the proletariat who built society only to be excluded from it. It is the proletariat who are dehumanized to the point of having their humanity denied altogether. It is the proletariat who the self-appointed guardians of 'civilisation' treat as 'barbarians' (the text cites the *Journal des Débats* article noted above).[16] The sociopolitics of Rome could be transposed quite easily to contemporary sociopolitical groups, interests and struggles, Blanqui again claims in 1855. 'We represent neither the patricians nor the praetorians. We are their common enemy, the people of the catacombs, digging beneath them the tomb that must engulf them all.'[17]

The people do not have 'the right to live' a life of freedom and happiness.[18] The people are treated as slaves by the law.[19] The people, in short, 'are nothing, they count for nothing'.[20] So begins a cycle of political exclusion and material suffering. Under Louis-Philippe's 'government of the rich … the fate of the proletarian is similar to that of the serf and the Negro – his life is nothing but a long catalogue of misery, fatigue and suffering'.[21] The material realities of this deliberate and sustained deprivation, the everyday experiences of ordinary people, are crucial to Blanqui's social critique. He thus speaks of 'the existence of two very distinct classes of men, two great social categories': 'on one hand the pleasures of abundance, the advantages of civilisation and all the privileges of idleness; on the other hand the horrors of destitution, the ills of ignorance and the hereditary distribution [*partage*] of the toughest work combined with the most dreadful hardships'.²²

## France and Paris

Three further points should be established. First, in direct contrast to the cowardice and corruption of the bourgeoisie, Blanqui depicts the people as the true representative of France. Bourgeois egoism has no concern for *la patrie*. The bourgeoisie would soon sell the country down the river in favour of personal gain, as occurred after 1830.²³ The common destiny of the country is therefore inextricably linked to the common interests of the people. And while major revolutions and uprisings may occur elsewhere – and such events should be actively celebrated and supported – for Blanqui France alone remains the true beacon of revolution. The destiny of the continent as a whole, then, is ultimately determined by the political struggles in France, the primary battlefield and the vanguard of European politics. Since the causes of *le peuple* and *la patrie* went hand in hand, Blanqui's position is in this sense a double bind: to serve the country is to serve the oppressed and to serve the oppressed is to serve the country.

Does the nation-state mark the limit of Blanqui's conception of the people? At times a notion of international solidarity against a common adversary would suggest not. 'Workers of all nations are brothers, and they have only one enemy: the oppressor who forces them to kill each other on the battlefields,' concludes the *Instructions for an Armed Uprising*. 'Everyone, workers and peasants of France, Germany or England, of Europe, Asia or America – everyone, all of us have the same toils, the same forms of suffering, the same interests.'²⁴ No doubt here as elsewhere there is a certain international dimension to Blanqui's understanding of social conflict and political agency. Overall, however, there is a degree of tension in his thinking when it comes to this point. Take the 'Report to the Society of the Friends of the People' from 1832. At one level it speaks of two, antagonistic Europes – 'the Europe of the kings' and 'the Europe of the peoples'²⁵ – applying broadly the same analysis to Britain as it does to France and evoking an internationally interconnected struggle between the masses and the aristocracy.²⁶ But it also seems to suggest that social groups across Europe are largely confined by national boundaries and specific to the nation-states that produce them.[27] While forever expressing a clear interest in and solidarity with the struggles engulfing all corners of the continent, from Britain to Poland,[28] ultimately it is difficult to escape the political primacy – and exclusivity – of the *French* people within Blanqui's project.

Conceiving the people first and foremost in terms of a national body has certainly been a notable feature of many mass movements that have initiated often major international political sequences, as demonstrated by France itself in 1789 and 1848 but perhaps most clearly by the anti-colonial struggles of the twentieth century and again more recently during the Arab Spring of 2011. Marx and Engels are correct to argue that 'the struggle of the proletariat with the bourgeoisie is at first a national struggle',[29] and Blanqui's insistence on the mobilization and empowerment of the French people is no doubt strategically astute in this respect. But what Blanqui lacks, unlike Marx and Engels, is sufficient concern for political agency beyond the confines of the nation-state. Marx and Engels know that it is only after the proletariat acquires 'political supremacy' through constituting itself as 'the leading class of the nation' that universal emancipation can proceed. But the consequences of the first step are tied to and limited by the second; again, the experience of the twentieth century clearly demonstrates this point. 'United action, of the leading civilized countries at least,' so the *Manifesto* states, 'is one of the first conditions for the emancipation of the proletariat.'[30] We might suggest that it is with the national struggle that Blanqui tends to be primarily, if not often solely, concerned. And although such thinking is perceptive, politically speaking, it nonetheless remains a limitation: 'one of the first conditions' of one project is the final goal of the other.

Just as France and the French take precedence over Europe, we must also remember that Paris and Parisians take precedence over France. As we saw in Chapter 1, for Blanqui the people of Paris are the revolutionary agent par excellence. Why? Because they are enlightened. The 'principal strength' of the 'Parisian workers' is their 'superior intelligence and adroitness'.[31] Free from the ignorance holding sway over most of the country, the people of Paris together have the concentrated enlightened thought, the material resources and the collective force capable of overpowering any oppressive regime and liberating

France from tyranny. Blanqui consequently accords primacy to the capital as representative and determinant of the nation as a whole.

## The actor's political action

The final point worth noting in this initial overview of Blanqui's subject is of particular importance since it concerns the constitution of the people as a political actor.

Referring in 1832 to the conflict between three competing groups and interests, after the aristocracy and the bourgeoisie Blanqui deliberately places 'the people last because they have always been the last, and because I count on an imminent application of the Gospel maxim: "the last shall be first".[32] Frantz Fanon would later appeal to the very same biblical phrase as the essential meaning of decolonization: the aim of national liberation from imperial domination is to realize this fundamental change in the balance of power.[33] Such imagery also exemplifies a view of the oppressed that echoes the well-known words of *The Internationale*, 'We are nothing, let us be everything.'[34] Blanqui's conception of the people, though not an international class, nonetheless similarly stands for those who count for nothing, those dismissed as capable of nothing. Revolution inverts this logic; it is the moment at which the people prove themselves capable of completely transforming the country, of subverting all existing hierarchies and established orders, of shattering all presuppositions and prescriptions. To become all or to remain nothing – in Blanqui's eyes this is the essence of revolutionary politics, as July 1830 revealed.

A truly radical intervention, an event of immense beauty and wonder, July marked the rebirth of the people, Blanqui insists. Dormant for fifteen years, the people finally awakened in 1830. On Thursday 29 July, the third consecutive day of fighting in Paris, 'the people emerged victorious'.[35] In the streets and on the barricades, the last became the first. Through their action the people showed both to others and – perhaps most importantly – to themselves what they are collectively capable of achieving. In this sense, we might say that for Blanqui popular power is the actualization of a potential or possibility. When he speaks of 'the force of the masses',[36] the term 'force' denotes the collective power of the people as an active political agent; their force is their potential capacity – actualized through their own collective political action – to realize radical change, to make their own history.

It is in this sense that one might distinguish between an actor and a subject.[37] Across his writings Blanqui usually employs the term 'subject' in the pejorative sense of individual and collective subjection and submission to oppression. 'Capital', he writes, for example, 'wants to overpower the audacity of its subjects.'[38] To be a subject is to be externally controlled and dominated; it is to be neither active nor self-determining. A manuscript note that classifies political vocabulary according to meaning and usage offers further insight into this issue. Blanqui first groups together what appear to be synonyms of domination and disempowerment: 'Force, violence, constraint, oppression, enslavement, subjection or constraint [*assujettissement*], authority, coaction, coercion, intolerance, yoke, subjection or constraint [*sujétion*], tyranny'. One then finds another, seemingly opposite, set of terms: 'Force, power [*pouvoir*], strength [*puissance*], faculty, potentiality [*virtualité*], vigour, energy, effort, intensity'.[39] What defines the latter from the former is the individual and collective capacity to act deliberately and consciously, the ability to undertake a process of popular empowerment through determined voluntary action. Collective political action is, to cite Rousseau, 'the act by which a people is a people';[40] it is the act that creates the actor.

Blanqui knows that a collective actor will not overcome its domination through a single, isolated act, however. A collective actor must discover ways to consolidate its initial action, to persist and advance through and beyond any rupture it itself creates. The action required to impose and sustain popular power is, in other words, the decisive issue. Again, for Blanqui 1830 clearly demonstrates this point. Once the street battles had ceased the bourgeoisie emerged from hiding to grasp the reins of power, reasserting their supremacy over the people. Domination, hierarchies, prescribed places and positions all returned. 'To each his role: the men of the workshops had withdrawn, the men who work behind the counter now appeared.'[41] Most significantly of all the outcomes of July, 'the people, who did everything, remain nothing, as before.'[42] The revolution and the opportunity it presented – and briefly realized – was lost. Why, Blanqui accordingly asks, was this initial popular victory, a victory 'that should have marked the end of the exclusive reign of the bourgeoisie as well as the advent of popular power', not sustained and ultimately triumphant?

How could one account for the hijacking and betrayal of a revolution 'made by the people alone', for the stark distance between the immediate achievements and long-term possibilities of July on the one hand, and the realities of its aftermath on the other?[43]

A mass revolutionary mobilization presents at once a triumphant opportunity and a perilous uncertainty. The task, as Blanqui sees it, is to ensure that a revolution is indeed a revolution.[44] This gave rise to a question – a version of the one Machiavelli poses – that would persist across his whole political project: how to be, how to remain, victorious. Crucial to resolving such a problem, alongside the development of the militant forms of leadership and organization that underpin a broader strategy of decisive mass action, is a sustained sense of confidence in the possible. Indeed, Blanqui maintains that, in spite of the socio-political realities of Orléanist rule, 'a tremendous act [*fait*] was accomplished' in July. 'The people had suddenly entered onto the political stage like a thunderbolt, taking it by assault; and, although driven from it at almost the same instant, they nevertheless acted with mastery and put an end to their resignation.'[45] That he describes the unexpected constitution of a combative popular actor as the primary accomplishment or 'revelation' of the revolution – July is hailed as 'a sudden and fearsome revelation of the power of the masses'[46] – is telling. Unanticipated outcomes should not, Blanqui insists, invalidate mass political action or the potential it holds. This popular revolution may have resulted in bourgeois despotism, greater impoverishment for the many and further national decline. But in the face of incredulity, despondency and defeat, Blanqui's voice is one of enduring confidence. That the revolution did not remain a revolution must not give way to disillusionment with the original act. For July 1830 is, if nothing else, the confirmation of a possibility. That the last became the first, the slave became the master, however ephemeral such a transformation may ultimately have been, commands a continued confidence in this potential and an unwavering commitment to re-actualizing it, which means discovering and harnessing the means to do so.

We can now begin to piece together some of the basic, defining traits of Blanqui's actor. The proletariat are the ordinary or common people, the anonymous masses without wealth or power, property or privilege. Born to work, to suffer, to die, the people have nothing, they count for nothing, they are nothing. Yet through their conscious political action they prove themselves capable of doing and becoming everything. The gap between nothing and everything, between outside and in, can only be overcome through the sustained mass action of conscious popular forces.

## Interpretations

For many of his readers Blanqui's proletariat is a contentious construction. Since the social analysis clearly has no bearing on the reality of contemporary socio-economic conditions, so runs the common line of criticism, here 'the proletariat', particularly as depicted in the 'Defence Speech' of January 1832, is a mere restatement of the eighteenth-century idea of 'the people', which is far closer to the 'unsophisticated Babouvist dichotomy of "rich and poor"' than it is to the Marxist conception of 'a true industrial proletariat'.[47] For V. P. Volgin, Blanqui's proletariat designates 'the worker in general'; Blanqui ascribes it 'the same meaning that democrats gave to the notion of "people"', in which 'the distinction between "the aristocracy of wealth and the people", or indeed between "the bourgeoisie and the people"' – a characteristic of contemporary social thought – attested to an 'imprecision in terms' that 'reflected the insufficient level of capitalist development in France' and led Blanqui to confuse 'the proletariat' with 'the poor'. Such shortcomings, Volgin tells us, are symptomatic of a crude analysis of capitalism in which capital is synonymous with usury (profit derives from the inequality of exchange) and capitalism is denounced principally in terms of moral and rational judgement (capitalism is incompatible with justice and logical reason). It follows that Blanqui's 'petit bourgeois' analysis of exploitation – which is 'profoundly mistaken' and rooted in a conflation of the proletariat and all social groups living from their labour – is incapable of understanding and explaining the class structure of capitalist society.[48]

Samuel Bernstein, who, commenting on the thirty million proletarians depicted in the 'Defence Speech', maintains that 'neither the term nor the number could withstand economic analysis', joins Volgin in seeing the conception of social class outlined in the 'Report to the Society of the Friends of the People' (1832) as equally 'schematic and superficial'.[49] Bernstein notes that the 'prerequisite situation of a revolution' is something that 'forever escaped [Blanqui's] analysis'. Such an analytical limitation, according to Bernstein, results from an inability to 'get inside the economic structure to study its dynamics'. Consequently, while a 'romantic rebel' and a 'Titan of revolt', Blanqui's 'weapons were museum pieces', a deficiency which left him 'poorly equipped to give history a push'.[50] Philippe Vigier, meanwhile, suggests that Blanqui never offered a 'rigorous' definition of the proletariat, and the term certainly could not apply to his own social background.[51] It therefore falls to Alan Spitzer to show that while such interpretations, particularly the eighteenth-century-influenced conception of 'the people', are validated by some of Blanqui's writings, 'there is considerable material which shows that Blanqui's idea of "the people" contains implications beyond the vague democratic dichotomy of "the many and the few". His writings and speeches evince a theory of economic classes more precise and more sophisticated than the one implied by his self-identification [in January 1832] as a "Proletarian … one of thirty million Frenchmen."'[52] Spitzer then goes on to offer a concise overview of the development of Blanqui's thinking on class and class struggle that is particularly instructive and so worth our consideration before we proceed.

Ideas expressed in the 'Defence Speech', for example, 'contain the germs of a fairly sophisticated theory of historical development based upon the conflict of economic and social classes', Spitzer writes.[53] But Blanqui's analyses in both the 'Defence Speech' and the 'Report' shortly after it '[do] not define in economic terms the social categories of "bourgeois" and "proletarian" whose conflict was to decide the political configurations of the future'. Spitzer accordingly draws readers' attention to the writings two years later from *Le Libérateur*, in which one discovers Blanqui's first allusions to exploited workers, to the ownership of the instruments of production and to the antagonism between wages and profits. The result is a 'somewhat clearer statement of the economic relations among the contending classes'.[54]

It is only later, however, in the 'Letter to Maillard' (1852), that Blanqui gives a more 'precise' definition of the two opposing social groups, Spitzer claims. Blanqui describes to Maillard the existence of a class that, although 'less well defined perhaps than the nobility and the clergy', is nonetheless 'very distinct and perfectly well known to everyone under the name: the bourgeois class'.

> It includes most of the individuals who possess a certain amount of affluence and education: financiers, merchants, property-owners, lawyers,

doctors, legal professionals, civil servants, rentiers – all those living from their revenues or from the exploitation of workers. Add to this quite a large number of country-dwellers who have some wealth but no education, and you reach a maximum of perhaps four million people. There remain thirty-two million proletarians, who own no property, or at least no significant property, and who live only from the meagre product of their hands.[55]

The thirty-two million proletarians Blanqui evokes here, as in the 'Defence Speech', 'would still have included a small proportion of industrial workers and an overwhelming majority of those petit bourgeois elements which Marx considered essentially reactionary', Spitzer notes – 'the peasant proprietors, petty functionaries, shopkeepers, and self-employed artisans, who, after all, were "the people" evoked by any good Jacobin'.[56] But Blanqui's proletariat 'is no longer equivalent to "the people" of the eighteenth-century reformers. This honorable title he now bestows upon the "class of the workers" to distinguish them from the "third estate" '.[57] This brings Spitzer to his concluding remarks, which are worth quoting in full:

> When he applies this distinction to an analysis of contemporary political conflict, and especially when he relates it to control over the instruments of labor he has come quite close to the Marxian conception of class. However, the Soviet historian, Volgin, has correctly observed that the clearest distinction made by Blanqui is between the class which lives by exploitation and the class which supports itself without exploiting others. This is by no means the same as the basic Marxist dichotomy between the swelling mass of wage laborers and the dwindling number of those who reap the surplus value of the workers' industry through their control over the means of production.[58]

Later Spitzer offers what seems to be his overall assessment:

> Blanqui's conception of the relations between the class struggle and revolutionary politics is worked out with a heavy emphasis upon voluntarist and intellectual factors and virtually no reference to the long-run political potential of the industrial proletariat viewed as a specific socio-economic group. Blanqui's Parisian workers are virtually indistinguishable from 'the people' of Jacobin mythology.[59]

One can certainly agree with many of the points Spitzer makes in a sensitive reading of this issue. But let us take a step back. In the first instance, why is a notion of 'the people' only valid when it becomes 'quite close to the Marxian conception of class', as Spitzer claims, or completely invalid because it fails to meet this criterion, as Bernstein, Volgin and some of the other readers cited above argue? Is Blanqui's proletariat, even if – or perhaps precisely because – it is synonymous with the people or the oppressed in a Jacobin or voluntarist sense, really of no value or interest?

## A political logic

To respond to these questions we must first recognize that Blanqui's priority is to understand and explain the formation and mobilization of a popular actor in terms of the conscious and collective act of political struggle. Rather than a Marxian analysis of the manner in which the development of the forces of production generates the objective conditions and possibilities for subjective political action, Blanqui's primary concern is the action itself. We have seen that for Blanqui the proletariat or the people certainly are, broadly speaking, a social group shaped by material processes and realities (labour, exploitation, poverty, starvation and so on). But socio-economic considerations and factors – which, despite the imprecision and superficiality of their theoretical articulation, remain an important component of the overall analysis – that might make collective action possible, such as the forces and relations of capitalist production, are secondary to these strictly political concerns.

Ernesto Laclau's work on populism provides a stimulating point of comparison on some of these issues. Here the theoretical point of departure is not the class struggle but the popular struggle for hegemony within a heterogeneous social field. When a series of specific demands – be they for public services, civil rights or basic social provisions – are coherently linked and articulated together to form an 'equivalential chain', a popular identity, the people, is produced. As this collective subject is not a pre-constituted socio-economic class endowed with an a priori privileged role as a result of structural necessity, one must 'conceive the "people" as a *political* category, not as a *datum* of the social structure'. This contingent and broad popular identity 'designates not a *given* group, but an act of institution that creates a new agency out of a plurality of heterogeneous elements'.[60] For Laclau it is not a question of locating the positive content of the popular demands themselves but of the basic formal function of their collective articulation – that is, first, the construction of a universal political subject that transcends the actual content of the initial demands through which it emerged and, second, the creation of an antagonistic frontier within the social field between the two (necessarily heterogeneous) forces of the 'people' and the 'enemy'. 'This division presupposes', Laclau explains, 'the presence of some privileged signifiers which condense in themselves the signification of a whole antagonistic camp (the "regime", the "oligarchy", the "dominant groups", and so on, for the enemy; the "people", the "nation", the "silent majority" and so on, for the oppressed underdog – these signifiers acquire this articulating role according, obviously, to a contextual history).'[61] One of Laclau's crucial moves is to privilege form over content, to contemplate not 'systems of ideas *qua* ideas' so much as 'to explore their performative dimensions', from which follows the importance of signifiers, metaphors and rhetoric in the construction of political identities, if not of politics as such.[62] Naming a universality, the people, is, Laclau argues, the political act par excellence.

To place Laclau alongside Blanqui is to be confronted with some marked – and therefore illuminating – differences. Limiting myself to the most obvious points, first and foremost Laclau fails to offer any clear indication as to how rhetoric relates to or translates into collective force and popular power. Abstract articulation is privileged over concrete action in the construction of a 'hegemonic formation'. Blanqui, by contrast, insists that the people, like any decisive political actor, are constituted above all through their conscious thought, their collective will, their material power, rather than merely through the representative function of collective signifiers. Blanqui does place importance on naming an otherwise unnamed group and representing the unrepresented, as we have seen above and will again see below, but this is with the aim of initiating or sustaining the process of political empowerment that will enable their social emancipation. So follows the resolutely practical task – absent from Laclau's account – of an oppressed people's passage from passive submission to sovereign power. Rhetoric and signifiers therefore anticipate the beginning of, or support an ongoing, actual political struggle and are in no way its substitute or endpoint.

Although the question of representation is a complex one on which Blanqui and Laclau share certain similar limitations (an issue to which we shall return in Chapter 4), Blanqui would nonetheless reject Laclau's claim that naming 'a series of *heterogeneous* elements as "working class" ... performatively brings about the unity of those elements, whose coalescence into a single entity is nothing other than the result of the operation of naming'.[63] For Blanqui, and this leads on from the first point, political unity is not simply a 'performative act',[64] the product of the mere naming of a passive object. Unity is created, as Rousseau insisted before him, through an actor's deliberate and voluntary act of association.[65] Unity is then maintained through shared commitment and collective enthusiasm. Without militant organization and unwavering discipline, as June 1848 proved to Blanqui beyond any doubt, popular victory is inconceivable, popular power an impossible dream.[66] Blanqui is the first to recognize the tendency during revolutionary sequences for the struggle between opposing camps to intensify. He knows that this sharpening of antagonisms gives rise to a polarization of the entire political field, at which point everyone is forced to choose their side and commit to a cause, uniting with their allies and confronting their adversaries. But in every instance these choices and commitments are ultimately grounded in and sustained by real or material, not nominal, political practices.

Some instructive similitude does also exist, however. Laclau's notion of political actors not as 'pure class actors (defined by precise locations within the relations of production)', but as a formal political logic that cuts across specific, sectorial agents to designate, in consciously broad terms, 'the outsiders of the system, the underdogs' remains particularly useful.[67] No doubt Blanqui broadly follows a similar logic: insofar as 'proletariat', 'people', 'poor', 'multitude', 'masses' and so on all carry the same basic concepts and lived realities – dispossession, exclusion, domination, oppression, exploitation – the positive socio-economic content of each term or each different social group(s) they might designate is, if not completely irrelevant as in Laclau's account, certainly secondary to their political meaning and usage – that is, to clarify, unequivocally, the balance of forces and to establish both a common goal and a common enemy. 'We must establish a clear dividing line, an impassable dividing line,' Blanqui insists, 'between us and them.'[68] Such clarity necessitates a radical antagonism that delineates a conflict between two opposing camps. Indeed, Blanqui's whole approach, as we saw in the Chapter 2, turns on the age-old struggle of the poor and powerless many against the rich and powerful few. 'Aristocracy: the flowers.

The people: the manure that allows them to grow – this has been the structure of societies for centuries.'⁶⁹ In this sense capitalist exploitation merely intensifies age-old forms of social polarization. 'The gap between two distinctive castes, opulence and poverty, grows greater day by day,' Blanqui writes. 'Intermediary positions are disappearing.'⁷⁰ The reduction or 'condensation' of the social field and political space into a basic antagonism between two imprecise poles should not be dismissed out of hand as politically naive and immature but rather be seen as an essential political operation. 'There is in these dichotomies, as in those which constitute any politico-ideological frontier,' Laclau explains, 'a simplification of the political space (all social singularities tend to group themselves around one or the other of the poles of the dichotomy), and the terms designating both poles have necessarily to be imprecise (otherwise they could not cover all the particularities that they are supposed to regroup).'⁷¹ We might note that the authors of the *Communist Manifesto*, particularly in that very text, follow the same logic of reduction in the face of ostensibly complex social relations to present a struggle that over time tends to polarize into bourgeoisie against proletariat, oppressors against oppressed.⁷² Rousseau, too, had maintained that society can be basically divided into two contesting groups: rich and poor, conqueror and conquered. Needless to say, the respective accounts by which Rousseau, Blanqui, Marx and Engels, and Laclau arrive at these antagonisms are totally at odds, and the comparison is ultimately limited as such (the latter, to be sure, repeatedly rejects the claim, attributed to Marx, that collective actors are constituted by the social homogeneity that results from the 'simplification of the social structure under capitalism').⁷³ But the *strategic* political exigencies behind them are much the same. In their own ways and with varying degrees of success, taken together they reveal how broad, antagonistic dichotomies are inevitable in and crucial to processes of collective political action, both then and now.

## Blanqui with Rancière

Unlike the majority of Blanqui's readers, Jacques Rancière approaches Blanqui as a resolutely political thinker, his proletariat as a political concept, its usage as a political intervention. In so doing, Rancière – whose conception of politics shares certain key features and concerns with that of Laclau, a point the latter is the first to note[74] – provides a thought-provoking interpretation of many of the fundamental issues at stake in this discussion.

## Counting the uncounted

Rancière's interest lies in the exchange between Blanqui and the presiding judge at the start of the 'Trial of the Fifteen' of January 1832, before Blanqui gave his famous 'Defence Speech'. When asked to state his profession, Blanqui responded: 'proletarian'. 'That is not a profession', the judge objected. 'What do you mean, it is not a profession!,' retorted Blanqui. 'It is the profession of thirty million Frenchmen who live off their labour and who are deprived of political rights.'[75] According to Rancière, the disagreement over the meaning of the term 'profession' marks the point at which the unequal established order, what he calls the 'police', embodied in this case by the judge, and the radical equality of revolutionary politics, embodied here by Blanqui, come into conflict and thereby create a political subject.

> For the prosecutor, embodying police logic, profession means job, trade: the activity that puts a body in its place and function. It is clear that proletarian does not designate any occupation whatever, at most the vaguely defined state of the poverty-stricken manual labourer, which, in any case, is not appropriate to the accused. But, within revolutionary politics, Blanqui gives the same word a differing meaning: a profession is a profession of faith, a declaration of membership of a collective.[76]

In self-identifying as a proletariat, Blanqui subjectively *professes* an affiliation not to an occupation or to an existing social group or class, Rancière argues, but to 'the class of the uncounted that only exists in the very declaration in which they are counted as those of no account'.[77] Blanqui's proletariat is as such a radically egalitarian – and so a properly political – intervention: it asserts the equality of the non-existent part of a community whose founding 'wrong' is precisely that part's non-existence. Since the non-recognition of this class or part is the fundamental injustice or wrong of the status quo, Blanqui's proletariat creates 'a subject of wrong', Rancière writes. 'Blanqui, in the name of proletarians, inscribes the uncounted in a space where they are countable as uncounted.'[78]

When it comes to the active empowerment of this group, however, we immediately confront a shortcoming of Rancière's account to which we shall shortly return but that would benefit from some initial observations here (Rancière's problematic rejection of the sociological dimensions of Blanqui's proletariat will also be addressed below). By 'subjectification' Rancière means 'the production through a series of actions of a body and a capacity for enunciation not previously identifiable within a given field of experience, whose identification is thus part of the reconfiguration of the field of experience'.[79] Rancière discerns in Blanqui's proletarian subjectification a 'speech event' – a 'singular experience of conflict over speech and voice, over the distribution of the sensible'. The 'speech scene [*scène de parole*]' in the courtroom of January 1832 is in fact, for Rancière, nothing less than 'one of the first political occurrences of the modern proletarian subject'.[80]

For Blanqui himself, however, this is surely not the case. Proletariat is the name of the collective actor that actually appeared in July 1830 through its own insurgent force, initiating and driving the revolution before returning – and being made to return – to more or less dormant inaction. In Blanqui's eyes such a stark reversal compelled a searching contemplation of the necessary forms and practices of decisive mass action, of what a collective actor must do, concretely, to overcome its oppression. Proletarian nomination, in other words, is meaningless and inconsequential without proletarian empowerment.

## Division and unity

Rancière shows us that Blanqui's proletariat is at once a declaration of solidarity with and a recognition of the excluded as equal subjects, and a forceful attack on the order which denies that very existence and so denies that very equality. To reopen and expose this otherwise dismissed or obscured structural division and the injustice it carries is precisely the political function of Blanqui's intervention: the proletariat serves to clarify once again the essentially conflictual nature of politics.[81]

Blanqui's insistence on the divisive quality of the terms 'proletariat' and 'proletarian' was certainly not unique. Those who sought reform through social cooperation explicitly rejected them precisely because of the discord and division they created. 'Let the name "proletarian" – an insulting name that has become odious – disappear, and let us give help and assistance to those who bore it.'[82] So pleaded the Lyon silk workers' newspaper *L'Écho de la fabrique* in January 1832, for example. Blanqui subscribes to the same logic but from the inverse position, for if politics is conflict then it follows that the name 'proletarian' must be fully adopted and readily evoked. As Kristin Ross observes, adopting Rancierian terms herself, Blanqui's insistence in the 'Letter to Maillard' on speaking of 'proletarians' is precisely to create a gap, a division and rupture where the term 'democrat', having been appropriated by Napoléon III's Imperial regime, now created consensus in the service of continued inequality and domination. Proletarian, unlike democrat, still named 'the division to be overcome between those judged capable of governing and those judged incapable'.[83] Proletarian, unlike democrat, had not been deprived of its political function: to reflect and reveal the often concealed but no less real civil war and to name the two opposing groups waging it: proletariat and bourgeois.[84]

It is in this respect that Blanqui can be seen to hold a dual concept of popular unity. On the one hand there is the popular unity that is constructed around and serves as justification for a social order based on social hierarchy and inherited privilege. On the other hand there is a conception of popular unity that assumes the equality of all and that affirms and practices solidarity as the political translation of this principle. If the first form of unity creates and upholds the barrier to equality by means of consensual domination, the second form can shatter that consensus and overcome that barrier. But in all cases there must be no doubt around whom and what political unity is sought. 'The word "Union" has become the weapon of war of all the enemies of freedom,' Blanqui warns in *La Patrie en Danger*. 'Let it be known that concord, for republicans, does not mean enslavement to the counter-revolutionaries. [Republicans] want union for the salvation and not for the ruin of the Republic.'[85] Without clearly established and clearly stated political positions, the 'mixing' of 'disparate elements could only be dangerous for the cause', Blanqui later told Georges Clemenceau. Without clear choices, without clear sides and without a clear understanding of the interests and principles that underpin each side, the illusory unity of the adversary will absorb and weaken the cause of emancipatory unity, as occurred in 1848. 'It is this perfidious word, "union", that has been our ruin,' Blanqui duly remarked.[86]

The fundamentally divisive logic of Blanqui's politics again takes centre stage; again, between exploiters and exploited there is no third option; and again many readers have overlooked this political imperative. When commenting that 'whether or not Blanqui's conceptions of class struggle anticipated modern socialist theories, they did define the nature of socialist action for him',[87] Spitzer appears to hit on the crucial point, but he then fails to grasp its full implications: as far as political practice is concerned, creating a divide in order to expose conflict is itself of far greater importance to Blanqui than establishing precisely who or what compromises each side. Naming the subject of social inequality helps to establish the political divide between us (the people and those struggling for its emancipation, which is the emancipation of all) and them (the rich and those sustaining its domination over all). It is for this reason that Blanqui can, paradoxically it may otherwise seem, describe his usage of the terms 'proletarians' and 'bourgeois' as having 'a clear and distinct meaning; they state things categorically'.[88] 'Proletarian', for Blanqui, is a subjective position; it both presupposes and articulates a political choice and principle. 'Democrat', meanwhile, having been appropriated by all political camps, is 'a vague and banal word without any precise meaning, an elastic word, made of rubber'.[89] The word has been deprived of its strictly political functions – decision, allegiance, division – and therefore must be abandoned. Blanqui thus compels his interlocutor, Maillard: 'Choose your camp and fasten your cockade. You are a proletarian because you seek real equality between citizens and the overthrow of all castes and all tyrannies.'[90] The proletariat, in this sense, is not simply a social group, an objective category denoting a particular role and status that is assigned on the basis of one's background or occupation. To be a proletarian is also to side, subjectively, with labour over capital, emancipation over domination, us over them. Philippe Vigier's claim noted earlier that Blanqui's background is inconsistent with that of a proletarian completely overlooks this point. Blanqui is indeed well aware that 'by my background, by my education, I am bourgeois'. But that is not to say that a bourgeois by birth cannot join the proletarian camp out of conviction, uniting with and supporting their struggle.[91]

This is the point at which the sociological and political aspects of Blanqui's proletariat meet. On the one hand, the proletariat are – objectively – those who are born to work and must work to live, a group who are materially exploited as a result of their social position and function. On the other hand, the proletariat are *all* those who – subjectively – are conscious of this exploitation and voluntarily fight to overcome it. Collective actors are not, then, an inevitable result of historical processes or socio-economic development.[92] Whatever one's social background or occupation, political subjectivation is ultimately a matter of conscious volition. Blanqui's proletariat, his proletarian *profession* in the sense that it is a political affiliation, as Rancière instructively highlights, is simply an extension of the logic of making choices and taking sides outlined in Chapter 2. The term 'proletarian' expresses a political choice and a political commitment; it says whom you are for and whom you are against.

With Rancière we see that Blanqui's proletariat is, in many crucial respects, a subjective position – it articulates a decision, a side, a conviction. In this sense Blanqui's use of the proletariat and the people can be traced back to some of his most basic assumptions regarding conscious choices and principled engagement. The term 'proletariat' cuts through the veil of consensual domination to present politics in its most fundamental form: a conflict of two irreconcilable groups, interests and principles. It foregrounds questions of unity and division and highlights their role in the collective process of first recognizing and then overthrowing an order of domination.

Beyond such insights some problems nonetheless present themselves. Rancière, much like Laclau, tends to overemphasize the extent to which naming an unnamed group, the performative articulation or affirmation driving this 'process of subjectification',[93] alone creates a subject or actor. His radically anti-sociological conception of the proletariat fails to take sufficient account of the action constitutive of the actor and of the material realities of both the absence and the exercise of political power. For the purely nominal inscription of the proletariat's exclusion does not and cannot redress the concrete conditions of that exclusion.

## Blanqui beyond Rancière

Central to Rancière's reading is the claim that Blanqui's conception of the proletariat does not turn on work or the conditions of work. The proletariat, we are told, are not an identifiable social group; they 'are neither manual workers nor the labouring classes.' What is subjectified with Blanqui's proletariat, Rancière argues, 'is neither work nor destitution, but the simple counting of the uncounted.'[94] The wrong of the 'miscount', that which is subjectified with the name 'proletariat', is largely understood in terms of the distribution of who is and who is not audible or visible and the social order in which this distribution is assigned, structured and legitimized. Simply put, for Rancière, after Pierre-Simon Ballanche and Joseph Jacotot, to be among the 'uncounted' is to be unacknowledged as an equal speaking being; it is to be deemed incapable of rational argument, capable only of the animalistic expression of pleasure and pain. Injustice emanates from the perceived inequality of speaking beings and its manifestation in a social body in which one of its parts – the *sans-part* – is unseen and unheard, its equal participation in political life as equal speaking beings denied. Politics, by contrast, as Rancière conceives it, verifies the immediate intellectual equality of speaking beings; it manifests equality of intelligence, here and now.[95]

Such assertions require further consideration with greater reference to Blanqui's thought, for they represent at once a great strength and an ultimate limitation of Rancière's account.

## (In)equality of intelligence

A crucial difference between Blanqui and Rancière lies in the question of intellectual equality. Certainly, both ground their respective sociopolitical analyses in notions of equality of intelligences. But where for Rancière everything turns on the existing equal intelligence of all, for Blanqui such intellectual equality does not yet exist. Where Rancière presupposes intellectual equality in the present, Blanqui orientates everything towards its future possibility and necessity: equality of intelligence is both *possible* through equality of education and 'the universality of enlightenment',[96] and *necessary* insofar as 'there can be no lasting Revolution without Enlightenment', 'no emancipation without a basic level of intelligence'.[97] It therefore remains a goal to be attained, a task to be accomplished. Intellectual equality is not unheard or unseen and requiring its manifestation or verification in the face of its denial so much as deliberately stifled and repressed by the status quo; the possibility of intellectual equality can only be realized, as indeed it must, through a didactic process of mass intellectual cultivation and development, as we saw in Chapter 1. Rancière, in short, presumes the popular enlightenment to which Blanqui aspires. The former's point of departure is the latter's final destination.

The political implications of these contrasting anthropological assumptions are profound and decisive. Politics, as Blanqui understands it, is not simply the verification of an unrecognized or denied intellectual equality, a conflict over the affirmation or the denial of equality. Politics is the material work of overcoming the forces that impose and uphold the intellectual inequality of the present as the basis from which to launch a campaign for popular education that will develop and grow the critical faculties of everyone. Intellectual equality, in other words, is not the presupposition of politics but its outcome. Hence Blanqui's diagnosis – which establishes the very sociological distinctions between people on the basis of their intellectual capacities or incapacities that Rancière rejects as a matter of principle – of unprivileged masses forced to languish in uneducated ignorance; hence the need for an enlightened vanguard or elite to speak on their behalf until they are capable of speaking for themselves; hence the need for a revolution to inaugurate the process by which this enlightened thought and knowledge can be developed and the forces that currently stifle it can be suppressed; and hence Blanqui's broader concern with the necessary processes and concrete forms of revolutionary transition and popular transformation, an issue we shall address in Chapter 4.

On all of these points Blanqui and Rancière are totally at odds. Arguably Blanqui recognizes to a greater extent than Rancière what is fundamentally at stake in a process of collective empowerment and what overcoming the resistance to greater material equality will demand, practically and concretely, but neither's approach and solutions are entirely satisfactry. If Rancière seems to overlook the role of organized political action in overcoming the (also overlooked) gap between the status quo and the advent of a more just and egalitarian social arrangement, Blanqui often overstates the division between those who are presently capable of thinking and understanding – and therefore of decisively acting – and those who are not. Nor for that matter does he see any problem with classifying people on such grounds in the first instance.

## Perception

Under the Orléanist regime, so Blanqui argued soon after its establishment, the oppressed have no voice. The words and thoughts and ideas and beliefs of those who work day and night only to remain destitute are never heard. 'The spokesmen of the ministries smugly repeat that avenues are available for proletarians to voice their grievances, and that the law provides them with the regular means through which to advance their interests,' Blanqui notes, offering a characteristically blunt response: 'This is an insult.'[98] The people remain invisible, inaudible; they are, to paraphrase Rancière, only recognized and only exist through their very non-recognition and non-existence:

> The people do not write in the newspapers; they do not send petitions to the Chambers: it would be a waste of time. Moreover, all the voices that reverberate in the political sphere – the voices of the salons, those of the boutiques, of the cafés, in short of all the places where so-called public opinion is formed – are the voices of the privileged few. Not one belongs to the people; they are mute; they vegetate far from these high places where their destiny is determined.[99]

The struggle over who or what is seen and heard, written and read, in many ways goes to the heart of Blanqui's political theory. In the early 1830s he was emphatic that the Orléanist government's attempts to end press freedom – 'the most precious freedom of all' precisely because it is the freedom to think and write[100] – had to be resisted at all costs.[101] Almost forty years later, when Napoleon III was in power, he still decried 'the supposed equality before the law, which gives the rich the monopoly of the press and of speech [*la parole*], and which imposes silence and submission on the poor'.[102] Here Blanqui's proletariat clearly has a certain aesthetic dimension; it subjectifies, as Rancière argues, 'the difference between an inegalitarian distribution of social bodies and the equality of speaking beings'.[103] One finds this framing of political (non-)subjectivity in terms of perception elsewhere in Blanqui's writings. In 1834, for example, he describes how during the Restoration the people had remained a 'silent spectator', an onlooker, to the conflict between the middle and upper classes in which they had no stake.[104] It would therefore seem that a process of political subjectivation, as Blanqui sees it, is certainly in part the process by which the lone voices of individuals come to speak together as the collective voice of the people: 'Our isolated cries would get lost in the immense tumult of society,' so he explains; 'but, united as a solid mass of acclamation, they will form one great voice that will silence these charmers of tyranny.'[105]

But this issue – a key concern of Blanqui's early writings in particular – also raises some important questions about his project more generally. Consider the opening line of the 'But du journal' of *Le Libérateur*, which declares that 'of all the forms of exclusion that weigh down on the citizen without wealth, the most painful and bitterly felt is that which prevents him from publishing his thought'.[106] In a society in which the press is nothing more than the mouthpiece for the 'opulent classes' and political censorship means that 'an iron gauntlet smashes the words on the lips' of those militants devoted to equality, Blanqui seeks 'to defy the ban issued by the aristocracy of money against the poor person [*le pauvre*] who dares to think.' *Le Libérateur*, the self-styled 'Newspaper of the Oppressed', was therefore conceived 'to reveal, in simple, clear and precise terms, why the people are wretched [*malheureux*] and how they must cease to be so'.[107]

The problem here is obvious enough. No doubt Blanqui is right to highlight the basic material constraints on the people's freedom to speak – lack of resources, censorship, intimidation and so on – while Rancière's account is solely concerned with the perceived unintelligibility of speech itself. No doubt he is right to insist that what is visible, legible and audible is as much a matter of the distribution of power and wealth as it is the 'distribution of the sensible'. But to respond to the inaudibility of the poor by speaking on their behalf and to them, rather than providing them with a platform or creating a space from which they could speak for themselves (a position Rancière would most likely advocate) is indicative of the often excessively top-down nature of Blanqui's wider project. It could be said to reveal a lack of self-emancipatory practice within Blanqui's politics, informed by a belief in the necessity of instruction, of the – hierarchical – transmission of knowledge from the informed to the ignorant (recall from Chapter 1 that for Blanqui the practical importance of newspapers and propaganda is fundamentally rooted in a conception of intelligence as politically decisive and an insistence on popular enlightenment as the precondition for social emancipation).

## The untold suffering of work

Rancière's insistence on the aesthetic dimension of political subjectivity, though undeniably important and insightful here, nonetheless leads him to downplay or ignore other factors that inform Blanqui's conception of the proletariat, particularly the human suffering caused by political marginalization and working conditions.

The 'Defence Speech', which Rancière takes as his point of departure, depicts the proletariat or the people not only as those with no voice and no recognized part in the social order but also as those who suffer and whose suffering goes unseen and unheard, the suffering excluded. Elucidating this point, much of the text first seeks to pull away the veil of democratic inclusion and representation. Blanqui derides the Orléanists' so-called representative government, a government in which 'one hundred thousand bourgeois form what is called, by a bitter irony, its "democratic element".'[108] The law, in turn, is nothing more than an ideological instrument of exclusion. 'The laws are made by a hundred thousand voters, applied by a hundred thousand jurors, enforced by a hundred thousand urban national guards,' Blanqui argues, before asking the court, and here we come to the crucial point: 'What do the thirty million proletarians do in the midst of all these manoeuvres? They pay.'[109] Through reasserting the gap between the politics of the established order and the plight of the oppressed multitude, the proletariat are seen to 'pay' not only in the literal sense of the unequal distribution of the fiscal burden. They also 'pay' materially and physically for their ever-increasing impoverishment.

How, if at all, do the rich respond to the suffering for which they are responsible? While most remain blind or indifferent, the more astute among them, sensing that problems are afoot, offer tokenistic gestures to alleviate hardship – not out of genuine humanitarian concern but as the minimal pragmatic measures necessary to save themselves from the potential threat posed by a starving and hopeless multitude. 'As for political rights, no one must speak of them. It is simply a matter of throwing the proletarians a bone to gnaw on.'[110] Social justice, as this metaphor suggests, is a matter of both material and political inequality. The proletariat are starved of food and rights. Any minor concessions will never end such structural injustice. Any form of recognition is solely the instrument of continued non-recognition: the privileged classes 'recognise in the people only the appetites of beasts, and thereby arrogate to themselves the right to distribute whatever food is necessary to sustain the animal vegetation that they exploit!'[111] Even when 'the tribune or the press lets slips some vacuous words of pity about the people's poverty, silence is quickly imposed in the name of public safety', raising such matters is reproached as risking anarchy, and any remaining dissenting voices are imprisoned. No one is allowed to pose the real, profound questions which might disturb the social order. So when the silence of subservience finally returns, the supporters of the government claim that 'France is happy, peaceful, order reigns!'[112] Meanwhile, the proletariat continue to be unheard, their suffering continues in silence and without end, and the conflict at the heart of French society remains concealed beneath the apparently 'tranquil waters'[113] of order. In a system that concedes nothing to the mass of the population, that is arrogantly indifferent to the injustice it creates, simply no opportunities or channels exist to break the very monopoly of power that only serves the imperatives of exploitation. No one is willing to 'listen to the screams and sobs of the vile herds who fall in their thousands into the abattoirs of history'.[114] 'These poor people die in silence; they are suffocated in darkness. There is no commotion, no fuss. We see nothing; we hear nothing. They disappear without a trace.'[115] This is untold – in both senses of the word – suffering.

What of the relationship between the proletariat, work and working conditions? Often evoked in the Saint-Simonian sense, worker, in Blanqui's lexicon, very broadly denotes the producers, the vast majority of the population (thirty or thirty-two million French people) who together form the working masses – artisans, peasants, labourers. This large group is distinct from the small group of rich, parasitic idlers whose wealth and power derives from the work of the (poor and powerless) majority.[116] Labour, in turn, is often valorized as an ideal or principle: together with intelligence, the two comprise the exclusive 'source of social wealth'; 'the soul or spirit and the life of humanity', together they form the banner of equality, contrasted with 'idleness and exploitation' of privilege. With intelligence and labour society 'lives and breathes, grows and develops'; without them society is doomed to dissolution and collapse.[117]

However broad and imprecise, for Blanqui the proletariat unquestionably does imply, contrary to Rancière's insistence, a social group. It unquestionably does imply, again contrary to Rancière's insistence, both work and, more importantly, the destitution and hardship caused by that work. Here as elsewhere, Blanqui's analysis foregrounds the *human* impact of capitalist production: he locates in the social relation between capital and labour a major source of human suffering. A political actor, whatever its collective noun, is therefore formed when individuals consciously and directly unite in the name of their collective humanity, of their right to live a life free of the pain and misery inflicted upon them solely as a consequence of their lack of wealth and power. We should also note that Blanqui explicitly uses the word 'victim',[118] a term Rancière rejects, to highlight the brutality of everyday life for the poor. This also serves to establish a unity between the victims of social forces and the victims of state repression in popular revolts against these very social forces, as we saw in the previous chapter. 'To work, suffer and die for the new masters – this is the duty that is imposed upon the plebs, by means of grapeshot, the guillotine and the penal colony.'[119] Overall, then, we might say that the proletariat are – negatively – those who suffer, who endure destitution and hardship, and – positively – the conscious and organized, committed and resolute movement to overcome this suffering and to realize universal peace and happiness. The emancipation of this group will bring an end to all social distinctions and 'class differences',[120] to all forms of domination. 'Doing away with' the categories of 'rich and poor, powerful and weak, exploiters and exploited' is 'the true form of progress that we should pursue.'[121]

Where does this leave Blanqui and Rancière? We have seen that for Rancière to be among the 'uncounted' of an existing social order is to be unacknowledged as an intelligible being; this excluded part of the community is perceived only through its animalistic voicing of pleasure and suffering. But does inequality not amount to more than speech and the injustice of its miscount? Is it not also a matter of what that miscount materially produces so long as it is sustained, of how being unseen, unheard and uncounted denies the expression of what it concretely means to be among the unseen, unheard and uncounted, of the realities of the everyday existence of those deemed non-existent? What about the material inequalities of wealth, power and resources that produce and reproduce the perceived inequality of speaking beings? Therein lies the importance of suffering, as well as pain, misery and deprivation, alongside issues of intelligence and speech, in any account of inequality. The proletarian may at present only be recognized as a figure of passive suffering; it may at best only receive empty words of pity from those who ultimately seek to maintain its social position and role. But that is not to say that emancipatory politics should not seek to expose, fully and forcefully, the status quo's structural imperative of dehumanization and suffering, to bring into focus the misery and impoverishment of the excluded and unheard, for it is precisely these material forms of inequality that shall have no place in a truly free and humane society. 'The day when, through the universal transmission of thought, the whole human species will feel, electrically, the grievances of its most humble members,' Blanqui writes – 'on that day the absolute sovereignty of weakness shall be proclaimed, and the newborn child shall be king, for it is the weak being par excellence.'[122]

According to Blanqui's analysis of 'the war between rich and poor' the oppression of the proletariat therefore seems to take two principal forms. First, there is the material reality of injustice itself: the proletariat go hungry and are dying of starvation while the rich lead a life of opulent excess, and indeed society is deliberately structured and organized in such a way that the latter is dependent on the former, hence exploitation serves inequality. Second, there are the forms of oppression that enable this suffering to go unseen, unheard and unrecognized. Dispossessed from the land, the instruments and the fruits of their labour, and disenfranchised from the political sphere, the proletariat are discarded to the periphery where they face deprivation and misery. Each form of oppression therefore reinforces the other in a self-perpetuating cycle. Injustice is the condition of exclusion, exclusion the condition of injustice – both are symptomatic of inequality, both the condition of the proletariat.

It will now be clear that Blanqui's proletariat are the anonymous masses, the invisible or forgotten multitude, the excluded 'barbarians' and 'brutes' whose struggle to assert their equality in an order in which they count for nothing will necessarily bring them into conflict with that very order. Blanqui's fundamental distinction is always between the rich – the privileged few, those with wealth and power who produce nothing but own everything – and the workers – the majority, those without wealth or power who produce everything but own nothing. This division can in turn be reduced to two antagonistic principles: privilege versus equality. The precise, positive socio-economic content of these categories and principles is secondary to their strictly political functions – namely, to create a divide between oppressors and oppressed and to compel a choice between them. In this sense we have seen, with the help of Laclau and Rancière, how Blanqui's use of the people and the proletariat is an extension of the politics of conflict and principled commitment outlined in the previous chapter. To be a proletarian is to affirm, subjectively, one's commitment to the emancipation of the oppressed. A political actor is constituted, first and foremost, through conscious, reasoned choice and deliberate, voluntary action.

Such an emphasis on the political dimensions of Blanqui's proletariat should not lead us, however, to overlook the importance of socio-economic factors in this analysis. We have seen that Blanqui conceives the proletariat or the people as a broad social category. The proletariat does denote, in socio-economic terms, workers and work, toilers and toil; the proletariat and the people are the toiling masses and the impoverished workers, those who must work to live, whose prescribed socio-economic position and function necessarily excludes them from wealth and power. We must therefore acknowledge the extent to which the material deprivation, hardship and suffering caused by real forms and processes of exploitation and domination underpin the broader political project. No doubt it is as a result of these very immediate material concerns that Blanqui, further and more forcefully than Laclau and Rancière, insists on the sustained exercise of collective power and the decisive political practices this will require (association, organization, discipline, unity and so on) as irreducible to the material empowerment and social emancipation of the people.

It is to the practice of this political action itself, of how an actor acts, that I shall turn in Chapter 4.

4

# Volition

*It is with the lever of enthusiasm that we can change the world. All the insights of science, all the refinements of theory, all the calculations of mathematical economics will never create even the smallest fragment of this irresistible force that arises from enthusiastic hearts and exalted minds.*[1]

We can now begin to piece together some of the constituent elements of Blanqui's project. The previous three chapters revealed a politics that is based on a theory of a conscious and committed actor. Enlightened thought, Blanqui assumes, precedes decisive action. Unenlightened, unguided and uninformed political action is doomed to manipulation, appropriation and disintegration – to failure, in short. What, then, are the characteristics of effective political action itself? We have considered who will participate in and lead these forms of popular mobilization, but we have only begun to consider how and why those actors will do so. This brings us to the question of collective conscious volition.

'The principle of every action is in the will of a free being,' Rousseau affirms. 'It is not the word *freedom* which means nothing; it is the word *necessity*.' Rousseau insists as a matter of course that man 'is free in his actions,' and 'if man is active and free, he acts on his own.'[2] A process of collective self-determination therefore begins when 'each of us puts his person and all his power in common under the supreme direction of the general will'. A group of individuals' conscious act of voluntary association produces a 'moral and collective body', the people, of which all willing individuals are part and through which a unified, general will, whose object is the common good, is declared and exercised as sovereign.[3] Blanqui's conception of a common or collective will broadly follows some of the most salient features of Rousseau's.

For the former as for the latter, this is a process that presupposes enlightened intelligence and rational choice; it is a process of deliberate action and collective assembly that seeks to formulate and impose a common goal, cause or principle and that will require duty and devotion in order to inspire and sustain it.[4]

The aim of the first half of this chapter is to reconstruct Blanqui's conception of collective volition. After developing some of the initial observations outlined in Chapter 1, I then return to what seems to me as a major shortcoming of Blanqui's voluntarist politics: the overprivileging of enlightened consciousness as a precondition of volition. Insofar as those deemed unconscious and unenlightened are by extension incapable of genuine voluntary action, Blanqui displays a certain lack of confidence in the mass of the people as self-determining political actors, I suggest, as illustrated in the problem of post-revolutionary transition and the temporality of sociopolitical change.

# How to begin

### A conflict of wills

Recall that Blanqui's political theory begins with a broad division between the realms of nature and humanity. Reason is what distinguishes human beings from nature and animals. The capacity for enlightened thought enables humans to understand the present organization of society and affords them the potential power to reorganize that society on the basis of reason itself. Together these assumptions underpin Blanqui's notion of conscious volition. 'The works of nature are fated or fatal, and are carried out according to immutable laws,' he claims. 'The works of human thought are changeable like thought itself, and depend on will, on energy or on weakness.'[5] Enlightened thought is powerless to change society without the active will to realize it materially, hence Blanqui privileges 'intelligence and will' as the principal force behind sociopolitical change.[6] The growth and improvement of the brain through education is precisely how a conscious will can be actively cultivated and developed, as we have already seen.

Although the philosophical grounding of Blanqui's voluntarism only received substantial elaboration in the 1860s, its core organizing principle can be traced back to his formative political engagements of the early 1830s. Already in 1832 Blanqui knows that 'we can do it, if we will it! [*nous le pouvons! si nous le voulons!*]'.[7] By linking *vouloir* and *pouvoir*, willing and doing – a move that offers greater precision to the claim a year earlier that when it comes to freedom 'we want it, and we will have it [*nous la voulons et nous l'aurons*]'[8] – Blanqui ties collective will to collective capacity. By maintaining the importance of *pouvoir*, of the actual capacity or the doing, he makes clear that we can will only what we are collectively capable of doing. People cannot achieve anything, anywhere, at any time, then. To have the collective will to realize a common goal or aim is to have the actual collective capacity to realize it; but this realization remains at every moment dependent on the collective willing of it.[9] A collective actor is therefore capable of achieving its chosen goal so long as it is prepared to do what it takes – so long as it has the necessary resolve and commitment – to achieve it.

Blanqui assumes that all forms of hegemonic power, whether that of the rich or of the people, are the product of conscious thought and of conscious will – of organized political force, in other words. All social orders deploy consciously conceived means in the active pursuit of consciously conceived ends. Blanqui even summons a maxim more commonly associated with revolutionary movements in order to foreground the deliberate practices and strategies of the established order. 'Whoever wills the end wills the means,' he notes. 'Stupefy in order to exploit, make man as docile as a horse' – such is the oppressor's vision for society and how it goes about realizing it.[10]

A will is exercised in the service of specific interests and imposed by means of political power. The law, as we have already seen, in the human realm means 'the will of whoever has force. It remains to be seen if this will conforms to right.'[11] By the same token, then, under an egalitarian popular government the people 'indicate their will … through the law, which is nothing other the expression of the general will'. The duty of each citizen, Blanqui declares after Rousseau, is to 'obey the general will' as the sovereign authority.[12] Under the existing order, however, shaped by the private interests of the rich, 'the triad of Sword–Money–Altar is still sovereign, and [it] can only maintain itself through violence and debasement'.[13] The will of the rich acts in the name of oppression, the will of the people in the name of justice; both wills emanate from an intellectual conception of humans and society, both serve a particular set of social interests: the private interests of the wealthy few on one hand, the common interests of poor majority on the other.

Political struggle reflects this balance of social forces. And the established order, having imposed its will on the people, will not readily relinquish that dominance – quite the contrary. 'Capital will never consent to relinquishing even one iota of its power'; 'it will not, it cannot make concessions.'[14] Why, for example, Blanqui asks, did the Société Populaire, an association of ribbon workers formed in Saint-Etienne in 1848, cause such fury among the city's manufacturers? Quite simply because this 'new', rival 'power' curbs that of the manufacturers and thereby threatens the most basic existing social relation: the domination of labour by capital. In Blanqui's eyes the wider lesson is certainly clear: 'Capital commands but does not obey', for it requires 'absolute power' and will accept 'no other relation with labour than that of master and slave'.[15]

An oppressive order's crucial ruse, however, is its ability to pursue its own private interests 'under the pretext of general interests'.[16] More serious and damaging still is the conflation – propagated by the rich and accepted by vast swathes of the people – of a deliberately imposed social order with a form of natural fate or providential design. Blanqui notes how this strategy of presenting the contingent as necessary, of insisting on either blind, natural forces or transcendent, disembodied wills as determining humanity's social and economic arrangements, has been so successfully achieved that any form of conscious human agency therein is totally obscured: a contingent act of human volition is turned into and duly becomes perceived as an inevitable 'fact' of nature or the preordained will of God.[17]

Politics begins with the recognition of and engagement in this conflict of wills. Emancipatory politics means consciously constituting, organizing and imposing a popular will that is capable of overcoming any particular wills. 'The worker,' Blanqui insists, 'through the force of union, no longer has to endure the will of his former rulers.'[18] How, then, is a common will constituted in the first instance? And how can the will of the people overcome the will of the rich?

## Collective volition as positive and practical exercise

One of the root causes of the ultimate defeat of July 1830, according to Blanqui, was that 'the masses had not formally expressed any positive political will. What moved them, what had pushed them into our public squares', he suggests, 'was their hatred of the Bourbons, their firm resolve to overthrow them. There were traces of both Bonapartism and the Republic in their wishes for the government that was to emerge from the barricades.'[19] Two main consequences follow from this claim.

First, an upsurge of defiant indignation or general opposition, anti-Bourbonism in the case of 1830, is inadequate when it comes to the subsequent, decisive work of formulating a clear, common goal and then realizing it as an act of sovereignty.[20] Opposition to hereditary monarchy is not in itself an affirmation of justice, freedom and equality, as the people discovered in the wake of July when their fellow opponents of Charles X, the bourgeoisie, simply replaced one government of wealth and privilege with another upon seizing power. A process of collective self-determination, Blanqui reasons, is capable of articulating what it stands for and then realizing it. Clearly stated principles also force the taking of sides, demarcating friends and foes alike. In July, however, the people did not go beyond anti-Bourbonism in order to form, declare and then enforce their collective will as sovereign power, nor, more critically, did they believe or know themselves to be capable of constituting and sustaining that power themselves – hence their inability to distinguish between their genuine friends and foes; hence their readiness, having offered alliance with and accepted the leadership of their adversaries, to put down their arms and willingly surrender their collective power to the bourgeois usurpers; and hence their transformation, following the bourgeois betrayal, from a concentrated, active force into a dispersed, passive spectator to the drama in which they previously had the leading role.[21]

Crucial to this basic capacity to formulate a common goal is the question of political leadership and popular consciousness. As Blanqui argued in 1834 when looking back on the political sequence that began four years earlier: 'The various popular demonstrations, far from seeking to overthrow the [new Orléanist] dynasty, only sought to enlighten it. In December 1830, as in February, June and September 1831, one thing remains constant: the idea of destroying the new monarchy did not enter into the people's head.'[22] During 1830 and its aftermath the people, lacking consciousness of and confidence in their power, dispersed their concentrated collective force, willingly surrendering their position of strength to the bourgeois usurpers. This fatal mistake, Blanqui claims, would not have happened if the people had had time to find their 'natural leaders, those who would have led the way to victory'.[23] A popular force, if it is to form and impose its collective will successfully, cannot be blind and unconscious energy. The people require awareness, encouragement and guidance. The people must know that the exercise of their power is sovereign and they must know how to exercise that power. The role of leadership is therefore to inform the people of their 'real position' and 'interests', to 'teach them how they can conquer and then preserve their rights'.[24] It is to make the people aware of the possibility of their own power and to guard against those who might seek to manipulate that power.

Many of these principles inform a broader – and particularly stimulating – critique of resistance to injustice as a minimal form of political action. Depending on the context, Blanqui often evokes 'resistance' as a necessary though ultimately inadequate endeavour; it is often symptomatic, for the revolutionary movement, of passivity and resignation.[25] Resistance must be linked 'to the practice of emancipation. If resistance is defined first and foremost as resistance to oppression, domination or coercion', Hallward has argued more recently, 'then engagement in resistance would itself involve some appeal to the normative criteria of freedom and the work of self-liberation'.[26] A strike, Blanqui writes, illustrating a similar point, 'is the simple idea of resistance to oppression. Everyone rallies around it'. Blanqui even goes so far as to describe a strike as 'the only really popular weapon in the struggle against capital'.[27] And yet, precisely because it can but remain a temporary form of mass resistance to the wider structures and processes of capitalist exploitation and oppression, a strike – much like revolutionary seizures of power – is not an end in itself so much as a beginning, an initial popular mobilization that provides a basis for the possibility of popular power. 'Employing a strike as a provisional defensive tactic against the oppression of capital,' Blanqui explains, 'the popular masses must concentrate all their efforts towards those political changes that alone are capable of carrying out social transformation and the redistribution of goods and products in accordance with justice.'[28] At stake in emancipatory politics is far more than an ephemeral rupture with structural oppression. Emancipatory politics in its most meaningful sense is the process of actually organizing and exercising a collective power capable of overthrowing and transcending structures of oppression. This is why the concentrated will of 'the popular masses' poses such a threat to the established order.[29] This is why the forces of oppression seek to maintain the worker in his 'atomic individuality, to deprive him of any form of collective action that might protect his interests'.[30] Exploitative social relations can only be imposed on an uninformed, passive and divided population; the existing social order therefore relies on actively creating such a population and maintaining it in this state of political impotence.[31]

By the same token, emancipatory politics is not a matter of making demands to and receiving concessions from an established power but of the people seizing power and realizing their own goals themselves. History teaches us that those with power and privilege will not voluntarily compromise an order from which they prosper. In 1789 had the people 'humbly begged' the nobility to relinquish their feudal rights they would have been punished for insolence. Hence the people 'went about things in a different way'.[32] For Blanqui, again the lesson is clear and simple: direct popular empowerment means direct popular action. From his early writings on the student movement, Blanqui insists that young people – just like any group of ordinary people – 'have the right to join together in order to guide their efforts towards a common goal, and they will use this right'.[33] History shows that 'an exercise in political will involves taking power, not receiving it, on the assumption that (as a matter of "reason" or "natural right") the people are always already entitled to take it'.[34]

The second, and no less important, point that emerges from Blanqui's analysis of the defeat of July 1830 links to the first: what is most fundamental to a process of popular self-determination and the formation of a collective will is the practical exercise of willing itself. Blanqui's 'positive political will' denotes the actual, collective willing of an end or goal. Recall that, according to the maxim 'we can do it, if we will it!', the capacity to realize freedom and equality is tied to the willing of this realization. Insofar as a collective group is unified and organized, determined and resolute in the willing of a common goal it is capable of realizing it, Blanqui assumes.

After the revolutionary seizure of power and the work of popular education had been completed – a problematic issue to which we shall return below – a general will would govern society through the active and informed citizenry of whom it would be constituted. 'All the workers, transformed from passive instruments into enlightened citizens,' Blanqui writes, reaffirming the centrality of conscious volition to the dual process of empowerment and emancipation, 'would spontaneously bring into association all their intellectual and physical capacities, and the problem of organising labour in accordance with justice would be resolved.'[35] This form of 'gradual and progressive general association'[36] that is developed through active and ongoing popular participation would enable general interests to prevail over private interests in the arrangement of social and economic life. 'Industrial creations, public works, will be the fecund work of the general will, and no longer the ruinous game of speculation or of absolute power.'[37]

Communism, Blanqui maintains, is the name of the only possible form of social organization which can establish 'absolute equality – the sole means by which to reconcile everyone's demanding claims with those of everyone else', for if freedom implies 'social parity among individuals' it follows that 'equality is the limit to freedom'.[38] Therein lies the relationship, also outlined by Rousseau, between the individual and the social body: only the 'full, integral association' of all individuals can both enable individual freedom to flourish and protect every individual from the egoist private interests of individualism.[39] Like Rousseau's balance sheet on the civil state,[40] Blanqui sees the loss of natural freedom and unlimited right as the means to gain civil freedom and the rights of a citizen. Just as Rousseau maintains that 'to be driven by our appetites alone is slavery, while to obey a law that we have imposed on ourselves is freedom',[41] so too does Blanqui prioritize the freedom from oppression and domination over the so-called freedom to enrich oneself through the exploitation of others. This does not mean, of course, that egalitarian forms of economic and political association can be the result of coercion or compulsion. Across all his writings Blanqui is emphatic that genuine political subjectivity begins with genuine freedom – that is, with individual conscious volition. The act of collective association is a product of individual voluntary choice and conscious decision, or it is not. The 'common undertaking and work'[42] of association is, by definition, a collective activity, and anyone who joins will always do so 'out of their full and free will'.⁴³

A voluntary and collective process of willing cannot therefore predetermine its end results or foresee the eventual form(s) it might take. Only on the road to the new society, only in 'acting towards the triumph of equality as the final goal',⁴⁴ will its actual form become apparent. It is on this basis that Blanqui consistently rejects any calls to 'provide a formula, a form of administration, a system, a set of regulations'⁴⁵ for an imagined future society in the manner of Fourier, Saint-Simon and Cabet – indeed the latter and the Icarian movement 'made the mistake precisely of conflating the regular ideal of the future with the empty hypotheses peddled by [these] tin-pot revealers'.⁴⁶ For Blanqui as for Marx and Engels, communism cannot be imposed 'by fiat, as an abstract a priori principle'. 'We simply predict that it will be the infallible result of universal education', he notes.⁴⁷ For Blanqui as for Machiavelli, the 'fantastic mirage of programmes, these fogs of the kingdom of Utopia', must be well and truly abandoned; revolutionaries had to 'leave the domain of fiction so as to return to reality', focusing all their energy and efforts on the work of organized political action here and now.⁴⁸ Anything outside of these immediate practical concerns, Blanqui insists, 'is not within our competence'.⁴⁹

Emancipation, in this sense, is a series of conscious decisions and deliberate actions. 'It is the process of actively willing or choosing that renders a particular course of action preferable to another', Hallward writes. 'It is the active willing which determines what is possible and what is right, and makes it so.'⁵⁰

## How to continue

### Overcoming obstacles and resistance

Blanqui seeks to foreground the paths to an unknown and unknowable destination. Understanding the approaching obstacles and barriers these paths will present, and the requirements for their successful negotiation, are therefore vital considerations. If an emancipated, egalitarian society, Blanqui argues, 'is the work of everyone, a project that proceeds over time, through trial and error, through gradual and progressive experience, through an unknown, spontaneous current', the 'river thus slowly takes shape from the confluence of a thousand springs, of billions of drops of water'. So the role and task of revolutionaries is clear: 'We can remove the obstacles in its path, and help to carve out a downward slope, but we should never pretend that we can create the river itself.'[51]

The emergence of obstacles and resistance to popular power is indeed a crucial issue for Blanqui. Rousseau had of course already recognized that 'the sole means that [men] have of preserving themselves is to create, by combination, a totality of forces sufficient to overcome the obstacles resisting them, to direct their operation by a single impulse, and make them act in unison'.[52] But Blanqui's attempt to account for both the inevitability of this resistance and the demands of overcoming it arguably goes further than Rousseau – and no doubt the century separating the two thinkers, the differing pressures and priorities of two distinct historical contexts, drove Blanqui to pursue the point to a greater degree than Rousseau before him. The political struggles, and failures, of the nineteenth century informed and continually reinforced Blanqui's persistent preoccupation with the question of how to organize a mass mobilization and achieve a common goal in the face of those dominant groups and private interests that will inevitably work, with all the abundant resources at their disposal, to impede, contain, deceive and divide it.

Political analysis, as Blanqui sees it, essentially boils down to comprehending the balance of forces between the people and the rich. The response to the – real or imagined – threat of popular power is therefore of particular interest to him. Fear of the 'rabble', he wrote in the wake of 1848, is the key to understanding the manoeuvrings of those like Ledru-Rollin whose personal interests are threatened by the 'prospect of a revolution from the streets'.[53] To understand the politics of the July Monarchy, he similarly told an audience in 1832, is to identify the spectre that haunts it: the people of 1830. One popular victory is all it took in July, and all it would take again, for the established order to break.[54]

This explains why it was imperative for the new regime to delegitimize insurrection – the (inconvenient) origin of its own power. Blanqui describes at length the Orléanist government's attempts to derail the advance of the popular movement and its concern not to appear openly hostile when working, both independently and with its foreign allies, to contain the threat posed by 'the people of July' so as not to provoke another uprising.[55] Attempting to establish its control and satisfy the European monarchs' demands to disempower the French people, the government tentatively began 'to stifle enthusiasm, to discourage patriots and to instil mistrust and discord across the nation.'[56] The kings of Europe granted Louis-Philippe time 'to deepen the people's discouragement, to make them lose their taste for revolution, and to strike them with inertia.'[57] In short, the depoliticization of ordinary people was the order of the day. And Blanqui regretfully recognizes the government's success in containing this popular power and neutralizing this revolutionary passion, thereby preventing the possibility of a second revolution.

What we discover here, in the positive implications of these reflections on popular disempowerment, is crucial for Blanqui's political theory as a whole. Unity, confidence and enthusiasm, Blanqui reasons, are all essential for the people to become a revolutionary force capable of overpowering their adversaries. A process of popular empowerment requires collective enthusiasm to initiate and then to sustain it thereafter if the stagnation, containment and division to which defeats are often owed are to be successfully avoided.

The extent to which revolution would invariably incite counter-revolution remained a key concern of Blanqui's in the wake of the July Revolution. His response to this question was both clear and consistent. Just as barriers will continue to block the popular movement's path, so the people must continually work to surmount them. For the obstacles and resistance to the realization of a given goal can only be overcome when directly confronted and actively negotiated. 'We must march on', Blanqui declares. 'When the masses encounter an obstacle they stop, gather themselves together, and overturn it. This is the history of the past; it is also that of the future.'[58] Such resolute determination in pursuit of a common goal is precisely the great achievement of February 1848, when, 'after three days of resistance', the people – those ordinary people without wealth or power who are dismissed as 'the rabble' – had, through their collective action, 'forced the bourgeois guard to submit to the Republic'.[59] But 1848 would also demonstrate that as an initial mass mobilization takes hold, as a popular movement advances, radicalizes and the stakes are raised, resistance to it will intensify. In the wake of a political revolution those who seek to exploit, oppress and manipulate the people for their own personal gain will reappear and attempt to reassert their control. And where manipulation and deceit are not employed, the force of arms readily will be. April 1834, June 1848, March 1871 – all showed the brutal resistance that a popular movement threatening the power and privilege of the established order would face.

1848 taught Blanqui that the only political force capable of overpowering this counter-revolutionary resistance is the conscious and organized Parisian proletariat. This is the key message of the *Instructions for an Armed Uprising*. No government forces, Blanqui argues, can withstand the power of the organized people of Paris – 'a well-organised Parisian army' – collectively working towards the same goal and prepared to do what is necessary in order to achieve it.[60] Or as he put it in 1851: 'In the presence of armed proletarians, all obstacles, resistances and impossibilities will disappear.'[61]

## Moral duty, resolute commitment

Such emphasis on actively working towards a common goal raises the question of the subjective motivations and requirements, both individual and collective, of this activity itself. If emancipation is achieved only through concrete action, action that must confront and overpower direct and persistent opposition, then one must be prepared to see to this task of practical realization with all the resolve it will continually demand. The overcoming of obstacles and resistance must be nourished by a clear conviction and an unyielding determination to prevail. Let us explore this point further.

Blanqui's insistence on duty and devotion – so central to and characteristic of his politics – alongside resolute commitment and a sense of purpose, arises from an acute awareness of the major difficulties facing radical movements. The 'Initiation Ceremony of the Society of the Seasons' of 1837 readily acknowledges that the 'realisation' of the principles of popular sovereignty and equality 'is not easy'. 'Our enemies are numerous and powerful', the text continues. 'They have all society's forces at their disposal; we, republicans, whose very name is proscribed, we have only our courage and our rectitude.'[62] Individual and collective political engagement is, to be sure, guided by a set of fundamental moral principles and qualities. 'Sobriety, courage, force, devotion' – these, according to the 'Formulaire de réception de la Société des Familles' of 1834, are the 'virtues' of a true republican.[63] 'Knowledge, intelligence, magnanimity, devotion, virtue' – all of which constitute, Blanqui later insisted, 'all that is great, noble and beautiful' in humanity – are in fact the principal 'enemies' of those who seek to repress, divide and deceive the people both before and after the revolutionary rupture.[64]

Certainly, the moral dimension of Blanqui's conception of duty is essential. As we shall see in Chapter 5, Blanqui assumes that morality is 'the foundation of societies'.[65] But he also assumes that there is no such thing as eternal or fixed morals or morality. Morality, Blanqui argues, 'is a resultant, which can always change and vary, of the intellectual movement that people make.'[66] History reveals morality to be always, first, a direct emanation of – and so proportional to – the wider level of intellectual enlightenment and, second, acquired and achieved not through divine revelation but through the didactic process of human cognition and thus through humanity itself. Since morality is 'strictly dependent on education', it follows that 'if enlightenment is extinguished, morality' – which is to say, for Blanqui, a kind of enlightened, collective morality – 'disappears with it'.[67] Contrary to spiritualist claims regarding the invariability of morality and duty, Blanqui maintains that both morality and duty change and can be changed through the material process of cognition outlined in Chapter 1.

Here the role of an intellectual elite seems to reappear. Those who have already achieved the necessary level of enlightenment, Blanqui appears to suggest, are able to act with devotion and a sense of duty to their cause, which is itself the cause of engendering enlightened morality through enlightened instruction. In fact, the radical contingency of human affairs is such that 'one only arrives at equality through devotion. Devotion alone gives thought this irresistible power that rules the world.'[68] Enlightened thought and resolute duty are the very means through which equality will be animated and achieved, converting the ideal into the real. The conscious and active commitment to equality, this dedication and devotion, is precisely how the principle itself 'unites and brings men together; it is through intelligence alone that it governs them and that it leads them to coordinate their efforts towards a common goal, which is the well-being of all.'[69]

Morality, and humanity with it, can therefore be lifted to great heights through enlightened education, achieving the 'feeling of justice' and social solidarity, or be plunged to the depths of egoism through the propagation of ignorance.[70] Hitherto immorality has widely prevailed, Blanqui argues after Rousseau, because of the systematic mis-education and deception of the people by the rich. Those who have already attained the necessary level of intelligence and knowledge to be able to see through such deceit, who know and understand that injustice presupposes ignorance of its existence, are thus morally obliged to expose and overcome this state of affairs. And so a practical imperative, a revolutionary duty, emerges: 'We must struggle relentlessly against ignorance in order, first, to maintain morality at its present level, and second, to elevate it further by developing our existing knowledge and advancing the conquests of thought.'[71] A revolutionary must indeed be willing to sacrifice wealth and well-being, to face imprisonment, even to lay down their life in their commitment to their convictions. To carry out one's 'duty' is, necessarily, to 'carry it out in full'.[72] Anticipating Fidel Castro's famous injunction, 'the duty of every revolutionary is to make the revolution',[73] Blanqui certainly does not shirk from assuming the full implications of this principle. 'The duty of a revolutionary', he declares, as a sort of guiding maxim, 'is always to struggle, to struggle no matter what, to struggle to extinction.'[74]

Moreover, Blanqui assumes that strength of conviction confers political strength. Unlike government troops fighting under constraint and compulsion, in the popular ranks 'they fight for an idea. There, they are all volunteers who are motivated by enthusiasm, not fear.'[75] It is for this reason that Blanqui rejects the accusation that Gustave Tridon and the other militants who comprised 'the political and philosophical movement of the Latin Quarter' in the 1860s were 'automatons' or 'machines, blindly obeying a watchword or slogan'. All these young people, Blanqui affirms, 'have ideas, characters, passions'.[76] If individual conscious volition towards a common goal is an essential characteristic of a collective political actor, the 'essential quality' of a government soldier, by contrast, is 'passive obedience, the renouncement of all individuality'. Never seeking explanation of their orders, never passing comment on the situation, the distance for Blanqui between the government soldier and the revolutionary militant is striking. 'Under the pretence of training soldiers, [the army] seek to create machines that walk and strike, deaf and blind rifle-carriers, automatons without memories or future, without country or family, without mercy or remorse.'[77] Militants devoted to an idea have, precisely by virtue of their voluntary decision to become militants and to persevere resolutely as such, all the political resources necessary to bring about the triumph of that cause. 'They are superior to their adversary not only through devotion,' Blanqui claims, 'but even more so through intelligence. They have the moral and even the physical upper hand as a result of their conviction, vigour and resourcefulness, their vitality of body and mind; they combine stout hearts with clear heads. No troops in the world are equal to these elite men.' Blanqui indeed insists that the 'zeal, ardour and intelligence of the volunteers will compensate for' the insurgent army's lack of military cadres to form and train it.[78] The underlying assumption of all these statements, and which is again one shared by the Cuban revolutionaries,[79] is very simple: a popular force that possesses a resolute conviction and a clear strategy has the capacity to overthrow an oppressive force.

We might infer at least two interlinked points from the elements above. First, any true sense of duty can be in no way involuntary. Revolutionary duty and the courage, self-sacrifice, discipline and honour it inspires must be a product of conscious volition, of rationally acquired knowledge and deliberate action, for this will be its source of decisive power when confronting difficulties and resistance as they inevitably appear. Second, a voluntary sense of duty emanates from and is guided by an enlightened morality, which is itself developed through a process of enlightened instruction. To qualify the first point, then: one can certainly act out of a sense of duty, or with a sense of passion, towards reactionary, unenlightened causes. But here we should recall the conflict of wills outlined earlier. For Blanqui, there is an essential difference between the voluntary duty to act in the name of freely acquired and developed ideas and the (often involuntary) duty to act in the name of corruption, deceit and oppression (the latter, to be sure, is reproduced as much by the unconsciously manipulated as by the conscious manipulators themselves). In many respects the question of duty, of truly and faithfully 'serving an idea' or principle,[80] goes to the heart of what it means to be a free and conscious human being, for 'glory lies in voluntarily facing danger for the triumph of one's convictions; it does not lie in danger suffered as a result of constraint and fear.'[81]

## Politics as faith

Politics, according to Blanqui, is as much a matter of logical reasoning as it is of subjective passion. Such is the meaning behind his repeated invocation of the unity of head and heart: whether drawn from the bourgeoisie or the masses, a revolutionary conceives the ending of injustice and inequality as a conscious duty and task guided by humanist compassion (heart) on the one hand and cerebral rationalism (head) on the other.[82] It is not a case of separating material (suffering and well-being) from cerebral (ignorance and enlightenment) concerns but of thinking the two together as the basis of a critique of the present and a guiding ideal for the future. A rationally conceived and passionately avowed commitment to freedom and happiness are the sine qua non of a voluntarist actor, triggering both the decision to begin and nourishing the resolve to continue. If freedom is the 'immortal motto', the 'sacred cry' for which all revolutionaries enthusiastically act with fervent devotion to realize, as they must, this is because, as Blanqui explained in January 1831, 'its echo alone stirs our hearts; it alone has a right to our love, our devotion.'[83] He later professed in 1834 that 'equality is our faith; we march with ardour and confidence beneath its holy banner, filled with veneration and enthusiasm for the immortal defenders of that faith, animated by the same devotion, and ready, like them, to spill our blood for its triumph.'[84] Like Buonarroti, who described equality as his 'religion' and his life its 'testimony',[85] Blanqui often frames politics and political commitment in terms of a struggle of opposing faiths or, worst of all, of a struggle against those who either avow no political faith whatsoever or who enthrone the golden calf.[86] The accusation of apostasy that reappears across Blanqui's writings[87] – already in 1834 he pours scorn on the 'apostates' who commit the 'crime' of abandoning intelligence, who 'blaspheme' or attempt to 'enchain' it and thus show that 'they no longer march along the road of humanity'[88] – is likewise informed by similar principles.

But how can Blanqui simultaneously claim that 'the rule of equality and fraternity' is 'our sole religion', 'our social faith',[89] while maintaining that communism is 'the last word of social science'?[90] Is there not a tension between the insistence on emancipation as a work of faith and the conception of communism as an Enlightenment project? He himself states that there is a 'complete contradiction in every respect between faith and reason. Society must abandon one of these two principles. They can no longer live together.'⁹¹ How does Blanqui reconcile his vehement anti-spiritualism with his own avowed political faith?

Reminding ourselves of the fundamentals of Blanqui's sociopolitical theory can shed some light on this issue. 'What is materialism,' Blanqui asks, 'if not the doctrine which declares the universe to be infinite in time and space, and the mind an inseparable property of the nervous or neural substance, in life as in death?'⁹² The human mind is an emanation of, and so in no way distinct from, the materiality of the human brain. As we saw in Chapter 1, Blanqui insists as a matter of principle that thought cannot be immaterial or disembodied; thought, he writes, is 'only a product of the brain', it 'exists only through matter' and is therefore 'enclosed in the brain'.⁹³ To champion collective faith, then, is not to abandon the primacy of objective matter, of the human brain, from which this cerebrally cultivated morality, faith, passion and sense of duty appear, as does spiritualism in its distinction between spirit and matter. Blanqui indeed states that while Catholicism represents 'the death of intelligence, of thought, of the brain', Protestantism, for its part, marks 'the death of conscience, of sentiment, of the heart'.⁹⁴ It follows that, in order to avoid its 'degeneracy' at the hands of 'mysticism', 'sentiment' must remain 'supported and held up by' reason.⁹⁵ Blanqui's project, in this sense, seeks to develop and defend a form of enlightened, materialist morality. Enlightened reason produces an enlightened morality, a conscious passion for freedom and equality born of the knowledge that all human beings are born free and equal. Socialism, Blanqui accordingly explains, 'is not just scientific truth, it is also the highest morality'.⁹⁶

To say that communism is the most logical, rational form of social organization does not in itself offer the means for its establishment. As Blanqui recognizes with regard to religion: 'Science and history have handed down their sentence. All that remains is to execute it.'⁹⁷ Religion may be irrational and anachronistic. But that does not mean that collective human action is no less necessary in order to end it. Equality, Blanqui stresses, can only be realized through collective human action. And this action requires belief – belief that equality is right, belief that it is just, belief that it is true. Reflecting on Che Guevara's death, Fidel Castro – another figure who repeatedly insists on the decisive role of belief and faith in political struggle – argued that 'without this type of revolutionary and human being, ready to do what they did; without the spirit to confront the enormous obstacles they faced; without the readiness to die that accompanied them at every moment; without their deeply held conviction in the justice of their cause and their unyielding faith in the invincible force of the peoples, against a power like Yankee imperialism' – 'without these, the liberation of the peoples of this continent will not be attained.'[98] Only this profound and resolute subjective commitment is capable of advancing the cause of freedom in the face of successive defeats, in the knowledge that history and historical processes will not provide the solution sooner or later, on the assumption that people can rely on nothing but themselves as the bearers of their own destiny. 'Through persecution and violence we will march firmly, unshakably, towards our goal,' Blanqui declared in 1831; 'we are young, we are patient; we will not easily give up on freedom.'[99] Defeat is not definitive, then. It is the summons to begin again, to ensure victory next time.

## Voluntary servitude

Underlying Blanqui's voluntarism – and of major importance to his politics as a whole – is the conviction that to surrender voluntarily the capacity to will is to become an agent of oppression and domination. Of course the will to overthrow servitude presupposes consciousness of that servitude in the first instance, as we have seen. Nonetheless, since Blanqui defines humans first and foremost in terms of their potential capacity for voluntary self-determination, it still follows that to obey passively is to renounce voluntarily one's most basic natural ability: to will freely. 'To renounce our freedom is to renounce our character as men, the rights, and even the duties of humanity', Rousseau states. 'It is incompatible with the nature of man; to remove the will's freedom is to remove all morality from our actions.'[100] This conjunction of free volition as the basic characteristic of humanity and moral duty as decisive in the triumph of freedom or tyranny is fundamental for Rousseau and Blanqui alike. Since for Blanqui the brain alone 'makes man what he is',[101] tyranny indeed requires 'abjection, rampant submission, the abdication of all dignity, voluntary stupefaction [*l'abrutissement volontaire*]'.[102] Recall Blanqui's assumption that oppression and servitude are not natural, preordained or inevitable, but the result of the consciously formulated and actively imposed will of the exploiter. Any form of resignation, of accepting an externally prescribed or historically imposed 'fate', must therefore be dismissed as a matter of course – the political stakes are simply too high. 'When a nation that is afflicted with a bad government no longer has the will or the force to change it', that nation 'gradually falls into a sepulchre'.[103]

Blanqui does not stop there, however. In the face of systematic oppression and ubiquitous injustice, his response is to extend and radicalize the role of duty within his voluntarism in line with his notion of political morality outlined above. As Spitzer puts it, in Blanqui's eyes 'the passive victim of a violation of natural rights [is] as guilty as his oppressor, for the acceptance of injustice [is] its sanction. ... Therefore everyone [is] morally bound to the struggle against injustice, no matter what the cost'.[104] From his very first public text, a call to arms written in the heat of the *Trois Glorieuses*, Blanqui sets out this fundamental choice between passive compliance and principled defiance. 'Do we consent to becoming a herd of slaves under the lash of the Jesuits?', he asks. 'No, no! Sooner death.'[105] Politics conceived as moral duty allows no room for ambivalence, indecision or purported impartiality: either you reject the injustices and oppression of the status quo and work with all your energy to overthrow them, or you are complicit in injustice and oppression. For a reactionary force like spiritualism derives its 'strength' precisely from the 'impunity' conferred upon it; impunity is precisely how it remains 'inviolable', empowered by 'the humility of its victims', Blanqui notes, before adding: 'Woe to those who suffer abuse without returning it! Their fate is sealed.'[106]

We might say, then, that for Blanqui all power that commits injustice is illegitimate; all illegitimate power is empowered by voluntary obedience; all those who empower illegitimacy consent to injustice; and all justice is achieved through the defiance and overpowering of illegitimate power.

## Collective volition and revolutionary transition

Blanqui's reflections on the necessity of a post-revolutionary transitional power – first outlined in his writings in 1837[107] – arose from a set of questions that, to his mind, became particularly urgent following the defeat of 1830 (and would remain so in the wake of 1848): What would happen the day after power had been seized from the ruling government? What is the relationship between political and social transformation? Who would continue the revolution, pushing and guiding it forward? How would they do so? These are questions – questions that confront all revolutionary thinkers – we shall now consider.

## A patient realism

Surprisingly for a figure often dismissed as an impatient adventurist, when it comes to the construction a new post-revolutionary social order and the question of social change more generally, Blanqui calls for patience and caution. Once political power had been seized, priorities would have to be made and struggles carefully chosen. 'There are too many obstacles that will require years of siege or trench warfare for us to distract ourselves with a full-scale attack on a hurdle or a hedgerow that could be cleared with a single leap,' Blanqui explains. 'The army, the magistrates, Christianity and political organisations – these are mere hurdles. Ignorance is a formidable bastion. One day for the hurdles; twenty years for the bastion.'[108] To evoke a metaphor unfamiliar to Blanqui, we might say that therein lies the relation between the base and superstructure of society (although Blanqui of course assumes the opposite of Marx – that ideas and consciousness determine the material reality and social existence of man). Ignorance is the intellectual foundation or base, so to speak, upon which the material exploitation and inequality of the existing sociopolitical order are established; ignorance is the primary source of the deception and manipulation that enable social domination and political oppression. Conversely, as Blanqui repeatedly insists, universal enlightenment is the base of equality, freedom and justice – of communism. Blanqui's communism, we have seen, posits the end of domination and inequality on an informed, conscious population; the advent of communism will occur when 'no man, thanks to the universality of enlightenment, can ever again be the dupe of another' and 'judgement will become the prerogative of all.'[109] To think that radical social transformation can be achieved immediately, without the protracted work of ending ignorance through mass enlightenment, is therefore 'the dream of impatient people'; it is 'a dream that cannot be realised before the transformation of minds'. Without mass enlightenment, the 'will of even the whole of France would still be powerless to hasten the moment of this transformation, and any attempt to do so would lead to failure'.[110] Popular ignorance, it seems, is the one obstacle that cannot be overcome by force of will alone. Such a claim is certainly consistent with the primacy Blanqui accords to consciousness in his conception of conscious volition: at all times and in all circumstances, intelligence and thought are the basis of decisive action. This is precisely why, as has already been made clear, 'community cannot be improvised, because it will be a result of education, which cannot be improvised either'.[111]

Blanqui has no illusions about the difficulty of transforming society's ruling ideas and consciousness. He is brutally frank about the time and work required to reach an emancipated society and the distance between now and then. 'A prerequisite of communism is the universality of enlightenment, and we are yet to reach this.'[112] To quote phrases in which, without this wider contextualization and the essential qualifications it holds, Blanqui appears to suggest that communism is an order-in-waiting, brought to light through the force of events alone, is therefore somewhat misleading.[113] Political revolution can occur immediately, social revolution cannot. One need look no further than 'Communism, the Future of Society' (1869) to find a clearer statement of this point. 'The day after a revolution, a *coup de théâtre* occurs,' Blanqui writes. 'It is not that a sudden transformation takes place all at once. Men and things remain the same as before. It is just that hope and fear have changed sides. The chains fall, the nation is free, and an immense horizon opens up before it.'[114] The *horizon* of communism certainly appears for the first time in the wake of revolution, then, but not communism – not the abolition of 'all forms of exploitation of man by man'[115] – itself.

It is worth recalling what is at stake here. Like Rousseau, Blanqui knows that humanity can be corrupted or elevated, debased or ennobled. And again like Rousseau, for Blanqui the ultimate goal of revolution is indeed to change human nature – to develop and perfect it, both intellectually and morally. It is only through destroying 'prejudices and the carefully maintained habits of servility in which the people are kept' that human nature can be remade.[116] Such fundamental changes are nothing new, of course. Humanity has already changed its 'mores, character, habits, laws, religions, morals' so many times that we cannot really know what 'its limit in this path of transfigurations' will be.[117] But without transforming human nature, any attempt to create a new and enduring social order will fail and the old order will return. Thus the horizon opened up by revolution presents less an immediate or an assured eventual triumph than a further injunction: to begin the work of real social transformation.

## Transition and transformation

Blanqui is entirely correct to insist that political revolution, the overthrow of the old state apparatus and the seizure of political power, in reality constitutes the beginning of a much longer, more profound period of transition and transformation. He reminds us that emancipatory politics is not reducible to a single moment of rupture – a view that not only overlooks or downplays the inevitable practical problem posed by counter-revolutionary forces, as noted earlier, but that also ignores or evades the question of how an oppressed people become capable of genuine 'self-government', to use Blanqui's own term.[118] In the case of the latter point, the disregard is in fact often quite explicit, predicated on the belief that the people are already capable of self-rule. Blanqui, however, like a whole series of thinkers from Rousseau through Jefferson to Lenin, maintains that the practice of democracy requires a change in human nature. As Michael Hardt affirms with Lenin and Spinoza (and the same applies to Blanqui): 'If the population is ignorant and superstitious then establishing democracy would merely mean instituting the rule of ignorance and superstition. The multitude will not be spontaneously or immediately transformed by the revolutionary event. It is the role of the transition to accomplish this task: to make a multitude capable of democracy, with the skills, talents, and knowledges necessary to rule themselves.'[119] Any attempt to resolve this problem therefore rests on how one conceives the relation between the mechanisms of transition and the transformation of the people. What is Blanqui's proposed solution, and how does it compare with that of these other political theorists?

Before examining Blanqui's proposals let us first consider Hardt's reflections on this subject a little further, for he highlights some of the fundamental tensions and advances some solutions – and in my opinion convincing ones – to the problem of revolutionary transition.

Hardt begins by outlining the concept of transition as fundamental to thinking revolution as a process – the initial revolutionary event 'opens a period of transition that aims at realizing the goals of the revolution' – and yet also as one of the major impasses of revolutionary politics. 'The (often authoritarian) means employed during revolutionary transitions frequently conflict with and even contradict the desired (democratic) ends; moreover, these transitions never seem to come to an end.'[120] Historical experience, particularly that of the twentieth century, attests to the need to re-engage with this at once contentious and vital concept.

Hardt then traces Lenin's analysis as the most insightful and significant contribution to this discussion. Against the social democrats, who believe that the rule of the people is impossible and so seek to maintain the state as a mediating force in the necessary division between rulers and ruled, and against the anarchists, who think that the rule of the people is possible now and that the exercise of humanity's (presently supressed) natural capacity for self-rule only requires the abolition of the state, Lenin, Hardt explains, posits that while the state is antithetical to democracy and must be abolished, democracy cannot simply be established through the immediate abolition of the state. A process of transition is therefore necessary during which a dictatorship of the proletariat completes the work of popular education, eventually arriving at democracy and the withering away of the state altogether. Lenin's reasoning derives in part from the practical need to wield the power of the state in order to defend the revolution against the counter-revolution. But what is most important here is the issue of human nature and humans' capacity for self-rule. The central strength of Lenin's analysis, Hardt suggests, is the recognition that a transitional period is needed in order for the people to learn how to rule themselves; human nature must be transformed so that the people become capable of self-rule.[121]

The major weakness of Lenin's schema, however, according to Hardt, 'lies in the radical division it requires between means and ends, between the form of transitional rule and the revolutionary goals.'[122] Enter Thomas Jefferson. Hardt discovers in Jefferson's concept of participatory democracy a corrective to the attempts of Lenin, as well as of Ernesto Laclau and Slavoj Žižek more recently, to present the source of popular transformation as emanating from an authority standing outside of or above the people rather than from within the people themselves. An externally imposed transformation becomes a *self-transformation*. While Jefferson agrees with Lenin that a new human nature must be created through popular education, training and the establishment of democratic habits, and that this new humanity is 'the *outcome* of the revolutionary process' rather than its 'prerequisite', Jefferson's decisive move is not to separate the means and ends of the transitional process but, rather, to present them as one and the same.[123] In Jefferson, writes Hardt, 'democracy is the goal of the revolutionary process and, paradoxically, democracy is also the means of achieving it.'[124] Therein lies the crux of Hardt's argument. 'A transition ruled by a hegemonic figure does not teach people anything about self-rule,' he claims, 'it only reinforces their habits of subservience and passivity. People only learn democracy by doing it. The necessary transformation – learning to rule ourselves without a master – can only take place through practice, in action.'[125]

Turning now to Blanqui, three notes from the late 1860s and 1870 reveal the premise and reasoning, as well as the solutions and outcomes, of his own concept of revolutionary transition. Writing in 1870 Blanqui sketches out, with the austere simplicity and directness that so often characterize his unpublished notes, the fundamental elements of his approach:

> Education – necessary and rare. Inability of the people to rule themselves. It would be a mere façade. Universal suffrage – disastrous in 1848. More disastrous would be government of the people by the people. Prey of schemers, gossips, charlatans, Tartuffes. Whatever they decided would always be a mere echo of someone else – they would parrot them, act as their mouthpiece. Bad government [*Le gouvernement mal*] – necessary until [the process of popular] education is complete. Government of the people – a lie and an illusion today, as impossible as a trip to the moon. … Parisian dictatorship, as a national representative – only reasonable and possible government. Rapid development of education – the sole instrument of salvation.[126]

The people's insufficient level of enlightenment at present excludes the possibility of genuine democracy, Blanqui believes. Without the transformative effects of education and the enlightened consciousness it engenders, far from popular self-rule based on common interests any new government would merely reflect and reproduce the structures and interests of the old order – that is, oligarchic rule based on private interests. The sole practical means to bridge the gap between what is and what ought to be is thus the negation of direct, popular self-rule: dictatorship.

The necessity of Paris's temporary supremacy is outlined in a second note:

> Paris, the national representative, gives France its strength by concentrating all its intellectual forces in one point. This can be a good way to constitute a country and give it both external and internal energy. But this situation is not a normal state of affairs. A people must live by themselves and not through representation. Today Paris is the whole of France. The whole of France must become Paris, and Paris will then cease to be a vital necessity for the nation. The nation is in a state of minority, under the tutelage and natural authority of a parent of greater intelligence. But the child cannot remain a minor forever. It must come of age.[127]

In Blanqui's project the primacy of Paris is symptomatic of the primacy of intelligence and ideas. The 'bastion' of ignorance that props up tyranny and prevents democracy can only be overthrown through exercising and extending the concentrated intellectual supremacy of Paris over France. Paris, in this sense, is both representative and creator of the people; Paris instructs the people, developing its critical capacities and, thereby, its capacities for self-government, to the extent that the work of this central authority, once complete, results in its own abolition. 'Paris will abdicate when France has come of age.'[128]

This brings us to a third note, which expands on the results and goals of the transitional process. Just as in 1793 Paris represented, Blanqui writes in a curious phrase, 'the autocracy of all [*l'autocratie de tous*]' – which is to say, equality – instead of 'the autocracy of one [*l'autocratie d'un seul*]', so Paris in the nineteenth century remained and would remain the representative of equality until France as a whole had adopted the principle (any curtailment of the centralized power of this revolutionary force before that point was a counter-revolutionary measure). Although the precise details of this future egalitarian social arrangement were of no interest or concern to Blanqui, its essential contours could nonetheless still be traced:

> There will then be no more monarchy, nor patriciate, nor clergy, nor bourgeoisie, nor plebeians, nor Parisian dictatorship, nor centralisation, nor

federalism, nor class differences. These words will belong to history. The nation – one, free, master of itself, without millionaires and without beggars, without exploiters and exploited, above all without idlers – will have the real form of self-government that does not yet exist anywhere.[129]

The third part of this schema, then, is the end of all forms of authority and the emergence of the rule of the people and a unified, truly free and equal society. Enlightenment through dictatorship to democracy – these are the three components of Blanqui's concept of transition.

We can now see how Blanqui's reframing of the temporality of revolution anticipates the two central pillars of Lenin's theory: on the one hand, maintaining state power as the practical means through which simultaneously to enact transition and to defend the revolution from its enemies; and, on the other hand, the necessity of transforming the population in order to make it capable of self-rule. Blanqui is useful, if not rather prescient, in conceiving, like Lenin after him, 'the revolutionary event as both rupture and duration, an historical break that opens a new historical process.'[130] Blanqui's attempts to respond to the dilemma of how to achieve democracy also display an admirable level of political realism – 'a concrete analysis of a concrete situation', to borrow Lenin's own oft-quoted maxim – in assessing an actual state of affairs and advancing resolutely practical solutions. 'One should bear in mind,' Machiavelli advised new princes, 'that there is nothing more difficult to execute, nor more dubious of success, nor more dangerous to administer, than to introduce new political orders.'[131] Blanqui, too, is certainly mindful of these difficulties and dangers.

Ultimately, however, Blanqui's conception of transition comes up against the same hurdles that Hardt identifies in Lenin. And, again like the Bolshevik leader, Blanqui offers no obvious means of overcoming them. Instead of training the people in democracy through the practice of democracy itself, Blanqui's thinking is properly dialectical: the transition to democracy requires the negation of democracy. In this sense Blanqui does not go beyond Lenin, or rather, strictly speaking Lenin fails to go beyond Blanqui. Predating the dictatorship of the proletariat, in Blanqui's account it is the dictatorship of Paris that stands above the people and forms the central, hegemonic power directing the education of the population. The democratic social arrangement Blanqui proposes under the name of 'community' or 'association' is deferred until the process of enlightenment is complete. Blanqui is indeed quite explicit about the division between the means of popular education and its goals of universal enlightenment and communism. Having noted, for example, 'the consequences of the universality of enlightenment', he insists that 'communism will figure as a mere effect, not as a cause. Communism will arise inevitably from generalised education, and it can arise in no other way'.[132] The strict incompatibility here between causes and effects, between means and ends, necessarily results in delay and deferral. Communism cannot 'impose itself suddenly'[133] because, as we have seen, enlightenment is 'the sine qua non of communism'.[134] Only when universal instruction is finally complete can its fruits be enjoyed. Communism thus conceived excludes by definition any form of self-transformation, a communism or democracy produced through its own practice, since education – the sole means of achieving communism and democracy – is posited here on a fixed hierarchy of intelligence and knowledge, on an irreducible master-student relation.[135] To act otherwise is, in Blanqui's eyes, to short-circuit the necessary process of the proper dissemination of enlightened intelligence and critical thought.

The problem of transition reveals one of the major structural problems of Blanqui's political theory as a whole. The price he pays for his insistence on *conscious* volition is extremely high and opens the door to accusations of vanguardist elitism. Across his writings Blanqui tends to suggest that, lacking enlightened instruction and the basic level of intelligence and consciousness it produces, not all the people are presently capable of freely willing, or at least that this capacity is severely stifled or repressed – whether internally or externally – to the extent that it cannot be properly exercised as it can and must. Only an external, hegemonic force or figure can correct this. Only under the tutelage of the educator can the masses be educated. But is it not necessary to 'educate the educator himself', as Marx claimed?[136] As a result of the strictly dialectical process by which he conceives transition and change, does Blanqui not overemphasize this pedagogical prerequisite, the conscious thought necessary for decisive voluntary action, thereby delaying – unnecessarily, no doubt – the exercise of a truly democratic, participatory collective will? In short, does Blanqui's conception of conscious volition not display a certain lack of confidence in the people, in their capacity for *self*-development and *self*-transformation?

Consider the following passage from the *Critique Sociale* on workers' cooperatives and associations, which is generally illustrative of Blanqui's thought on this issue. Blanqui argues that the problem facing such associations is, again, the wider level of ignorance among the population. As a result of religious mis-education 'the majority of proletarians do not have the sufficient knowledge to manage a company by themselves'.[137] Likewise, since only a small minority of workers possess the 'necessary [intellectual] capacity' to undertake the self-management of production, their doing so in an unenlightened society risks separating them from the ignorant and impoverished majority and becoming a 'new caste', an enriched 'half-bourgeoisie' that would henceforth pursue their own private interests over collective emancipation. These societies for production would therefore cream off from the mass of the people its 'natural protectors'.[138] Without the necessary critical faculties required of egalitarian socio-economic practices – to repeat, without the 'necessary capacity' – any form of direct, popular participation must be delayed. Blanqui is explicit about this. Only after a programme of mass public education 'based on science' and 'rational teaching' would the intellectual transformation of France be 'complete'. So while Blanqui describes how, as a result of this process, which he speculates would last 'less than ten years', 'all the workers, transformed from passive instruments into enlightened citizens, would spontaneously bring into association all their intellectual and physical capacities, and the problem of organising labour in accordance with justice would be resolved', even this depiction of an enlightened citizenry actively and collectively participating in the ruling of society is then immediately qualified as a distant reality – 'unfortunately, we are not yet at this point'[139] – a qualification which only serves to reinforce the present state of passive ignorance for which, regrettably, no instant solutions could be offered.

The same text also reaffirms that popular emancipation can not take place through '*small* cooperative companies. ... The people can only escape serfdom through the impetus provided by the *great* company, the state,' Blanqui writes. 'For the state has no other legitimate task.'[140] The post-revolutionary state alone possesses the knowledge and power to liberate the people, it seems. Only the government can simultaneously direct popular education while protecting the people against 'the race of vampires' that is ready and waiting to 're-establish exploitation behind new masks'.[141] To return to a point evoked in Chapter 3,

Blanqui and Laclau are in this respect quite close in prioritizing forms of representation over direct popular empowerment (Blanqui for the non-elite sections of the people in the provinces, Laclau for the people as a whole) and are accordingly both limited in their own ways.[142]

Peter Hallward suggests that appeals to 'the virtue of patience' are characteristic of those 'who lack confidence in the people' and who instead insist on 'the time of ongoing "development"'. 'It is always too early, from this perspective, for equality and participation,' Hallward writes. 'Only when they "grow up" or "progress" might today's people become worthy of the rights that a prudent society withholds.'[143] Blanqui certainly cannot be accused of substituting 'confidence in the people' for 'confidence in historical progress,'[144] as we shall see in Chapter 5. But his stringent conception of *conscious* volition does assume that so long as an actor is not intellectually conscious it remains incapable of exercising the rational will that animates a free, egalitarian society whose object is the common good. The result is in many ways an undeniably elitist and/or substitutionist conception of transition and change: only those with the requisite knowledge and intelligence can act to create a society in which all are informed and so all are actors. It is less a question of direct popular *self*-empowerment than of representing and eventually giving power to the people when, but only when, they have 'come of age' – 'as soon as' they 'reach the age of reason', as Rousseau similarly puts it[145] – under the tutelage of a superior intelligence.

## The legislator

A possible explanation for Blanqui's limitation in this respect might be found in Rousseau's claim, noted in Chapter 1, that the general will can only be exercised 'when [the people are] properly informed'.[146] 'The people, being subject to the laws, must create them', Rousseau explains (a point Blanqui reiterates, as we have seen); 'it is the associates who have the right to determine the conditions of society. But how are they to determine them?', Rousseau then asks. 'Who will give [the body politic] the foresight it needs to produce acts of will and publicize them in advance, or how, in time of need, will it make them known? How can the blind multitude, often ignorant of what it wants, because it seldom knows what is good for it, accomplish by itself so large and difficult an enterprise as a system of legislation?'[147] How, moreover, is it possible to explain such a project to the people?[148] For under the existing order each individual, driven only by their own particular interests, 'has difficulty in perceiving the advantages he must gain from the deprivations that are continually imposed on him by good laws.'[149] And like Blanqui, Rousseau maintains that the means and ends of popular government certainly cannot be conflated – to do so would be to put the cart before the horse. He explains: 'In order that a people in the process of formation should be capable of appreciating the principles of sound policy and follow the fundamental rules of reasons of state, it would be necessary for the effect to become the cause; the spirit of community, which should be the result of the constitution, would have to have guided the constitution itself; before the existence of laws, men would have to be what the laws have made them.'[150] Earlier, in the *Discourse on Political Economy*, Rousseau had similarly argued that a truly popular government, 'which has as its object the good of the people', must 'follow the general will in everything'. In order for the general will 'to be followed', however, 'it must be known' and, as such, 'it must be clearly distinguished from the particular will.' Making this distinction is 'always very difficult', Rousseau acknowledges, 'and only the most sublime virtue is capable of giving the necessary enlightenment.'[151] Rousseau accordingly advances a form of popular sociopolitical education as the basis upon which the general will can be clearly known and so can be properly exercised.[152] Citizenship in this sense is a didactic construction: it must be taught and 'trained' though its instruction and subsequent practice.[153]

A discussion of who or what might 'preside over this form of education, which is certainly the state's most important affair',[154] is left to the *Social Contract*, where the figure of the 'legislator' appears. Society, like all creations, requires solid and durable foundations, Rousseau insists. It follows that 'the wise creator of institutions will not begin by drafting laws good in themselves, but will first consider whether the people for whom they are intended is capable of receiving them.'[155] And since these people are indeed deemed incapable on this score, the legislator is presented with its task – a task whose importance that cannot be overstated. 'The man who dares to undertake the establishment of a people has to feel himself capable of changing, so to speak, the nature of man', writes Rousseau; the legislator 'must deprive man of his own strength so as to give him strength from the outside, which he cannot use without the help of others. The more completely these natural strengths are destroyed and reduced to nothing, the more powerful and durable are those which replace them, and the firmer and more perfect, too, the society that is constituted'.[156] This wise man has the intellectual power to understand the mechanisms of enduring sociopolitical change, to transform the nature of each individual in such a way as to make possible the constitution of the social body. The legislator anticipates popular power and paves the way for the empowerment of an oppressed people, initiating the process through which the sovereign body is constructed and the general will exercised. The legislator, in short, is a creator – of a new society, of a new humanity.

Blanqui takes up and in certain ways extends these assumptions, focusing his attention on the role of enlightened thought and knowledge in the construction of a voluntary political actor. The result is twofold: he often appears, first, to conclude that not to be 'properly informed' is to form part of the 'blind multitude' incapable at present of conscious volition; and, second, to conceive the enlightened revolutionary elite of which he forms a part and the revolutionary power they wield as a form of Rousseauist legislator. This is perhaps best seen in the 'Initiation Ceremony of the Society of Seasons' from 1837. On the question of whether the people can 'rule themselves immediately after the revolution', the text states that the 'social state has been rendered gangrenous' and 'heroic remedies are required to reach a healthy state'.[157] Hence, 'for a certain period of time' the people will 'require a revolutionary power'; a revolutionary power, the text repeats, 'must be employed to enable the people themselves to exercise their rights'.[158] The task of this transitional power, in other words, is to transform the people, to make them capable of self-rule.

Now, that is not to suggest that Blanqui dismisses the political agency of everyone but himself and his small revolutionary vanguard. Blanqui maintains that a part of the people – the atheist workers, students and intellectuals concentrated in Paris – is properly informed, to the extent that the part (Paris) acts in the name of and represents the whole (France).[159] Nor is this to claim that we are dealing with an egalitarian society that is conceived a priori and imposed from above. Blanqui is emphatic that association is a common project collectively undertaken by free individuals; he repeatedly insists that 'the new social organism cannot be the work of one single person, nor of a few people, nor simply of good faith, nor of devotion, nor even of genius'.[160] But on the question of *when* exactly all ordinary people will be properly informed and thus capable of actually carrying out this work themselves and exercising voluntary self-determination more generally, the tendency towards a paternalistic and hierarchical conception of action, education and transformation is often all too apparent. Before Blanqui, Rousseau had similarly claimed that 'as soon as [man] reaches the age of reason, he alone is the judge of how best to look after himself, and thus he becomes his own master'.[161] But how soon is 'soon'? How long actually is this seemingly indeterminate 'certain period of time'?

Let us conclude. We have seen how Blanqui's politics is built on a concept of conscious volition. Political struggle, according to Blanqui, is a conflict of wills. Blanqui conceives popular will in terms of the rational and deliberate collective action that is necessary in order for a group or people to realize its stated common goals and aims. This is why he is so insistent on the practical dimensions of this collective political action and, in particular, on the manner in which a popular movement will have to overcome the resistance that it will inevitably face. Blanqui maintains that if a conscious collective actor has the organized, unified and resolute collective will to prevail then it can do so. And contrary to his 'utopian' contemporaries, he also maintains that it is only through the process of collectively willing its realization that the actual form of the project itself will become clear. Moreover, we can now appreciate the role of duty, morality, conviction and faith within Blanqui's politics as the subjective resources that sustain a process of collective self-determination, to the exclusion of any form of renunciation or resignation. All such points no doubt betray, in their own ways, a certain theoretical lucidity.

On the question of post-revolutionary transition and the temporality of sociopolitical change, however, certain limits of this theory appear. Although analytically lucid and practically astute in some key respects, a theory that generally tends to conceive of an enlightened elite that presides over the transformation of the ignorant and passive masses in many ways prefigures the practice – and failures – of twentieth-century communism: purportedly temporary and exceptional initial periods became the permanent state of things and the state, far from withering away, grew ever stronger. Jefferson, but also Rousseau in his concern for a government's inevitable tendency to usurp the sovereign power of the people, both offer useful correctives to these problems.

Despite such limitations with regard to the temporality of transition, Blanqui's reflections on historical time more generally are extremely rich, as we shall now see in the final chapter.

5

# History

*The interconnection or succession of human things is not inevitable, like that of the universe. It can be changed at any moment.*[1]

Questions of history and progress have generated more interest and discussion than all other aspects of Blanqui's thought – and with good reason. Blanqui's writings on historical time and the temporalities of political struggle are among his most intellectually stimulating, particularly when considered within the context of their author's own often embattled life. But the attention has not always resulted in convincing interpretation. Indeed, perhaps no other facet of Blanqui's project has been so misrepresented as his conception of history and human progress.

In what follows, I seek to reconstruct the relationship between philosophical and historical change in Blanqui's thought and consider how these assumptions shape his political project as a whole. I note the distance between Blanqui's view of history, rooted in his notions of intelligence, ideas and human consciousness, and that of Marx, in order to explore the former's overall merits and flaws, particularly with regard to issues of determinism, fatalism and the historical role of human agency.

All these issues are present within *Eternity by the Stars* (1872), Blanqui's most enigmatic text. Against a persistent misreading, first proposed by Walter Benjamin, that in this late work Blanqui finally admits political defeat and abandons any prospect of revolutionary change, I argue that *Eternity* is entirely consistent with Blanqui's most basic assumptions regarding the capacity of humans to make their own history and determine their own destiny. I aim to show that, through insisting on the primacy of politics within Blanqui's general outlook, we can appreciate both the central meaning of *Eternity* itself and its place within his wider body of work.

# What is history?

## Philosophical primacy

We saw in Chapter 1 how Blanqui ascribes primacy to philosophy, ideas and thought in 'governing' the world and the societies it contains. Social change, according to Blanqui, is the result of philosophical change.[2] When it comes to the history of those societies and that world – a matter of great importance to Blanqui – it follows that, as well as denoting in a conventional sense the occurrence of events and the passage of time, history in a more fundamental sense is the account of the ideas, thought, consciousness and morality that have defined and determined humanity's material social arrangements. 'To philosophise is to study thought and consciousness. To write history is to recount the role of consciousness and thought in the lives of peoples.'[3] The foundational role of philosophy in Blanqui's project thus leads him to conceive historical change as philosophical change; any given social transformation across history was, fundamentally, the result of a transformation in the ruling philosophy of that society.[4]

A fascinating manuscript note sheds a great deal of light on the consequences of Blanqui's claim that 'the omnipotence (the power) of philosophy' constitutes the basic force in human history and is therefore worth quoting at length. In essence, historical change, Blanqui believes, denotes the supersession of an old philosophy with a new one. In the necessary transitional period of struggle between the two opposing philosophies the primacy of philosophy itself may be called into question; seemingly under attack from 'extra-philosophical forces' and subordinate to the sociopolitical influence of other 'sciences', philosophy may appear destined to disappear altogether as the determinant of social structures, to be replaced 'by new powers of an entirely different order'. This is a 'profound error', Blanqui suggests. However much they might otherwise appear, 'these new forces are simply the elements of a new philosophy' that will, in turn, become 'the public thought and the sovereign power of society'.

Antagonistic ideas, the overcoming of a seemingly stable philosophy and its corresponding social order, the emergence and the eventual establishment of a new philosophy and a new social order – one might suggest that there is a certain dialectical motion to historical change here. Blanqui continues: 'What we call periods of transition are precisely nothing but periods of war between two philosophies – the one that is coming and the other that is going.' Rather than a negation of philosophy as such, historical change is a process of philosophical struggle between conflicting ideas and then of the synthesis of the new philosophy and the real, material structures of society, he concludes.[5]

Philosophies, Blanqui argues, govern humanity's social arrangements, but they cannot influence or alter societies by themselves, of course. Philosophies are conceived by humanity and realized in a war that can only be waged by the militants of those philosophies. It is in this sense that Blanqui's primary concern is *human* history; history is first and foremost the realm of human thought and activity, of human intelligence and consciousness. And like Hegel, so Spitzer notes, Blanqui sees humanity as 'both the agent and the product of endless change'.[6] Against Charles Fourier, whose doctrine is built on the 'false basis' of 'the fixedness of instincts, the constant identity of man with himself', Blanqui sees the development and perfection of humanity as the most basic historical task.[7] If Fourierism's central contradiction is its attempt to construct 'a definitive or final organisation based on the permanence of penchants and passions' – a move that is in fact entirely consistent with its failure on the social question to offer anything other than the conservation of the existing order[8] – Blanqui's thought is animated by transformation and change at the level of people and social arrangements alike. History recounts the process of humans progressing 'through the continual improvement [*perfectionnement*] of the brain'. Developments on earth, therefore, take place through

> perpetual and imperceptible change, the progressive mutation of beings. Man is the product of a continuous transformation that is as slow in its effects as it is persistent in its forward march. Mankind abandons and it acquires. It is renewed in its instincts and in its faculties, like the body is in its tissues.[9]

The development of human consciousness through the exercise of human thought and the improvement of the brain is, Blanqui claims, the primary motor of historical change and progress. For the collective capacity to arrange social and economic relations in line with morality and justice is the corollary of collective self-consciousness. Only in thinking and understanding ourselves as free, in other words, can we actually become free. But between the consciousness of freedom and its realization forever lies political action. And history certainly recounts the political struggle that accompanies this process of human self-transformation. History is indeed as much the account of humanity's cerebral progress and improvement as it is the account of the forces that actively prevent, undermine or undo this process through mis-education, deceit and manipulation. 'Historical experience has shown that education is the sole agent of progress, that enlightenment springs (almost) only from the exchange (and clash) of human thoughts; consequently all that encourages and increases this exchange is good, all that suppresses or hinders it is evil.'[10] The whole effort of Blanqui's project is to contribute to this historical struggle for freedom – the freedom of the people, as equals, to determine the organization of their social, political and economic life themselves.

To be modern is to be conscious of one's freedom, conscious of oneself as a self-determining actor capable of moral judgement; it is to strive for the collective realization of this freedom as the foundation of an egalitarian, self-governing social order. Blanqui sees the exercise of conscious volition as the criterion from which to plot and judge the sociopolitical development of peoples and civilizations. Genuine historical judgement can be attained, then, but the capacity to judge history itself presupposes consciousness. History, in other words, is the result of the history it recounts – both historical change and its accurate narration are realized and attained through the development and exercise of consciousness. 'In the trial of the past by the future, contemporary *memoirs* are the witnesses, *history* is the judge, and the verdict is almost always an iniquity, either because of false or missing evidence, or because of the ignorance of the court,' Blanqui notes. 'Fortunately, the appeal remains forever open,' he adds, 'and the light of future centuries, cast into the distance, onto past centuries, denounces the sentences passed by the darkness.'[11] True to his Eurocentrism, in Blanqui's eyes the far East exemplifies how the absence of conscious thought results in the absence of freedom and progress. 'Europe has never been able to equal the Hindus' cashmere weaving,' he writes. 'As artists, as artisans, the Chinese are at the very least our rivals. And yet what degradation! Why? Because thought is absent.'¹² Blanqui's essential position is again clear: it is the development of and changes in human intelligence and consciousness, not economic modes of production, that are the yardstick of historical progress.

Insofar as the realization of communism is presented as the goal, the 'final stage' of human association,¹³ Blanqui's conception of history can be said to have several broad stages of development. Writing under the title 'Communism, the Future of Society', he depicts a 'constant forward march of the human species' in which the future will clearly reveal that

> every instance of progress is a victory for communism, and every regression a defeat for it; … that all the problems successively posed over the course of history by the needs of our species have had a communist solution; and that the unresolved questions we are wrestling with today – those that are the most difficult, the most bound up with war and unrest – can have no other solution than communism, without making things worse and descending into the absurd.¹⁴

All progress in human affairs, from taxes and various forms of commercial and industrial associations to schools, armies and governments, are 'communist innovations'; all have been achieved as stages on the 'path' towards communism. The idea of communism, Blanqui accordingly notes, 'has barely begun to stammer its first words. Before it utters its last, it will have changed everything. As yet we are still nothing more than barbarians.'¹⁵ With self-consciousness – and this is a crucial point – we locate ourselves within an ongoing movement, a wider process of achieving sociopolitical progress through the realization of self-consciousness. The level of collective association, which is itself tied to the level of popular enlightenment, provides 'the true instrument and barometer of progress' and marks out the 'stages of humanity'.¹⁶ (On this score the Middle Ages – 'the era of blood and darkness' which 'was nothing other than the reign of Christianity' – marked a period of profound regression that was only brought to an end with the advent of the printing press.)¹⁷ Blanqui's insistence on contemporary's society's relative barbarism therefore serves to reinforce self-conscious human activity as history and historical change in two coupled respects: realizing self-consciousness is humanity's self-narrated history and the self-conscious task of the historical actor as such.

Since cerebral transformation is the causal factor behind social association, the notion of a 'communism of primitive man',[18] or the suggestion that 'communism has ever characterised the initial stages of any form of society', are dismissed as 'diametrically opposed to the truth'. Blanqui certainly recognizes that 'in every era there have been communist theories', for 'great intellects can discern in communism the ideal of social organisation. Application of the ideal, however, has always failed in the face of ignorance.' Why? Again, Blanqui repeats his most basic maxim: because 'enlightenment is the sine qua non of communism. Communism only becomes possible through enlightenment; it is its necessary end-point.'[19] Communism, in other words, will be the future sociopolitical form of the enlightenment achieved through universal instruction.

This in no way implies that history is an invariable, linear sequence or that communism is humanity's natural fate or inevitable destiny, however. On the contrary – there is no 'steady filiation from one event to the next', Blanqui maintains; every era is not 'the product of the previous era'.[20] We shall explore the question of historical determinism at greater length below. For now, it is enough to note that at every stage of his political and intellectual project Blanqui insists on political possibility over historical necessity. To reject historical necessity, according to Blanqui, is to affirm the primacy of collective self-determination over purportedly immutable forces, laws, tendencies or processes in shaping – and so in changing – humans' social arrangements; it is to explicitly open the door to alternatives and bifurcations, to contingency and discontinuity, in our social and economic life.

So Blanqui's response to the problem of social progress as a historical possibility is political voluntarism. 'Our misdeeds or our virtues can certainly slow down or accelerate the advance of civilisation,' he states, 'which means that our destiny is entirely in our own hands.'[21] History as possibility is at once a task and an opportunity. Humans have the capacity, if not the duty and obligation, to create their own history. But only conscious, decisive collective action here and now can create and continue to create the path to future emancipation; only through this active and deliberate process can humanity arrive at its ultimate realization – the definite outlines of which are unknown and unknowable, of course, and as such of no concern to Blanqui.[22]

## Historical materialism?

Some readers have advanced Blanqui's view of history as, if not a forerunner, then at least broadly similar in orientation to that of Marx and Engels.[23] This can be seen, it is claimed, when, building on passages from the 'Defence Speech',[24] the 1832 'Report to the Society of the Friends of the People' affirms the class dimensions of the civil war in France, describing a country gripped by a conflict between three groups: the upper class, the middle class and the people.[25]

Blanqui does indeed depict a class war that is also a historical struggle between oppressor and oppressed, with July 1830 as merely its latest manifestation, a battle that punctuates an ongoing war. As he insists at the beginning of the speech: 'No new party emerged during this revolution or as a result of it.'[26] Yet perhaps save for Walter Benjamin's Blanqui-inflected 'materialist conception of history', to which we shall return later, to suggest that in Blanqui one discovers the seeds of historical materialism is misleading on three counts, two of which can be seen in the 'Report' itself, the other finding clear refutation in later writings.

First, such a claim overlooks the explicitly national dimensions of Blanqui's thought, as already noted and discussed in the preceding chapters. For Blanqui, France in the early 1830s is witnessing a struggle between two groups: on the one hand the people, the true representatives of the nation, and republican 'patriots'; on the other the bourgeoisie and 'royalists', the lackeys of the Holy Alliance. His key reference point here is of course the French Revolution, while his central concern is the political and intellectual dynamics that define and differentiate national struggles. Second, and following the first point, it overlooks the lack of a critique of political economy, Marxian or otherwise, in both France and elsewhere. Blanqui depicts a class conflict that emanates primarily from political history, not from the historical evolution of the mode of production, as historical materialism would of course later advance as determinant of class relations in any given society. (July 1830, for example, is described as a 'political crisis' provoked by Charles X's ordinances,[27] and indeed throughout the speech the revolution is explained first and foremost in political terms.) In Blanqui's eyes the war between republicans and royalists that began in 1789 is still the principal battle line in France and, by extension, in Europe. Blanqui does suggest the bourgeoisie is driven by commercial imperatives while the masses seek to end their exploitation, and class clearly has some socio-economic bearing for him, as we saw in Chapter 3. But as we have also seen it is the primacy of politics in general, and national politics in particular, that are key to understanding Blanqui's conception of class struggle and the historical dimensions of that struggle. Finally, and most significantly, to conflate Blanqui's and Marx's views on this point is of course to overlook the foundational role for the former of intelligence and consciousness in history and historical change, as developed at greater length in his later work. Political struggle and class conflict, as Blanqui conceives them, are the manifestation of a more fundamental war of ideas and principles.

What does this mean for Blanqui's project? No doubt here as elsewhere Blanqui's particular position has both its strengths and flaws. As we shall see below, Blanqui avoids forms of determinism (economic, natural, scientific, providential…) that may downplay the role of collective conscious volition in the making of human history and may, therefore, lead to popular disempowerment. Likewise, we have seen how Blanqui's notion of the proletariat emphasizes the extent to which collective actors are first and foremost the result of collective action. Blanqui reminds us that socio-economic exploitation and domination do not in themselves inevitably engender the agency through which their redress can occur; ultimately it is conscious and determined action that creates a collective actor – an assumption that in turn serves to reaffirm the importance of organizing this collective action so as to make it most decisive and effective.

What about the – equally important – analysis of the objective grounds on which this subjective action takes place? To be clear, Blanqui is not ignorant of the constraints of circumstance. He does not think that collective action takes place or can be made to take place *ex nihilo*, without any consideration of when and why it might do so. The enduring image of a reckless adventurist, forever insistent on taking power 'no matter how, no matter when, no matter by whom'[28] is unfounded. 'We need courage,' Blanqui states, 'but not temerity.'[29]

Spitzer provides a useful survey of this point, highlighting Blanqui's support for non-insurrectionary tactics among the masses (electioneering, strikes, propaganda) alongside what he instructively calls Blanqui's 'reluctant putschism'.[30] As Spitzer shows, after May 1839 Blanqui consistently rejected his supporters' calls to seize power. Any attempt to seize power 'by a bold assault' without popular support, he warned in February 1848, would risk being overthrown itself soon after. 'What we need is a mass of the people, the *faubourgs* rising up in revolt, a new 10 August [1792].' Only this form of mass 'revolutionary force' could create the sustained popular power necessary to implement far-reaching social reforms.[31] For similar reasons Blanqui would later advise his supporters in April 1866 to 'remain within the limits of great prudence, not adventuring into vague and ineffectual attempts at action that are both powerless and without any prospect of success'. A revolutionary strategy adapted to the severe political constraints of Imperial France was required. And since, in such a context, 'the group can only gain influence through the pen', the order of the day was to embrace 'persuasion, activity and prudence all at once' and to renounce forms of aimless and reckless action that could lead to arrest, imprisonment and the disintegration of the vanguard group as a whole. Mass propaganda alone, Blanqui believed, provided the means to spread the revolutionary ideas that would lead to revolutionary action.[32] On 15 May 1848 and again on 14 August 1870, however, Blanqui was compelled against his own better judgement to participate in or lead ultimately unsuccessful coup attempts. The unpropitious circumstances, he argued, would lead to failure, as indeed duly occurred.[33]

Although the basic tenets of his philosophy could be said to have pushed Blanqui towards a top-down conception of political action, the specific political contexts in which he operated clearly played a significant role in shaping his conspiratorial politics that must also be acknowledged. Recall, for instance, that Blanqui's Société des Familles was formed at a time when the association law of April 1834 required any club, regardless of size or political goals, to be officially authorized. Soon after, the September laws of 1835, passed in response to Giuseppe Fieschi's assassination attempt on Louis Philippe in July 1835, sought to crack down even further on conspiracy and sedition, granting far greater powers to the judiciary (which overall made it easier to try and convict suspects) and outlawing any discussion of the king, the July Monarchy, the Bourbon dynasty or republicanism in the press.[34] Faced with this political repression, and unable to engage openly and directly with a mass audience because of the absence of a free press, for Blanqui and those like him who sought to persist with a revolutionary project the alternative was simple: conspiracy or capitulation. Not willing to resign themselves to the established order, they were effectively forced to undertake clandestine organization and activities. And as with other underground groupings, from La Chabonnerie in the 1820s to the Maquis in the 1940s, they recognized that secrecy and strict internal discipline were necessary if they were to evade the authorities and survive as a political force.

In any case, whether underground or not, revolutionary voluntarism does not mean a form of unconscious reflex. Any decisive political intervention, Blanqui maintains, requires serious contemplation and careful planning. 'Our duty, the duty of every one of us, is to commit ourselves without hesitation,' a letter from 1879 affirms, though not without then adding the essential qualification, 'as soon as circumstances call for it.' At this moment, but only at this moment, one must devote one's entire force and energy to the task at hand in order to seize the opening as it presents itself: ' "Do what you must, come what may." There may be no other opportunity. This maxim alone is always timely.'[35]

Evidently, then, Blanqui recognizes that successful revolutionary activity presupposes the existence of certain conditions. Revolutionary strategy, in turn, has to adapt to and reflect these conditions. But for all this lucidity he still does not go far enough, and in many crucial respects his overall analysis remains inadequate. In large part this is because he is far more concerned with political contexts and conditions than any underlying economic considerations. His disdain for the 'pseudo-science' of political economy is indeed explicit, a corollary of his renouncing any worldview that fails to take sufficient account of rationally acquired moral judgement, justice, as the ultimate means by which to assess human affairs. An economist, Blanqui claims, 'is interested in what is and has little concern for what should or could be. For him, "justice" and "inequity" are hollow words. Facts are everything; right [le droit] counts for nothing.'[36] Here the essential idealism of Blanqui's socialism, and the manner in which it informed his political project, becomes clear. Analysis of what (materially) is provides no obvious account or means for achieving what (socially) could or should be. Rather than the contradictions inherent *within* capitalism itself that might enable working-class consciousness and organization to emerge – 'with the development of industry the proletariat not only increases in number,' the *Communist Manifesto* explains; 'it becomes concentrated in greater masses, its strength grows, and its feels that strength more'[37] – only the idea and the militants of the idea are able to realize a new social order, Blanqui believes.

Its scientific pretentions may be contentious, yet for a militant political theory to do away with a serious and substantive critique of political economy is without question a glaring omission. Taking sufficient account of the processes that, though not ultimately determinant, certainly shape political struggles and the actors waging them is a necessary component of any emancipatory project.

## Equality or catastrophe

Six months after July 1830 it was clear that the popular movement had not triumphed. But all was not lost. 'Legitimate right and the future belong to us,' Blanqui declared in January 1831; 'the day of justice will arrive.'[38] With these assurances of future victory in spite of short-term defeat, Blanqui set the agenda and tone for his defence speech a year later at the 'Trial of the Fifteen' following his arrest, along with fourteen other members of the Société des Amis du Peuple, for conspiracy and press violations in July 1831.

A popular revolution can be suppressed, Blanqui told the Parisian court, but one cannot suppress the truths borne out by the event. 'It is easy to point the bayonet at the chests of men who surrendered their arms after victory. What will be less easy,' he insists, warning his adversaries and emboldening his allies, 'is to erase the memory of this victory. ... No human force can reduce to nothing what was achieved.' Something happened in July. Something was achieved that cannot be undone, forgotten, covered up or destroyed. Further defeats may occur, the forces of reaction may return. But all such efforts cannot prevent the birth – however prolonged, however painful – of the new republican order and the rule of the people. And so concludes the speech as it begins, in uncompromisingly combative style:

> You confiscated the guns of July. Yes, but the bullets have been fired. Each of the bullets fired by the Parisian workers is now making its way around the world. They strike without ceasing, and they will continue to strike until not a single enemy of freedom and the happiness of the people is left standing.[39]

With an audacious forcefulness these lines encapsulate the essential message of the speech as a whole: where injustice prevents freedom and happiness, where inequality and suffering are enforced through violence, no consensus will be found, no compromise will be offered. Accepting the realities of the social conflict, the people will take their struggle for victory to the end – and they will be victorious. 'With their arms of a giant' the people, Blanqui repeated barely a month later, in terms that echo, if not complement and complete, the remarkable denouement of the 'Defence Speech', 'will overthrow the allied bourgeoisie and aristocracy. The revolution is under way; nothing can stop it.'[40]

A pronounced conviction strikes us in these early writings: the revolution, the principles of freedom and equality, *will be triumphant*. For all his 'ultra-voluntarism' Blanqui seems strangely deterministic, at least in the sense that a final victory appears to be beyond doubt. How can this be so?

Following these texts from 1831–32 one of the most intriguing features of the articles from 1834's *Le Libérateur* is indeed the sustained reflection on the inevitable future triumph of equality. Blanqui's point of departure is the conviction that in the struggle between equality and privilege only one side can be victorious, leaving the other to perish. The obvious question follows: who will win? How and why will they do so? Equality's seemingly certain victory appears to rest on four modes of reasoning: moral judgement (the 'moral superiority' of equality, its alliance with the cause of justice, ensures its triumph over privilege, which is the triumph of 'good' over 'evil');[41] logical deduction (workers ultimately hold power since society could not function without their labour; the idle landowners are ultimately dependent on the workers);[42] political analysis ('we can, without any illusions, rest assured that all nations are advancing, with the French leading the way, towards the definitive conquest of absolute equality');[43] and the study of historical tendencies (the morals and ideas of the nation's past revealed that the 'social transformation' republicans propose is one that 'France so urgently calls for and which is its density').[44] Taken together, these factors enable Blanqui to conclude confidently, and with a generous dose of intellectual optimism: 'Today it is easy to see that the principle of property is in decline.'[45]

It would be easy to dismiss this as either empty rhetoric, naive supposition, hopeful projection, or perhaps a combination of all three. But if we look beyond these assurances and unqualified claims of future victory, the basic assumption – one which underpins all these early writings – is that equality will be victorious because it *must* be. This insistence derives from the threat and fear, indeed the very real possibility, of defeat and failure. It is unsurprising, Blanqui contends, that in this struggle between equality and privilege 'victory invariably goes to equality, since either it must triumph or humanity will perish'.[46] Equality is nonetheless still a 'necessary condition', in the sense of a state of affairs that must be achieved through human action, 'for France to have a future'.[47] Equality certainly can and might be victorious, but if and only if the necessary struggle for that victory is carried out and won. Recall that for Blanqui to take up the struggle for equality – for it is in every respect an actual project and task, an endeavour and enterprise – is, as he affirms in the same article from 1834, to '[continue] an admirable movement of progress which has emerged with irresistible perseverance, smashing one after the other the obstacles that are ceaselessly reconstructed to hinder its forward march'.[48] The nineteenth-century revolutionary movement is therefore a product, continuation and extension of past struggles[49] that must confront and overcome the obstacles and barriers to social progress; and where privilege remains, hurdles and obstructions will continually and inevitably appear. This movement is 'admirable' in Blanqui's eyes precisely because it only emerges through perseverance and persistence in the face of ever-recurring difficulties and constraints. Far from the inevitable product of the inevitable movement of history, it is only through a series of forceful interventions that the principle of equality has ever been partially established or imposed, creating the possibility of its ultimate and full realization. Communism, in this sense, is a necessary task: 'Humanity began with isolation, with absolute individualism, and … as it proceeds through a long series of improvements, it *must* culminate in community'.[50] It is imperative to work, then, with resolute devotion, in order to realize equality and to avoid the catastrophic consequences of failure.

In contemplating the relationship between human history and human agency Blanqui is not alone, of course. Eric Hobsbawm's subtle reading of the *Communist Manifesto*, a text which contains similar claims regarding the seemingly 'equally inevitable' fall of the bourgeoisie and victory of the proletariat, confronts this very problem. 'The Manifesto,' writes Hobsbawm, 'has been read primarily as a document of historical inevitability, and indeed its force derived largely from the confidence it gave its readers that capitalism was inevitability destined to be buried by its gravediggers.' Rousing rhetorical flourishes proclaiming the certainty of victory also characterize much of Blanqui's early writings, as we have seen. And given the even greater political premium he places on the resolute determination to win, it is unsurprising that the tenor of this work would share in, if not go further than, the enthusiastic confidence of the *Manifesto*. 'Yet contrary to widespread assumptions,' Hobsbawm continues, 'inasmuch as it believes that historical change proceeds through men making their own history, it is not a determinist document. The graves must be dug by or through human action.'[51] The same is true for Blanqui. Emphasis on certain victory is, paradoxically, symptomatic of a deeper anti-determinist assumption that only through thinking and acting in line with the possibility of victory can it be realized. Blanqui knows that the starting point of any decisive political action must be its collective strength, its capacity to win. He knows that, in order to succeed, collective struggles must generate and sustain a sense of confidence and enthusiasm that they *can* succeed; hence the similar function in other contexts of slogans like '*Venceremos*' ('We Will Win') or '*El pueblo unido jamás será vencido!*' ('The people united will never be defeated!'). Those who appeal to mere resistance or protest, by contrast, start from a position of collective weakness; they concede dominance to their adversary and in so doing are more likely to consign themselves to continued domination.

In Blanqui's project historical change and social progress are likewise the result of instruction, organization and volition – of conscious and collective human action. 'It is not enough vaguely to declare that all men are equal,' Blanqui argues. 'We must convince proletarians that equality is possible, that it is necessary.'[52] Such is the essential political function of Blanqui's journalism and propaganda: to teach, to convince the people that equality is both possible and necessary – possible in that humans have the capacity to realize it, necessary in that failure to do so spells victory for injustice and inequality. This goes a long way in explaining why Blanqui would readily indulge in hyperbole regarding the certainty of victory. The written word must generate the confidence and conviction for the action required to realize the possible.[53]

The underlying political logic here is that of a radically contingent either/or. 'Humanity is not stationary,' Blanqui states, 'it either advances or retreats.'[54] Either victory or defeat, either emancipation or oppression – for Blanqui these alternatives articulate what is fundamentally at stake in political struggle. Again though, this gesture is certainly not unique to Blanqui. Like Blanqui, Marx and Engels depict a struggle between oppressor and oppressed that could end 'either in a revolutionary reconstitution of society at large, or in the common ruin of the contending classes'.[55] Like Blanqui, Rosa Luxembourg sees humanity as facing a clear choice between 'socialism or barbarism'.[56] Like Blanqui, Fidel Castro and Che Guevara have no illusions that in a revolution 'an entire people [will] either triumph or fail', that 'either we are all saved or we all sink'.[57] Like Blanqui, Frantz Fanon insists that in the struggle for national liberation 'everyone will be massacred, or everyone will be saved'.[58] For all of these figures, in any given instance resolute dedication to and confidence in emancipation, equality and justice do not 'exclude the alternative: "common ruin"'[59] – on the contrary. It is precisely the lucid recognition of the real, ever-present possibility of the alternative that gives rise to the resolve to avoid it at all costs. 'The past and the future, privilege and freedom, the old world and the new world, immobility and progress are locked in an eternal combat', Blanqui writes. It therefore remains essential, whenever and wherever possible, to 'exclaim "Watch out! [*Alarme!*] They are the enemy!"', for the 'counter-revolution always stands before us'.[60]

Rather than an aberration or anomaly, then, these early statements prepare the ground for the anti-determinism that infuses Blanqui's mature thought.

## The poverty of positivism

'For a revolutionary,' Régis Debray once observed, 'failure is a springboard. As a source of theory it is richer than victory: it accumulates experience and knowledge.'[61] As with July 1830, the failure of 1848 provided Blanqui with such a theoretical springboard. No other event in his lifetime sharpened his early anti-determinist view of history as did 1848 and its aftermath. Though the intellectual consequences of 1848 may not have been immediately manifest, with Blanqui still assuring in November 1848, only five months after the June Days, that 'time will grant us victory without combat',[62] by the early 1850s, as Louis-Napoléon strengthened his grip on power, France slid back towards autocratic rule and the revolutionary party had all but disintegrated, the weight of events clearly compelled Blanqui to confront anew his avowed belief of 1832 that 'every revolution is a step forward [*un progrès*]'.[63] Combined with a searing critique of Auguste Comte's positivism, these events informed a sustained reflection on political fatalism and historical determinism that would dominate much of Blanqui's thinking during the Second Empire.

## Against fatalism

Just as Blanqui dismisses the claim that 'human affairs are entirely governed by the same fixed laws that preside over the general life of the universe'[64] and of nature, so he challenges attempts to impose absolute laws and logics on human history. His opposition to the 'supposed inevitability [*fatalité*] of the economic laws that govern society' insists in every respect that 'whenever human beings intervene, it can no longer be a question of law, but of caprice and arbitrariness'.[65] When it comes to understanding and explaining humanity's social arrangements, he rejects as a matter of course all forms of transcendent, immaterial laws or authorities, be they spiritual or scientific – and one note instructively links the two together for this very reason. 'Positivism is a demi-God that knows everything, that embraces everything, from the recent conflicts within higher mathematics to the slightest findings of *Sociology* past, present and future,' he writes. 'From the height of its omniscient throne, it contemptuously looks down on the pygmy who dares claim to be its equal and says to it, as it would to a tiny insect: "What do we have in common?"'[66] The mask of Comte's purported 'science' conceals the face of 'an ultra-aristocratic religion, the caste system, the enslavement of the masses, the absolute domination of the rich'. Comte's is indeed a pseudo-science for the status quo, offering the inviolability of empiricism and supposed 'scientifically proven truths' to guard against the threat of revolution.[67] God or the market, in the eyes of Blanqui's materialism both are no more than contingent intellectual constructions in the deliberate service of particular interests and aims. Such is the basis of Blanqui's politics of possibility, of cutting through the supposedly immutable (and therefore immensely complex) social field to present humans as the masters of their own destiny. For revolutionary and counter-revolutionary forces alike, political possibility, not historical necessity, created the past just as it will create the future. Scientific, spiritual or socio-economic claims to the historically inevitable and the socially immutable, meanwhile, merely serve to obfuscate the human agency consciously enforcing them.

This last point is key. Since Blanqui's central concern is *human* history his critique of fatalism operates a double movement: 'Execrable doctrine of historical fatalism, of fatalism in humanity.'[68] To champion historical determinism is to rationalize and condone all humanity's past afflictions as an inevitable part of an equally inevitable process; it assumes that 'what happens had to happen, because it happened'.[69] For Blanqui it follows, and even more critically, that positivism is an inadequate philosophical account of human history that legitimizes human suffering. The failure or refusal to consider human experience and moral judgement based on an enlightened sense of justice forms the thrust of his anti-positivist statements from the late 1860s, often written in response to articles from *La Philosophie positive*, a journal founded by Emile Littré and Grégoire Wyrouboff in 1867. Positivism, Blanqui claims,

> accepts only the law of continual progress regardless of what happens, of fatalism. Any event is excellent in its appointed time since it takes place in the ongoing series of improvements. Everything that occurs is always for the best. There is no criterion to evaluate the good or the bad. Any such criterion would be a matter of preconception, of the a priori, of metaphysics.[70]

Since positivism 'excludes the idea of justice both from its supposed science of sociology and from its philosophy of history',[71] in the eyes of these 'fatalists of history, worshippers of the fait accompli', Blanqui writes, 'all the atrocities of the victors, their long series of attacks, are coldly transformed into a regular and ineluctable evolution, like that of nature.'[72] Blanqui's socialist humanism, by contrast, is conceived in absolute opposition to 'the doctrine of the inevitability of social suffering'.[73] Outside of the natural world all must be conceived first and foremost in terms of humanity and social justice because all is human in cause and consequence. Since all forms of social organization are consciously conceived and established by humanity itself, nothing in human history is inevitable or predestined. Only the moral principles historically developed by humans themselves provide a worthy assessment of human relations past and present.

Blanqui applies this critique of historical determinism with no less force to his own political camp. To the extent that revolution reconfirms the power of the people and redefines the thinkable and the possible, Blanqui certainly forever sees it as a basic and necessary act of progress. But he does so not to the exclusion of regression and reaction. This conviction became far more pronounced after 1848. With the recognition that 'every failed attempt [at revolution] leads to an even more terrible reaction', as witnessed in the 'catastrophe' of Louis-Napoléon's coup d'état of 2 December 1851, the choice between perpetual domination or militant struggle acquired an even greater sense of urgency.[74]

Behind renewed practical and strategic imperatives lay more fundamental philosophical assumptions, however. It was in the fallout of 1848, when the promises of a 'popular victory' had been destroyed in mass bloodshed, political betrayal and a resurgent Bonapartism, that Blanqui penned one of his most effective attacks on the politics of positivist determinism. Writing in June 1850 from his cell in Doullens prior to his transfer to Belle-Île in October, Blanqui castigates the 'stupid fatalism of the revolutionary party' and its attempts to rationalize defeat, in all its human carnage, as merely part of the inexorable forward march of history. The revolutionary party, Blanqui writes,

> wins battles only for its own ruin, always quick and eager to hand power to the vanquished as soon as they are thirsty for vengeance. Then it consoles itself with hymns about the irresistible forward march of the human spirit and the certainty of its final triumph. Thirty or forty years of despotism, the blood of thousands of martyrs, the pain of millions of poor wretches – what does any of this matter to the serenity of these calm contemplators? What are two or three sacrificed generations to them? Two or three fallen leaves.[75]

For Blanqui, the philosophical error of fatalism, of the assumption that 'progress cannot be undone',[76] has the gravest sociopolitical implications, which explains the significant attention it is accorded in his writings: fatalism fails to recognize the basic need to seize and retain political power in order to initiate the process of social transformation and protect this process from its enemies; fatalism promotes a form of cold, dispassionate detachment, if not indifference, to the suffering caused in the name of supposedly immutable forces and processes; as such, while this human suffering, far from relenting, increases and intensifies, fatalism creates waiting over engaging, passivity over activity.

## The tradition of the oppressed

There is, according to Blanqui, a clear continuity between political struggle and historiographical practice. The historian, like the pseudo-scientific sociologist or political economist, is no 'objective' onlooker to the conflict between oppressor and oppressed. The fixation on the Jacobin Terror of 1793 and the overlooking or downplaying of the royalist repression that followed it, for example, proves once again that 'history is written by the executioners – which is to say, the rich and the powerful'.[77]

Blanqui's dismissal of positivist and determinist historiography is pegged at every moment to his humanist advocacy of social justice. The suggestion that there are political, social or economic laws of history is thus a 'bad joke'[78] in his eyes primarily because of its social implications. 'It is immoral, it is a crime to glorify the past despite everything, to justify it through supposedly immutable laws, to invoke the dignity of history, which commands respect or even indulgence for the horrors of times gone by.'[79] To denounce social injustice and oppression in the present is to do likewise for the past. Those, meanwhile, who insist on the causal relationship between past and present, precisely as the means by which to legitimize the present order, care not for the past. For them 'it amounts merely to a pile of dead leaves,' Blanqui notes. For these champions of teleology

> History is sketched out in broad brush strokes, in the most beautiful cold blood, with heaps of corpses and ruins. No butchery prompts a flicker of emotion across these impassive faces. The massacre of a people? Just part of the evolution of humanity. ... The whirlwind of Germans and Huns only stormed through the Latin world to purify its contaminated air. Providential hurricane! As for the populations of the cities that the cataclysm flattened on its path – that was a matter of necessity, the inevitable march of progress.[80]

In the eyes of positivist determinism, just as 'everything is worked out and scripted in advance' for future generations, those 'poor, puny automatons' deemed incapable of making history, past generations likewise merely endured history. Besides, we should in fact be thankful for this history, since 'anything that gave birth to the present – that is to say, to *us* – is good'.[81]

Blanqui, however, rejects any attempt to rationalize the oppression and exploitation of the past as essential to the present. Human history has no laws or logic. '*History*,' as the young Engels recognized, 'does *nothing*'.[82] Appeals to an inevitable process of historical evolution merely seek to present contingency as necessity, to turn social injustice into an inviolable social rule. Revolution is indeed condemned precisely because it subverts the most basic 'law' of history: 'Our role was to die, yours was to kill.' That the people might overcome their prescribed social position is the greatest fear of the established order. Fear of any violence this process might involve is certainly secondary to the fear of this fundamental change (this again explains why, compared to the Terror of 1793, 'the butcheries of the Thermidorian reaction' go unmentioned by supporters of the established order). Such is the essential meaning of the French Revolution: it marked the moment at which 'we stepped out of our appointed role'. In 1789, Blanqui writes,

> the victims ceased to lay their heads, with resignation, on the executioner's block. They rose up, and it was their turn to strike. They were struck themselves, but they returned each blow, and often with interest! What a strange turn of events! What an unprecedented scandal! The vassals of the gallows dared to raise their hand to their judges! What a reversal of all divine and human laws![83]

Across all these writings Blanqui's basic assumption is clear and simple: the people, the vanquished of history, are the cannon fodder of positivist historiography. Their experiences are meaningless, their lives expendable. 'Who is willing to listen to the screams and cries of these vile herds that die by the thousands in the abattoirs of history?,' Blanqui asks.[84] Poverty and suffering, famine and disease, slaughter and destruction – all must bow before the unending tyranny of teleology. For Blanqui the Comtean appeal to an inner logic of history, in which, like a form of Hegelian cunning of reason, humanity unknowingly becomes the instrument of history's rational designs, legitimizes the immoral injustice of the present by way of legitimizing the immoral injustice of the past. And just as in 1832 Blanqui noted the impression of the people as an 'instrument of the middle classes', as 'gladiators who kill and are killed for the amusement and benefit of the privileged',[85] these passages from 1869 exercise no restraint when characterizing the champions of historical necessity from the future perspective of the 'mechanical dolls' of history:

> In the history book of humanity, you are the page on cholera and the plague. The barbarities and foolishness of your forefathers can be attributed to their ignorance, and were the result of blind convictions. You, on the other hand, the harm you inflicted was deliberate, premeditated, driven by a dark selfishness. For you have never believed in anything other than your own self-interest, you ignoble sceptics, to this interest you were willing to sacrifice even your most distant descendants. Who gave you a mandate to speak in our name, to think and act on our behalf? Did we agree to the earnings you anticipated on the back of our labour? Hypocrites! On the pretext of ensuring our well-being, you devoured the fruits of our sweat in advance, doing your best to blind and deafen us so as to prevent us from seeing and hearing.[86]

Just as the past suffering, oppression and injustice inflicted against the people must speak through any account of history worth the name, the future emancipation of the people, as the task of that history, will avenge their historical suffering in a cry of 'vengeance to all centuries'.[87] Through consciousness the people, no longer passive objects but empowered, self-determining subjects, will be capable of historical judgement, and they will speak for themselves; they will recount their own history.

## Reappraising the astronomical hypothesis

The manner in which Walter Benjamin's late writings, particularly the 'Theses on the Philosophy of History', echo the lines above has caught the attention of several readers – and rightly so.[88] Blanqui in many ways seems to synthesize 'the discontinuity of historical time; the destructive power of the working class; the tradition of the oppressed' that are advanced as the basis of the materialist conception of history in a preparatory note of the 'Theses' and translated into the conceptual framework of the work itself.[89] But it is with the 'astronomical hypothesis' Blanqui penned in 1871 while imprisoned at the

Château de Taureau, following his arrest a day before the declaration of the Paris Commune, on 17 March, that Benjamin is most associated.

Benjamin makes two claims regarding *Eternity by the Stars* of import for Blanqui's politics. First, he argues that the text signals a political surrender. With *Eternity*, Benjamin tells us, Blanqui offers a 'resignation without hope' that was to be 'the last word of the great revolutionary'.[90] Second, he suggests that Blanqui rejects any notion of progress. According to Benjamin, although in *Eternity* 'Blanqui displayed no antipathy to the belief in progress; between the lines, however, he heaped scorn on the idea' – a position that was, in fact, entirely consistent with 'his political credo'.[91]

Both claims are misleading, and yet both have shaped and continue to shape the interpretation of Blanqui's politics. The Blanqui–Benjamin encounter is indeed a problematic one, such that it is necessary to make a detour via Benjamin, via the stars, in order to address these issues.

The argument Blanqui outlines in *Eternity by the Stars* is at once complex and simple: to comprehend the text as a whole requires systematically working through each of its constituent assumptions, yet once these are established it generally reads as a straightforward and internally coherent (if scientifically flawed) exercise in deductive reasoning. In what follows I trace the steps by which Blanqui builds his analysis in order to arrive at an understanding of the text itself and to consider how we might interpret its wider significance within his project.

## The finite, the infinite

The opening line of *Eternity by the Stars* advances the first of three basic theses that will underpin Blanqui's overall argument. 'The universe is eternal in time and space – eternal, boundless and indivisible.'[92] Since comprehension of infinity exceeds the limits of human intellect, the infinity of the universe remains and shall remain an enigma to us.[93] Such incomprehension should not call into question the knowledge that we cannot know, however, or lead us to claim that the universe must therefore be finite. Contrary to our presumptuous tendency to think otherwise, earth and humanity are but a minute part of this immense interstellar system. Human beings are 'mere intruders in the very group that our vainglory pretends to see bowing before its supremacy'.[94] Even the sun, the supposed centre of the universe, 'is no more than an imperceptible point in the expanse of space'.⁹⁵ All cannot escape the finitude of their material forms. Relative to the infinity of the universe, the course of finite material life, whatever its form, 'amounts to not even one-thousandth of a second. Eternity does not distinguish between a star and something ephemeral.'⁹⁶

To this conception of an infinite and eternal universe Blanqui then adds the assumption, taken from the contemporary findings of spectral analysis, that there are a finite number of material elements ('simple bodies'). The breakthroughs of spectral analysis show that these elements are not specific to the earth but are 'everywhere identical' in the material composition of all the universe's celestial bodies; the one hundred or so 'kinds of simple body that make up our Earth likewise form the basis of all the globes without distinction'.⁹⁷ The physical laws (gravitation and centrifugal) combining and governing these elements are in turn equally universal. The universe, Blanqui therefore writes, 'is nothing but a collection of families that are, in a certain way, united by flesh and blood. Everywhere we find the same matter, classified and organised by the same method, according to the same order. Its foundations and its government are identical.'⁹⁸ Taking these two assumptions together, Blanqui supposes that, because new atoms cannot be created and because the natural laws combining and ordering them are immutable, the material forms these atoms are able to produce are necessarily finite.⁹⁹ Across the universe this matter certainly takes multiple forms; the possible number of elemental 'combination-types' is indeed 'inexpressible', 'incalculably large'. But the basic matter itself, and, therefore, the total number of possible combinations, remains universally invariable.¹⁰⁰

On the basis of these first two assumptions a problem presents itself. 'Not one atom of matter can be created,' Blanqui notes, 'and if the deceased stars do not relight then the universe dies out.'¹⁰¹ Without the continuous rebirth and resurrection of matter the universe would be necessarily finite, too. A stark alternative emerges: 'the resurrection of the stars, or universal death'.¹⁰² Eternal rebirth and resurrection of the basic set of elements into new finite material forms are thus the means by which the universe's vitality is ensured and a vacuum avoided. Once a certain form of matter reaches the end of its finite existence, the elements composing it take on a new form through a process of shock and atomization. 'The metamorphoses follow one another without interruption,' Blanqui explains, but not without adding that at no point does this ceaseless, furious dying and rebirth, this 'pandemonium' of material regeneration, ever depart from or 'disobey the laws of nature'.[103] Such is the process through which elemental matter is transformed; it obeys 'the law common to all change' on the one hand while avoiding the 'eternal immobilisation' that would lead to the decomposition of the universe on the other.[104] Within the spatio-temporal infinity of the universe, then, 'the renewal of worlds through the collision and volatilisation of deceased stars takes place every minute across the fields of infinity'.[105]

Placing this finite material set and these immutable natural laws within the eternal universe leads Blanqui to suppose a process of eternal repetition; insofar as a finite number of elements are subject to an infinite process of shock, atomization and transformation within a spatially and temporally infinite universe, the logical consequence is the creation of infinite copies of the same finite number of elemental combinations or types. Alternatively put, spatio-temporal infinity decrees that once the limit of different original elemental combinations is reached and the number of types exhausted – as by definition it forever has been – new original combinations are unattainable, copies unavoidable. Therein lies the relation between the finite and the infinite: 'In spite of their vast numbers, these combinations have a limit and an endpoint. They must therefore be *repeated* in order to attain the infinite.'[106] Since 'the infinity of globes can only arise from the infinity of *repetitions*',[107] the universe is made and remade in an unending cycle. Repetition is matter's response, its only possible response, to the call of the universe's spatio-temporal infinity.

Strictly following the logic of these three propositions – an infinite and eternal universe, a finite set of material elements governed by universal natural laws, infinite repetition of the same elemental combinations – Blanqui does not hold back in affirming the full consequences of this process. It leads him to speculate that other worlds materially identical to our own world, 'from the day of its birth to the day of its death', have existed, currently do exist and will again exist within the spatio-temporal infinity of the cosmos.[108] The same applies to other humanities, too. Since human beings, like animals or things, are one possible form of elemental combination, every one of us 'has lived, lives, and will live endlessly' in the form of infinite identical twins, copies of ourselves who have lived, who will live and who are simultaneously living identical lives, at every second of our lives, across eternity. 'All human beings are thus eternal at every second of their existence,' Blanqui concludes.[109]

At this point Blanqui's basic argument becomes clear enough. Although separated by infinite times and distances, the universe nonetheless contains an infinite number of exact copies of our own earth, 'complete with all of its inhabitants, from the grains of sand to the Emperor of Germany', as well as an infinite number near exact copies, of course.[110] 'On each copy all the material things, all the organised beings, follow one another in the same order, in the same place, at the same minute as they do on the other Earths, its doubles,' Blanqui explains. 'Therefore, all the events that have taken place or that are yet to take place on our globe, before it dies, take place in exactly the same way on its billions of duplicates.'[111] Identical worlds and identical peoples lead to identical histories, both individual and collective, however great or small, from the assassination of Caesar through the Battles of Valmy, Marengo and Waterloo to Blanqui himself, sat at his desk in his cell on the Fort Taureau, writings these lines. Every moment of every life is played out again and again, for eternity.

## Fatalism against fatalism

But whereas these finite elemental combinations infinitely recreate the same species, peoples and worlds at a purely *material* level – and here lies the decisive, and often overlooked, point of the text as a whole – the same is not true at a *political* level. 'All identical at the outset of their journey, each of the Humanities follow, on their own planet, the road traced by their passions, and individuals contribute to changes in this road through their own particular influence.' In other words, humanity's capacity for choice and commitment means that biologically identical human beings are not destined to produce politically identical human histories. Humanity, Blanqui repeats, 'does not have the same personnel on all similar globes. Indeed, each of these globes has its own specific Humanity, so to speak, that emerged from the same source and began at the same point, but that was diverted along the way by a thousand alternations in the route, to culminate, in the end, in a different life and a different history.'[112] An Earth, therefore, 'is a genuine twin-Earth or Earth-double … up until today at least. For tomorrow, on each planet the events and the people will follow their own course. Henceforth everything is unknown for us.'[113]

To understand the underlying logic at work here, and how it does not contradict the assertions above regarding historical repetition, one must recall the foundations of Blanqui's thought, namely the division between the immutable laws and processes of the natural world and the contingent and changeable domain of human affairs. *Eternity* imposes the exact same division, with the exact same consequences. 'All natural laws are inflexible and immutable,' Blanqui states. 'So long as they govern alone, everything follows a course that is fixed and fated. But variations do begin to occur with animate beings that are endowed with will – or, in other words, caprice. Above all, as soon as human beings intervene, fantasy intervenes along with them.'[114] These lines, which constitute one of the pivotal passages of the text, simply reaffirm the basic principles of Blanqui's dualism as outlined in Chapter 1.

*Eternity*, then, in no way departs from the theoretical framework constructed before 1871. 'Fatality,' Blanqui insisted following France's allegedly unavoidable surrender to the Prussians in October 1870, 'is the law of the material universe and not that of humanity, which retains sole responsibility for its own affairs.'[115] A year later these assumptions accompanied Blanqui to the Fort Taureau where they would directly underpin his 'astronomical hypothesis'. For the restatement of this dualism does not constitute an obscure extract or passing inference in *Eternity* itself: Blanqui reiterates the point clearly and carefully lest its essential meaning be misunderstood or overlooked. Relative to the material composition of finite planets travelling through infinite time and space, he notes, even the greatest achievements of human volition are utterly inconsequential. Human activity 'never seriously disrupts the natural course of physical phenomena, but', he then immediately adds, and just as above the conjunction announces the key point, 'it does disrupt humanity.' Impotent in the face of nature's terrestrial laws and insignificant within the infinite history of the cosmos, human volition nonetheless does determine the course of human history. 'We must therefore take into account this subversive influence that changes the course of individual destinies, destroys or alters animal races, tears nations apart and topples empires.' Both individually and collectively, it is 'among themselves that men create victims and bring about immense changes'.[116] The division between nature and humanity, formally enacted in *Eternity* with the 'but', again attests to Blanqui's conception of human history as the site and product of human will and action, of struggle and conflict, of discontinuity and change. Impotence and insignificance within nature and the cosmos in no way denote impotence and insignificance within the realm of human affairs. If the natural world 'knows nothing of morality, and does not act in keeping with it', if nature acts 'unintentionally' and 'blindfolded',[117] it is because these are the very capacities – enlightened consciousness, deliberate action, the pursuit of justice – that only human beings can exercise. To cast aside necessity as nature's concern is to reveal the path of possibility, the only path humans ever have had and ever will have.[118]

Blanqui insists as a matter of principle that humans are not, as one note most likely written in the late 1860s puts it, the 'mere tools of the Eternal'.[119] Within the confines of our world we can shape our collective destiny; we are capable of deciding upon our future course. The past alone is a 'fait accompli'. The future remains unmade, unwritten. And we can make it; we can write it. As this unknown future unfolds 'each second will bring its bifurcation: the path we will actually take, and the one that could have been taken'. Decisions and action we do not take will certainly be taken by others in other worlds, creating in turn other possibilities and other histories. Blanqui's argument is indeed posited on every possible path having been taken infinite times, since the infinite 'knows nothing of alternatives and has room for everything'.[120] So while identical worlds and identical peoples result in the same individual and collective histories, the infinity of worlds and humanities does not fail to account also for the infinity of possible lives and histories, for the alternative paths and routes that we might have taken. In other worlds Napoleon may have won at Waterloo; by equal measure he may have lost at Marengo. Each of our twins follows the paths we ourselves did not, and vice versa.[121] That body doubles cannot warn each other of the consequences of their choices certainly constitutes the 'terrible' aspect of this universal system, Blanqui concedes, for if we were able to provide 'some sound pieces of advice' to those who had yet to live out these choices and actions then they would be spared 'a great deal of folly and sorrow' that we have had to endure and eventually overcome across the course of our history, and again the same applies vice versa.[122] But while this 'imprisonment of brother-worlds by the inexorable barrier of space' is no doubt 'melancholic' in principle, ultimately the impossibility of any common and cumulative human knowledge or experience across the universe's spatio-temporal infinity renders the point simply irrelevant. 'It does not matter much to us whether or not our doubles are our actual neighbours,' Blanqui therefore concludes.[123] Since we cannot ever anticipate the consequences of our choices and commitments the issue cancels itself out without in any way altering or diminishing the significance of choice and commitment in our world. Here lies the decisive point: even if on other worlds every path and every possible path has been and will be taken an infinite number of times before and after us, that does not alter or diminish our capacity alone, at every moment, to freely choose and pursue a course of action in order to determine what becomes of this world.

This is the lens through which we should read one particularly problematic passage on the fatalistic dimensions of this universal system. Reflecting on the cause of 'human variants', Blanqui again appeals to a logic of free choice when confronted by alternatives and bifurcations. 'What man has not at times found himself confronted with a choice of two possible paths or careers?,' he asks. 'The one he rejects would indeed change his life, while not altering his individuality per se. One leads to poverty, shame and servitude. The other leads to glory and freedom.' These sentences expand on and so should be read in conjunction with a preceding passage which likewise foregrounds the world's endless reproduction of voluntary choice and its corollary: voluntary relinquishment of all other possibilities. 'Every minute, every second, thousands of different directions are open to this human species. It chooses one of them, and forever abandons the others.' In this sense the claim that immediately follows, 'one cannot escape fatality',[124] simply means accepting the consequences of the initial choice. Just as we saw in Chapter 2, *Eternity* persists – with no less force and no less import – in the conviction that only through the fatalism of fully assuming all the implications of a free choice, of pursuing a course of action to the end no matter what the consequences, of remaining committed to a principle without recourse to concession or compromise, can the fatalism of externally imposed destiny be exposed as fallacious and duly overcome.

## The meaning of eternity

Given the clear consistency these statements share with Blanqui's wider understanding of history and politics, if not the simple fact that some of these phrases and their essential meanings are found, albeit slightly reworded, elsewhere in his writings, it cannot but seem somewhat surprising that *Eternity by the Stars* has been the subject of such persistent interest – and such persistent misinterpretation – to a far greater degree than any other of Blanqui's works. Why is this so? No doubt the text's seeming incongruity within the central preoccupations of Blanqui's life and thought is a contributing factor. Stylistically, meanwhile, *Eternity* is dense and oblique, demanding of its reader an investment seldom required (and intentionally avoided on the part of the author) for Blanqui's other writings.[125] Its astronomical theses afford little room for the immediate, incendiary prose of a 'Warning to the People' or an *Instructions for an Armed Uprising*. Even more atypical and unsettling is its apparent indifference to politics. These features, when combined with the circumstances of its conception, have invited a certain amount of speculation regarding the meaning of the text. With his trial impending in early 1872, did Blanqui, as Geffroy suggests, disavow or betray his political convictions in the hope that his scientific breakthroughs would spare him from further imprisonment (he insisted that copies of the text be sent to members of the Assembly, the Academies and the press), to the extent that 'if there is indeed a "Taschereau document" in his inflexible existence, then this is it'?[126] After the repression of the Paris Commune in May 1871, did Blanqui, as Benjamin and others claim, finally admit defeat and renounce revolution?[127] Did Blanqui, in short, abandon the political for the cosmological as a result of personal or political circumstances?

Close reading of the text can only lead one to answer such questions in the negative. We have seen that the politics of *Eternity* itself and their place within Blanqui's wider project, if not immediately obvious, become clear when his astronomical speculations are carefully examined and understood. Moreover, when *Eternity* is properly located within Blanqui's life and thought all other concerns regarding the possible anomalous status of the text, be they intellectual or biographical, are shown to be similarly inconsequential.

In the first instance, Blanqui's interest in this subject began long before 1871. His reflections on the infinite and the possibility of other worlds materially identical to our own have been traced back to 1841 during his imprisonment at Mont-Saint-Michel. Later, in 1857 when an inmate at Belle-Île, he wrote a short piece on humanity and the universe that might be seen as a precursor to *Eternity*.[128] Though the composition of the text served to divert his attention away from the physical and mental hardship of solitary confinement at the Fort Taureau – 'I am taking refuge in the stars,' he revealed in a letter from 21 June 1871, 'where it is possible to wander around freely' – that is not to say that the text itself was apolitical.[129] While its author was not a free political agent and was unable to act upon its conclusions, the same was not true of its reader. Moreover, as an intellectual intervention *Eternity* was not conceived as a direct response to events in the streets of Paris in May 1871, of which Blanqui remained ignorant as he wrote the text.[130] A more likely explanation for Blanqui's sustained interest in the universe would be his lifelong commitment to the Enlightenment ideal of understanding and explaining the world and human existence through reason (hence the passing observation that the text's scientific conclusions disprove the possibility of immaterial 'chimeras').[131] A desire to continue and advance the Enlightenment project certainly informs his assertion, when reflecting on the remaining lacunae in Laplace's cosmogony, that the 'enigma of the universe continuously confronts our every thought. The human mind seeks to decipher it at all costs.'[132] In turn, the characteristically combative writings and activities of Blanqui's final years put paid to any suggestion of a post-Commune defeatism, just as one cannot read this into *Eternity* itself. As this self-described 'poor prisoner engaged in the struggle against reaction'[133] wrote in July 1879, and summarizing the general sentiment of his correspondence at the time: 'We must join forces and regroup, size up the enemy and advance towards it.'[134] To suggest that by 1872 Blanqui had been defeated, that he had succumbed to his adversaries once and for all or that he had in any way renounced the central tenets of his political project is far from true.

The unique status *Eternity* has come to acquire within Blanqui's life and legacy arguably owes in large part to the interpretation of its most well-known reader. Walter Benjamin's discovery of this 'cosmic phantasmagoria' in late 1937[135] led him to become, as Hallward notes, Blanqui's 'most influential interlocutor', diffusing his own 'idiosyncratic patronage' of his subject.[136] Benjamin encouraged both interest in *Eternity* and in Blanqui as a major historical figure more generally, but at the price of the subsequent, and remarkably persistent, misunderstanding of the text as 'an unconditional surrender', the moment when its author, near the end of his life, finally 'yields to bourgeois society'.[137] Rather than a restatement of Blanqui's most basic assumptions about freedom and necessity, Benjamin's reading foregrounds the text's supposedly 'merciless speculations that give the lie to the author's revolutionary élan' in which 'basic premises [taken] from the mechanistic natural sciences' present a 'conception of the universe' that ultimately 'proves to be a vision of hell'. This conception of the universe, Benjamin suggests, is also 'the complement of' the social order that Blanqui simultaneously condemns and capitulates to: 'the terrible indictment he pronounces against society takes the form of an unqualified submission to its results' – 'an irony which doubtless escaped the author himself', Benjamin adds – leaving a feeling not of triumphant power but of 'oppression'.[138] As if to reinforce the 'infernal' quality of Blanqui's visions, in which the people are addressed 'as if they were apparitions' and 'natives' of this hellish world, Benjamin even cites the passages noted above on human will introducing variation and change in human affairs – passages which contain the basic meaning of *Eternity* as a whole – under the banner of 'Blanqui's misanthropy'.[139]

This is a puzzling ascription. Humanity certainly cannot determine or affect the course of the eternal and infinite universe. But that in no way means that humanity is 'damned' and deprived of a 'liberating solution' to the multiplying phantasmagorias of the 'commodity-producing' society.[140] It does not mean accommodation or resignation to the sociopolitical status quo. Humanity, Blanqui maintains throughout the text, makes human history – it forever has, it forever can. There is neither misanthropy nor 'mythic anguish', still less any 'melancholy' or 'pessimism',[141] to be found here – quite the contrary. *Eternity* is better read under the banner of Blanqui's voluntarism: within the sublime infinity of the universe we modest, finite beings can make of our society and our history what we will.

Like 'Warning to the People', like *Instructions for an Armed Uprising*, like all of Blanqui's writings, *Eternity* celebrates this empowering assumption. Those, meanwhile, who read *Eternity* through Benjamin's project rather than Blanqui's are led to reproduce the former's misunderstandings and misrepresentations.[142]

## Making progress

On the question of progress, whether in *Eternity* or in Blanqui's wider body of work, Benjamin's reading – and again those who follow it – likewise misses the mark.

One of the 'methodological objectives' of Benjamin's own research programme, he explains, is 'to demonstrate a historical materialism which has annihilated within itself the idea of progress', for unlike 'bourgeois habits of thought' historical materialism's 'founding concept is not progress but actualization'.[143] Benjamin repeats elsewhere: 'The belief in progress – in an infinite perfectibility understood as an infinite ethical task – and the representation of eternal return are complementary', comprising 'the indissoluble antinomies in the face of which the dialectical conception of historical time must be developed'.[144] This is all very well when confined to Benjamin's own thought, but Benjamin's appeal to Blanqui on this score is problematic. Actualization, boundless human perfectibility, moral task – these are all precisely some of the key elements of Blanqui's conception of progress; yet Benjamin explicitly separates Blanqui from them. 'The activity of a professional revolutionary such as Blanqui does not presuppose any faith in progress,' Benjamin claims, 'it presupposes only the determination to do away with present injustice. The irreplaceable political value of class hatred consists precisely in its affording the revolutionary class a healthy indifference toward speculations concerning progress. Indeed, it is just as worthy of humane ends to rise up out of indignation at prevailing injustice as to seek through revolution to better the existence of future generations.'[145]

Benjamin is only partially correct here, and his wish to detach contemporary struggles from any concern for progress creates a false dichotomy in Blanqui's politics. As we have seen, Blanqui certainly does not have 'faith in progress' in the sense of a blind optimism in its historical inevitability. Indeed, he explicitly insists that 'I am not among those who claim that progress can be taken for granted, that humanity cannot go backwards'.[146] Progress, as Blanqui conceives it, is in no way synonymous with the passing of historical time, with the mere occurrence of events regardless of their social content and consequences. 'These worshippers of success accept and celebrate as progress everything that happens, simply because it happens,' he acerbically notes. 'Time is progress, no matter what it brings.'¹⁴⁷ As the centuries progress humanity itself may well regress. By the same token, however, the assumption that 'the march of human things' is 'arbitrary', 'irregular' and varies 'according to the whims of billions of caprices'¹⁴⁸ does not by extension rule out the possibility of progress altogether. Blanqui does believe that progress is made possible *through* the determined struggle against present injustice. History does not beget progress. Progress is the result of popular education and human development, of forms of political and social association. It is neither cumulative nor achieved to the exclusion of regression, hence the importance noted earlier of sounding the alarm against this imminent threat. Where progress has occurred a conflict has been waged and won, a principle imposed and upheld. 'Victory,' Blanqui stresses, 'carries glory or opprobrium, freedom or slavery, barbarism or civilisation, in a fold of its dress. We do not believe in the fatality or inevitability of progress, that doctrine of emasculation and submission. Victory is an absolute necessity for right [*le droit*], on pain of no longer being right.'¹⁴⁹

In no way inevitable, human progress nonetheless forever remains possible. Rather than dismissing progress as the 'phantasmagoria of history',¹⁵⁰ Blanqui's conception of historical time in fact highlights the role of conscious, organized and sustained political action in confronting and overcoming the contingency of history in order to *make* progress, to *make* history. Political organization, present injustice and future progress are thus all linked, not divorced. 'Arms and organisation, these are the decisive elements of progress, the serious means of putting an end to destitution!'¹⁵¹ For Blanqui progress must be made; it must be made possible. To use Benjamin's own terms, progress *is* actualization.

At no point does Blanqui deviate from this assumption. His emphasis on the temporalities of the political struggle for social progress can already be seen in his early critiques of the law as sanctioning injustice. Regardless of 'the cry of hunger uttered by thousands of poor wretches', the 1832 'Defence Speech' notes, for the rich the sanctity of the law and the preservation of order is paramount. The only option for those who seek to end present suffering, so they are told, is 'to ask for legal reform; in the meantime [*en attendant*]', Blanqui adds, one must 'obey'.¹⁵² Note the shared passivity of the verbs here – ask, wait, obey – for the implication is telling. In the struggle for justice and equality there could, and so there would be no obeying of illegitimate powers, no asking for reforms that will never be granted, no waiting for progress that will never come. Just as 1789 had shown that the privileged few would not voluntarily relinquish their power, so 1830 had taught a new generation that 'when it comes to freedom, you cannot wait for it; you must take it'.[153] Any path to future justice must pass through a direct and immediate political confrontation with the social injustices of the present.

This central pillar of Blanqui's theory is perhaps best articulated by Gustave Tridon in his 1870 newspaper article already cited in Chapter 2, 'Hunger'. Declaring that the 'scandal' of exorbitant inequalities, of opulence living side by side with starvation must end, the text concludes with a maxim as remarkable for its rhetorical force as it is for its political insight: 'The hunger justifies the means' (*'La faim justifie les moyens'*).[154] Tridon's détournement of 'the end justifies the means' (*'la fin justifie les moyens'* in French, hence he plays on *la faim* and *la fin* as homonyms) in many ways cuts to the heart of his master's politics. For a project defined by the primacy of human agency, by the rejection of social or economic laws and the inevitability of progress, it is the suffering here and now – 'the cries of distress of a starving population',[155] as Blanqui once said – that justifies, that indeed requires, our full, uncompromising engagement and devotion here and now. Imagining 'the end' is not the concern. Emancipatory politics is not a question of drawing up a vision of a future society or believing in the inexorable forward march of history as the means to get there. All are illusions, all blind alleys that do not confront the problem in hand. Perhaps nowhere else is Blanqui's voluntarism so clear and pronounced. Voluntarists, Peter Hallward writes, from Toussaint L'Ouverture and John Brown to Che Guevara and Paulo Freire, maintain that, if 'confronted with indefensible institution[s]', inequalities or injustices, 'when the opportunity [arises]' one must '[resolve] to work immediately and by all available means for [their] elimination'. Voluntarists affirm that 'an idea, like the idea of communism, or equality, or justice, commands that we should strive to realize it without compromises or delay, before the means of such realization have been recognized as feasible or legitimate, or even possible. It is the deliberate striving towards realization itself that will convert the impossible into the possible, and explode the parameters of the feasible.'[156]

Although the concluding section of *Eternity by the Stars* declares, in a seemingly dramatic rupture with all these previous assertions, that 'there is no progress',[157] the reader must again be sensitive to the purely astronomical realm to which this statement pertains. When Blanqui describes the belief that 'the past [represents] barbarism, and the future [means] progress, science, happiness' as an 'illusion', he does so in light of his discovery of infinite other worlds within the universe whose histories, as copies of our own, will return with them the same reactionary barbarisms of our past. The according assumption that 'the future will once again see the same ignorance, the same foolishness, the same cruelty of our previous ages' therefore applies to the futures of the infinite copies of our earth, not to our earth itself.[158] Tragically, all the barbarisms of our history that we presumed were forever buried and decisively overcome will be faced by our body doubles across their histories. But this does not mean that both we and our copies cannot still achieve progress for ourselves and do away with these barbarisms in our own times and worlds – as indeed we continually must in order to avert new or resurgent barbarisms. At stake is not our capacity for progress within our world, but the recognition that this progress can and will have no bearing or impact on the infinite copies of our world.

Progress itself is not the illusion, then; the illusion is eternal progress across the eternal universe. Because of the infinite repetition of the same planetary copies, the finite existence of each copy and our inability to communicate from one copy to the next, progress cannot be cumulative across each earth's lifetime. But even if the progress humanities achieve in their own histories through their own choices and commitments 'is shut away on each Earth and disappears with it' then so be it, for so long as we terrestrial beings remain concerned with the task, our only possible task, of shaping our history and changing our world, the relative insignificance this progress means for the cosmos does not diminish its significance for us.[159]

Since the central thesis of *Eternity* is entirely consistent with the philosophical tenets Blanqui had established in some cases long before 1871, adding an astronomical context that simply extends – albeit to an infinite scale, of course – the architecture in which the same political project still resides, should its place within that project not be reconsidered? What, in other words, is the meaning of *Eternity by the Stars* for Blanqui's thought and legacy? Above all *Eternity* represents Blanqui's most sustained exploration of the manner in which the radical contingency of human history is distinct from the necessity of the natural world and the infinity of time and space, from the eternal and boundless cosmos. However flawed its scientific claims now appear, its compelling force endures: *Eternity* is no less than an account of the universe and human life, as formidable and sobering in its scope as it is empowering in its political implications. As an exposition of Blanqui's thought its significance has been overstated. But as testament to the inspiring power and range of that thought its significance is undeniable.

Blanqui's overall understanding of history and progress will now be familiar. Beginning with the primacy of intelligence and ideas, Blanqui attributes historical change in human affairs to philosophical change. History is first and foremost the account of the role of human thought and consciousness in determining humanity's social arrangements. By the same token, however, the capacity of ideas or philosophies to determine the arrangement of humanity's social life forever depends on those willing to act in their name. These assumptions lead Blanqui, throughout his life and thought, to insist on the capacity of conscious human action to bring about radical social change. Across the course of human history social progress, as Blanqui conceives it, is the result of deliberate and decisive collective political action. But such progress is also, Blanqui importantly adds, forever exposed to its own undoing. History's contingency leaves it necessarily open to regression and new injustices. The alternative of 'socialism or barbarism' therefore presents itself at all moments of humanity's past, present and future. The choice is humanity's own, the path its own making.

*Eternity by the Stars* does not challenge or alter so much as reaffirm Blanqui's most basic philosophical assumptions. No less than any other of his writings, it is, to borrow Hobsbawm's formulation apropos of the *Manifesto*, a 'document of choices, of political possibilities rather than probabilities, let alone certainties'.[160] If at first the astronomical hypothesis seems to depart entirely from the politics of our earth, it is a detour via the stars from which Blanqui's militant politics return and reassert themselves with ever-greater force and ever-greater urgency.

# Conclusion

## I

My point of departure in this book was to consider what would it mean to return to Blanqui as a significant historical actor and, above all, as a serious political thinker. Across the declarations and articles, pamphlets and polemics, personal notes and correspondence that make up Blanqui's body of thought, I have sought to show that his fundamental aim, as Gramsci wrote of Machiavelli, is always to 'bring everything back to politics'.[1] Of course, politics here is not a matter of 'constitutional details' or government policies but of founding new social orders on the basis of a radical redistribution of wealth and power.[2] For Blanqui, everything turns on one basic issue: the empowerment of the powerless. What forms of collective knowledge and action, Blanqui asks, are necessary for the oppressed to overcome their oppression and to realize their freedom and happiness? How, in other words, can the people become capable of ruling themselves?

At the heart of Blanqui's project is the notion of conscious volition: it explains the primacy he accords to intelligence, ideas and education in determining the arrangement of human affairs; it explains the way in which he frames emancipation as a process of intellectual and moral development and transformation; it explains his insistence on resolute commitment to the principles of equality and justice; it explains his conception of the people as a collective political actor and proletarian as a subjective political position; and it explains, above all, the claim that humans have the capacity to determine the course of human history. Politics, as Blanqui conceives it, is in every respect a matter of rational, enlightened thought and deliberate, voluntary action.

To affirm the centrality of conscious volition is first to recognize philosophy and ideas as determinant of social arrangements. We have noted the foundational role of intelligence and thought in Blanqui's project. Human intelligence, as a product of the brain, can either be actively cultivated through free and enlightened instruction or deliberately suppressed and manipulated by means of institutional stupefaction and ideological mystification. Blanqui indeed maintains that 'every ignorant person is a dupe and an instrument of dupery, a serf and an instrument of servitude'.[3] Not only does mass intellectual stupefaction enslave and oppress, then. Those whose intelligence has been deliberately stifled unconsciously *reproduce* the injustice they themselves suffer. It follows that education and mis-education are decisive political mechanisms, the central means by which domination and exploitation are maintained or overcome.

One of the major tensions in Blanqui's political theory is precisely between this enlightened consciousness and the processes of popular empowerment. Insofar as Blanqui sees human will as a product of and conditioned by human intelligence, failure to have attained the necessary level of enlightenment precludes the exercise of conscious volition and, therefore, of decisive political action. Just as Rousseau claims that 'as soon as [man] reaches the age of reason, he alone is the judge of how best to look after himself, and thus he becomes his own master',[4] in Blanqui's eyes those who are deliberately mis-educated are also at present incapable of exercising the form of voluntary self-determination that will arrive at and govern a truly free and equal society.

No doubt Blanqui is right to insist on being properly informed as the prerequisite to making the free choices upon which voluntary action is based; no doubt he is also right that the deliberate dissemination of misinformation in the service of particular sociopolitical interests prevents this process. But he too often overstates this point. He too often creates a stark divide between an 'enlightened elite' and the 'ignorant masses', thereby downplaying or dismissing ordinary people's capacity for decisive political action. In many ways this is what would lead him to assume that a vanguard group can take action in the name of, rather than with, the people. His reflections on the role of a revolutionary transitional power derive in large part from the same basic assumption: those who have yet to cultivate enlightened intelligence are incapable of voluntary self-determination, for which enlightened instruction is the only remedy. It is in this sense of a strict division between the means and ends of an emancipatory process that Blanqui's proposals for a 'Parisian dictatorship', as we have seen, prefigure the problem that the Leninist project would in turn also confront and also fail to resolve of how to align political and social change. As Michael Hardt convincingly shows in his reading of Thomas Jefferson, to practice a politics of *self-*emancipation one must begin by thinking political and social transformation, the forms and goals of revolutionary transition, together, as inseparable components of the same process.

The failure to meaningfully influence and strategically reflect popular consciousness would certainly at times leave Blanqui 'a general without an army', as Gustave Geffroy suggests.[5] But it would also be inaccurate to claim, as does Geffroy, that Blanqui continually found himself in this situation or that he repeatedly advocated substitutionist action across the course of his life. Indeed, to reduce Blanqui's political theory to 'the fantastic idea of overturning an entire society through the action of a small conspiracy', as Engels once defined Blanquism,[6] is itself fantastic.

Two points challenge this view of Blanqui – a view that has persisted, largely unchallenged, since his death. In the first instance, secret societies should be understood primarily as products of specific political contexts, in which state repression often drove any meaningful political opposition underground. For those militants who were not willing to renounce their commitment to a project of radical social change, conspiracy seemed to offer the only viable alternative to capitulation. Conspiratorial tactics and organizing, in other words, were often conceived more out of practical necessity than an a priori political choice. Blanqui himself, of course, did not persist with these secret and isolated organizational forms once political conditions allowed for open agitation in and among the masses, as seen most clearly in 1848. And even when he did advocate or align himself with conspiratorial activity – this is the second point – he nonetheless maintained that to be effective any form of political action, including that of a vanguard, must have a mass impact and must initiate a much broader popular mobilization. As he warned supporters in the mid-1860s, a time when 'the government [would] not allow a revolution to develop or take form': 'Our action, in its current form, can only affect an imperceptible number of workers. They all may be quite advanced, quite well educated, but their wider influence is extremely limited. Nothing today has any great influence over the people. Everything is fragmented and fractured to an infinite degree. No one is in a position to act in a serious and general way on the masses.'[7] Blanqui's major mistakes often owed less to a disregard or rejection of such an influence as politically decisive than to its presumed existence. 'Should a spark ignite the gunpowder,' he once assured, 'eighty thousand armed men will appear on the public square.'[8] It was this false assumption, anticipating and therefore triggering an explosion only to discover the explosive was missing, and not the belief that revolutionary change could occur without a mass mobilization in Paris, that resulted in disastrously mistimed and misjudged action.

Voluntary choice and resolute commitment are at the centre of Blanqui's political theory. Politics, according to Blanqui, presupposes taking a side and precludes any semblance of impartiality or so-called middle ground. Whether through active affiliation or passive compliance, a side is always taken. Blanqui's own principled conviction famously endured across his life to the exclusion of compromise or capitulation. Across his writings, meanwhile, one discovers a persistent and profound contempt for vacillation and equivocation, for purported neutrality and unprincipled opportunism. Those qualities or virtues that sustain a principled choice and conviction, be they a sense of moral duty or an avowed political faith, must therefore be recognized as a key concern of Blanqui's thought, particularly since they inform his conception of the political actor.

Blanqui maintains the need for a leading actor, the enlightened workers and students of Paris, whose decisive political role owes first and foremost to their concentrated intellectual supremacy over the nation as a whole. Parisians' shared consciousness of their plight, their knowledge and understanding of the established social order as one of exploitation and domination, and their willingness to fight for the victory of their chosen cause – together these factors make them an unrivalled political force. Only a lack of organization and discipline can prevent this determined popular force from overthrowing the forces of the state, Blanqui insists.

An appreciation of the centrality of choice and commitment within this view of political agency indeed enabled us to comprehend Blanqui's contentious conception of the proletariat as, fundamentally, a political actor. Collective actors, Blanqui claims, do not inevitably or naturally emerge through historical or economic processes. They are above all constituted through conscious decisions and voluntary action. We have seen that Blanqui's notions of the people and the proletariat must be read, first, as political concepts, as expressions of conflict and commitment, and, second, as a very broad social category denoting those who live from their labour – impoverished workers, anonymous masses. Blanqui's concept of the people or the proletariat is indeed one that recognizes the everyday yet unseen suffering of all the exploited and excluded, whose exploitation and exclusion will end as a result of their active empowerment. For Blanqui's is, in every respect, a project rooted in the everyday lives of ordinary people and animated by a process of both individual and collective realization and transformation.

What distinguishes Blanqui's political theory above all from his 'utopian' contemporaries is the assumption – taken from the Jacobins and later taken up by figures like Lenin, Fanon and Che – that radical social change is first and foremost a matter of collective political action. It is only through mobilizing and organizing popular forces capable of overthrowing an oppressive power that the struggle to establish social equality can truly begin. Blanqui forever insists that emancipation is an actual project that, if undertaken, will require dedicated work, perseverance and resolve. During his formative political engagements he became acutely aware of the obstacles and resistance a movement for popular power will confront and have to overcome. July 1830 and its aftermath showed Blanqui that popular empowerment is not reducible to a single event but is a continuous process whose success will rely on harnessing an actor's concentrated collective capacities so as to simultaneously proceed and persevere while avoiding the ever-present risk of manipulation and fragmentation to which disempowerment and defeat are so often owed.

Of major importance here is Blanqui's rejection of historical necessity and any appeals to objective socio-economic laws, pre-determined natural fate or preordained providential destiny. From his proclamations during the *Trois Glorieuses* of 1830 to *Eternity by the Stars* of 1872, Blanqui maintained that social progress, understood as a collective project or task, is always and everywhere politically possible. The history of popular struggles shows that if a group is organized and willing to do what is necessary in order to realize a common goal then it can be realized – such is the basic assumption of Blanqui's voluntarism. This primacy accorded to popular mobilization would, however, lead Blanqui to neglect the importance of wider, socio-economic factors within such processes. We are left, then, with an account of the struggle for popular power that fails to take sufficient account of the historical grounds on which this struggle is waged.[9]

## II

Any attempt to draw direct parallels and equivalences between Blanqui's time and our own will soon run into trouble, of course. The largely pre-industrial social relations of a country still dominated by agriculture, small-scale commerce and artisanal production, to say nothing of the means of distribution and exchange, both nationally and internationally, are far removed from those of twenty-first-century global capitalism. And yet, for all the obvious contextual differences, one cannot fail to be struck by the extent to which, in certain basic respects, Blanqui's sociopolitical analysis does in fact resonate today. The depiction of a financial oligarchy, of a corrupted democracy and a so-called representative system that 'concentrates the [legislative, judicial and executive] powers in the hands of a small number of privileged people who are united by the same interests',[10] of an ever-widening gap between rich and poor and of ever more intensive forms of exploitation, could quite credibly be written today. The historical persistence of highly stratified social arrangements based on the concentration of wealth and power is certainly something Blanqui himself is keen to highlight. As he states, in a brutally reductive gesture: 'Aristocracy: the flowers. The people: the manure that allows them to grow – this has been the structure of societies for centuries.'[11] Similarly, it is not hard to see how his description of the ruling ideology of his age might seem somewhat familiar to contemporary readers. 'Equality is a chimera, and devotion foolishness,' he writes. 'Let each man be devoted to himself and he will not need the devotion of others. Our only duty in this world is to enrich ourselves. The strongest and most cunning have free rein. Those who dream of universal happiness are either madmen or fanatics.'[12] While the economic conditions and political forms today are immensely different from those of Blanqui's time, the social forces and interests that underpin them remain fundamentally the same.

What, we might then ask, is the significance of Blanqui for contemporary politics? In what ways might his political theory inform or serve as a corrective to contemporary debates about the politics of popular empowerment? Here I shall propose three points under the broad headings of *temporality*, *agency* and *strategy*. Needless to say, in all such respects it is not a matter of anachronistic repetition or unqualified affirmation of Blanqui's politics but of locating and extracting some principles or questions that may be effectively reaffirmed or reposed today.

## 1. Temporality

Blanqui's voluntarist rejection of historical or economic laws, of purportedly objective forces or processes pre-determining humanity's social arrangements, has been consistently rejected as Blanqui's voluntarist ignorance.[13] But it is precisely this open and contingent view of human history, its privileging of political possibility over historical necessity and its opposition to any form of fatalist teleology, that would mark some of Blanqui's most notable readers, from Benjamin to Bensaïd, who in the nineteenth-century revolutionary discovered paths out of the blind alleys into which twentieth-century revolutionary politics had been led.

The twenty-first century confronts these issues of the temporalities of political struggle with no less importance or urgency. Today, 'in our bleak age so adoring of every form of necessity',[14] in the ruins of 'scientific socialism' and any pretentions to have discovered the internal and immutable logic of history, Blanqui's anti-determinism and anti-positivism re-emerge with timely forcefulness. History in this sense is not something that happens to us, a process that we must passively submit to and endure. We can, we must, actively shape it ourselves. Blanqui knows that, within the radical contingency of human history, only the organized political action of today can advance the cause of equality and justice tomorrow. 'Revolutions do not happen by themselves,' he maintained in 1860; 'they are the work of men.' History will not bring deliverance. We cannot rely on the emancipatory potential of economic tendencies or technological developments. 'Our salvation depends solely on ourselves, and one must expect it only to come from ourselves.'[15] Collective political action, itself based on more basic assumptions regarding humans' capacity to rule themselves and to determine their own socio-economic arrangements, alone offers the possibility of radical social change. Blanqui's outlook, here as elsewhere, is not coloured by his own political experience. Despite nearly a decade of imperial rule, during which time the revolutionary party had disintegrated and popular resignation to the status quo had come to reign, he still stood by such a possibility. 'As long as we pursue this work in the future, as we have done for these past eight years, history will change course, in spite of whatever all the oracles of human fatalism might claim.'[16] There is no such thing as historical fate or inevitable future destiny. There are only the political choices and commitments of the present.

This is the urgent and empowering message that lies at the heart of Blanqui's writings. If it is sanguine it is not unrealistically so. For Blanqui has no illusions regarding the efforts required to realize this possibility. Collective emancipation is 'work', he makes clear; it is a project or task requiring great effort, perseverance, patience and discipline on the part of all those who undertake it in order to overcome all the difficulties and obstacles it will inevitably encounter. And history shows that such efforts are in no way beyond us, such possibilities always realizable, however remote they might at times appear.

## 2. Agency

Crucial to these assumptions about the temporality of collective action, then, is the exercise of this action itself. Most of the principal elements of Blanqui's account of militant political agency can be traced back to his early political engagements. July 1830 showed that only an insurgent popular actor is capable of overthrowing the established order of things. Such an actor must have a clear, common goal, a coherent strategy to realize it and the firm resolve to achieve it. For a dominant group will not grant freedom to a subordinate group – freedom from domination and exploitation will have to be forcibly won. Blanqui maintains that a united and organized collective actor, if sufficiently determined, has the capacity to overpower its adversary and to realize its stated aims – whether that be winning concessions from a dominant group or overthrowing it altogether. Understood in these terms, there are perhaps few more lucid expositions of some of the practical steps necessary to initiate and then to continue a process of popular self-determination.

There is, of course, no escaping the fact that all the major political sequences in which Blanqui participated, to say nothing of his own various political endeavours, resulted in failure. Simply put, the general tenor of his entire political experience is defeat. But, as Perry Anderson reminds us, 'to be defeated and to be bowed are not the same'.[17] Political militancy is as much a matter of encouraging and sustaining a process of popular empowerment as it is responding to a situation of generalized disempowerment. Across the nineteenth century each successive round of defeat and disappointment – 1830–4, 1839, 1848–52, 1870–1 – brought questions of commitment and renewal to the fore. In the 1870s, as in the 1850s and the 1830s, Blanqui's political experience repeatedly returned him to a related set of questions: How do you sustain a revolutionary project and commitment to principles of justice and equality in the face widespread political resignation and exhaustion, in a profoundly counter-revolutionary moment, a moment when, seemingly, 'there is no alternative' to the established order of things? How do you respond to the dispersal and disempowerment of a previously organized and combative collective actor?

Few of Blanqui's contemporaries rival the force and consistency of his own sense of conviction and purpose. In his life and work alike he shows that an informed, principled decision then requires principled, unwavering commitment; a politics of voluntary choice is meaningless without accepting the consequences – however difficult, however demanding – the initial choice will necessarily impose. But beyond the power of his own example,[18] here Blanqui no doubt often offers more in the way of questions themselves than answers. And yet it is precisely only through posing anew these and similar questions – what is the importance of clearly stated principles and goals? How might notions of dedication and resolve inform the approach to difficulties and defeats, obstacles and impasses, as they necessarily appear in the course of a political sequence, be it local or general, short or long? How is a sense of political confidence and enthusiasm created, harnessed and sustained, both individually and collectively? How is it stifled, repressed and extinguished? – that it might be possible to arrive at some answers.

## 3. Strategy

So far we have gone from the insistence on the possibility of social change to the political militancy that is necessary to realize, or simply to affirm, that possibility. The question of how that resolute militancy might be effectively channelled and directed forms of the basis of this third point.

Blanqui was one of the first socialist thinkers to reflect seriously on the question of political strategy. His strategic concerns derive from the recognition of a decisive factor confronting all movements for social change: political power. One of Blanqui's most significant and consistent insights is the understanding that without political power any attempt to enact far-reaching and lasting social change will bear no fruit. Power is certainly not the end in itself. But forms of collective action, no matter how inspiring, that downplay or ignore the problem of political power, of the means by which it might be collectively taken, retained and exercised, will be repeatedly contained and subsumed by the status quo, leaving little trace beyond a momentary rupture.[19] History shows, as Blanqui again learned in the wake of July 1830, that the realization of radical social change requires collective political action that extends beyond local, ephemeral disruption. Localized mobilizations, mass demonstrations and protests, strikes and occupations, must be concentrated and translated into political forms capable of constituting and exercising popular power. How, then, can localized practices be generalized? How do a people go from exclusion from to constitution of political power as the basis of enduring social change? How should we negotiate the apparent tension between popular empowerment and the concrete exercise of political power?

Questions of strategy lead to questions – and problems – of organization. To maintain, after Blanqui, that 'organisation means victory; dispersal means death'[20] is not to claim that a mere return to and repetition of past organizational forms would provide an answer. But it is to affirm that *forms* of organization remain necessary. Blanqui is right to insist that without responsive leadership and collective discipline, an oppressed group will remain incapable of ultimately transcending their oppression. He recognizes that there are no successful popular mobilizations without effective political organization. He correctly diagnoses this basic problem, even if his own remedies are, needless to say, far from satisfactory. The solutions remain ours to discover.

# Notes

## Introduction

1 Edward S. Mason, 'Blanqui and Communism', *Political Science Quarterly*, 44:4 (December 1929), p. 498; Maurice Dommanget, *Auguste Blanqui à Belle-Île* (Paris: Librairie du Travail, 1935), p. 7.
2 See 'Philosophical and Political Fragments', 19 or 29 September 1831, *BR*, p. 162.
3 'Philosophical and Political Fragments', 30 December 1868, *BR*, p. 129.
4 MSS 9592(3), f. 181 [c. 1868]; cf. MSS 9592(3), f. 50 [17 April 1868].
5 'Philosophical and Political Fragments', n.d. [1849–50], *BR*, p. 142.
6 'Notes on Positivism', 8 April 1869, *BR*, p. 239.
7 'Communism, the Future of Society', 1869, *BR*, p. 252. See also the claim that 'general ignorance' is the 'rampart of inequality. Only the spread of enlightenment will overcome any resistance and turn that which today seems like a chimera into a reality' ('Le Luxe', n.d. [c. 1860s?], *CS1*, p. 96).
8 'Report to the Society of the Friends of the People', 2 February 1832, *BR*, p. 33.
9 MSS 9588(2), f. 455 [c. June–July 1879].
10 'Introduction', in Gustave Tridon, *Les Hébertistes* (Brussels: Briand, 1871), p. 6.
11 'Letter to Blanqui's supporters in Paris', 18 April 1866, *BR*, p. 174.
12 'Letter to Maillard', 6 June 1852, *BR*, p. 119.
13 The most detailed biography available in English is Samuel Bernstein, *Auguste Blanqui and the Art of Insurrection* (London: Lawrence and Wishart, 1971); apart from Maurice Dommanget's multivolume study of Blanqui, the most thorough and informative biography remains Alain Decaux's *Blanqui l'Insurgé* (Paris: Perrin, 1976).
14 'Report to the Society of the Friends of the People', 2 February 1832, *BR*, pp. 24, 26.
15 'Lettre à Ferdinand Flocon', 18 August 1846, *OI*, p. 498.
16 I owe this formulation to Jonathan Beecher, who coined it with regard to Proudhon and 1848.
17 See Fidel Castro, 'The Death of Che Guevara', 18 October 1967, in *Fidel Castro Reader*, ed. David Deutschmann and Deborah Shnookal (Melbourne: Ocean Press, 2007), pp. 321–2. As Edward Mason notes, there is likewise 'an

extraordinary unity in the life of Blanqui: a blending of thought and action, a singleness of purpose and a monotony of experience which makes of him a figure clear-cut in its significance' (Mason, 'Blanqui and Communism', p. 501).
18  See Karl Marx and Frederick Engels, *Marx and Engels Collected Works*, Volume 10 (London: Lawrence and Wishart, 1978), p. 700, n.386.
19  Paul Lafargue, *La Rive Guache*, 1 July 1866; Paul Lafargue, 'Auguste Blanqui, Souvenirs personnels', in *La Révolution française*, 20 April 1879, both quoted in Maurice Dommanget, *Blanqui et l'opposition révolutionnaire à la fin du Second Empire* (Paris: Armand Colin, 1960), p. 51. See also Leslie Derfler, *Paul Lafargue and the Founding of French Marxism, 1842–1882* (Cambridge, MA: Harvard University Press, 1991), pp. 28–9.
20  See Maurice Dommanget, *Blanqui, La Guerre de 1870–1871 et La Commune* (Paris: Editions Domat-Montchrestien, 1947), pp. 145–7.
21  Karl Marx, *The Class Struggles in France 1848 to 1850* (Moscow: Progress, 1972), p. 117; emphasis in original.
22  Karl Marx and Frederick Engels, 'Introduction to the Leaflet of L.A. Blanqui's Toast Sent to the Refugee Committee', 1851, in *Collected Works*, Volume 10, p. 537.
23  Karl Marx, *The Eighteenth Brumaire of Louis Bonaparte* (Moscow: Progress, 1977), p. 17.
24  MSS 9588(1), ff. 205, 209 [*c.* April 1879].
25  Eugène de Mirecourt, *Blanqui* (Paris: Chez L'Auteur, 1857), pp. 7–8.
26  de Mirecourt, *Blanqui*, pp. 39, 59, 61.
27  Hippolyte Castille, *L.A. Blanqui* (Paris: F. Sartorius, 1857), pp. 56–7.
28  Heinrich Heine, *French Affairs: Letters from Paris*, Volume 2, trans. Charles Godfrey Leland (New York: United States Book, 1893), p. 394; translation modified.
29  Walter Benjamin, *The Arcades Project*, ed. Rolf Tiedemann, trans. Howard Eiland and Kevin McLaughlin (Cambridge, MA: Harvard University Press, 1999), p. 15.
30  Alexis de Toqueville, *Recollections: The French Revolution of 1848*, ed. J. P. Mayer and A. P. Kerr, trans. George Lawrence (New Brunswick: Transaction, 1987), p. 118.
31  Victor Hugo, *Œuvres complètes de Victor Hugo. Vol. 25: Choses Vues I* (Paris: Ollendorff, 1913), p. 376; Victor Hugo, *The Memoirs of Victor Hugo*, trans. John W. Harding (London: William Heinemann, 1899), pp. 291–2.
32  Paul Lafargue, 'Auguste Blanqui, Souvenirs Personnels', *La Révolution française*, 20 April 1879, quoted in Derfler, *Paul Lafargue and the Founding of French Marxism, 1842–1882*, p. 29. George Sand made the same comparison, describing Blanqui as 'the Marat of the present times' ('To Maurice Sand', 17 April

1848, in *Letters of George Sand*, Volume 2, trans. Raphaël Ledos de Beaufort (New York: Cosimo, 2009), p. 20).

33 'Blanqui is essentially a political revolutionist. He is a socialist only through sentiment, through his sympathy with the sufferings of the people, but he has neither a socialist theory nor any definite practical suggestions for social remedies. In his political activity he was mainly a "man of action", believing that a small and well organized minority, who would attempt a political stroke of force at the opportune moment, could carry the mass of the people with them by a few successes at the start and thus make a victorious revolution' (Frederick Engels, 'The Programme of the Blanquist Fugitives from the Paris Commune', 26 June 1874, at marxists.org).

34 Notable readings of Blanqui that appeal to such critiques in their depiction of an authoritarian – or indeed a 'totalitarian' – elitist whose project is clearly distinct from and antithetical to Marx's as such, include Richard Hunt, *The Political Ideas of Marx and Engels. Vol. 1: Marxism and Totalitarian Democracy, 1818–1850* (London: Macmillan, 1975), Hal Draper, *The 'Dictatorship of the Proletariat' from Marx to Lenin* (New York: Monthly Review Press, 1987) and Monty Johnstone, 'Marx, Blanqui and Majority Rule', in *Socialist Register 1983*, ed. Ralph Miliband and John Saville (London: Merlin, 1983), pp. 296–318.

35 Rosa Luxemburg, 'Blanquism and Social Democracy', June 1906, at marxists.org.

36 Leon Trotsky is the notable exception to this rule. See in particular chapter 42 of his *History of the Russian Revolution*, entitled 'The Art of Insurrection', in which, reflecting at length on the link between conspiracy and popular insurrection, he describes Blanquism as 'the revolutionary essence of Marxism' (Leon Trotsky, *History of the Russian Revolution*, trans. Max Eastman (London: Penguin, 2017), p. 746).

37 V. I. Lenin, 'The Dual Power', April 1917, in *Collected Works*, Volume 24 (Moscow: Progress, 1974), p. 40. This is the same Lenin who insisted on 'the initiative and energy of class-conscious fighters' as a decisive force in political struggle (V. I. Lenin, 'What Is to Be Done?', March 1902, in *Collected Works*, Volume 5 (Moscow: Progress, 1960), p. 392) – a version of Blanqui's claim that socialists have the capacity to make revolution if they 'know what they want' and they have the 'vigour and initiative' to realise it ('Philosophical and Political Fragments', November 1853, *BR*, p. 167).

38 Walter Benjamin, 'Theses on the Philosophy of History', in *Illuminations*, ed. Hannah Arendt, trans. Harry Zorn (London: Pimlico, 1999), pp. 251–2.

39 Maurice Dommanget, *Les Idées politiques et sociales d'Auguste Blanqui* (Paris: Marcel Rivière, 1957), p. 67.

40 Quoted in Miguel Abensour, *Les Passages Blanqui: Walter Benjamin entre mélancolie et révolution* (Paris: Sens & Tonka, 2013), p. 29 and Peter Hallward, 'Blanqui's Bifurcations', *Radical Philosophy*, 185 (May–June 2014), p. 40.
41 'Philosophical and Political Fragments', 1868, *BR*, p. 136.
42 Antonio Gramsci, 'The Modern Prince', in *Selections from the Prison Notebooks*, ed. and trans. Quintin Hoare and Geoffrey Nowel Smith (London: Lawrence and Wishart, 1971), p. 123.
43 Niccolò Machiavelli, *The Prince*, trans. George Bull (London: Penguin, 2003), p. 50. As Gramsci notes, 'Machiavelli wrote books of "immediate political action", and not utopias.' Machiavelli's worldview 'bases itself entirely on the concrete action of man, who ... works and transforms reality' (Gramsci, 'State and Civil Society', in *Selections from the Prison Notebooks*, p. 248).
44 Trotsky, *History of the Russian Revolution*, p. 742.
45 Blanqui uses this phrase in his 'Letter to Maillard', 6 June 1852, *BR*, p. 119. Elsewhere he speaks of his 'essentially practical mind', insisting that he is 'highly impatient with theories that come to nothing' ('Premier Texte Autobiographique', n.d. [*c.* 1849–52?], *OI*, p. 41).
46 'Instructions for an Armed Uprising', 1868, *BR*, p. 206.
47 Niccolò Machiavelli, *The Prince*, trans. Russell Price (Cambridge: Cambridge University Press, 1988), p. 21; translation modified.
48 'Concerning the Clamour against the "Warning to the People"', April 1851, *BR*, p. 103.
49 Machiavelli, *The Prince*, trans. George Bull, p. 58.
50 Machiavelli, *The Prince*, trans. George Bull, p. 47. According to Gustave Geffroy, *The Prince* was Blanqui's bedside book while he was an inmate of Sainte-Pélagie prison in the early 1860s. See Gustave Geffroy, *L'Enfermé* (Paris: Bibliothèque Charpentier, 1919), p. 244. As far as I am aware there are no positive references to Machiavelli in Blanqui's writings, however.
51 'Instructions for an Armed Uprising', 1868, *BR*, p. 207.
52 Machiavelli, *The Prince*, trans. George Bull, p. 47.
53 See Jean-Jacques Rousseau, *Discourse on the Origin of Inequality*, ed. Patrick Coleman, trans. Franklin Philip (Oxford: Oxford University Press, 2009).
54 Jean-Jacques Rousseau, *The Social Contract*, trans. Christopher Betts (Oxford: Oxford University Press, 2008), pp. 54–5; translation modified.
55 'Rapport gigantesque de Thiers sur l'assistance publique', 1850, *CS2*, p. 247.
56 Rousseau, *Social Contract*, p. 54.
57 Rousseau, *Social Contract*, pp. 55–6.
58 Rousseau, *Social Contract*, p. 57. Rousseau insists that 'sovereignty, being only the exercise of the general will, can never be transferred, and that the sovereign,

which cannot be other than a collective entity, cannot be represented except by itself' (*Social Contract*, p. 63).
59 'T140', 8 July 1841, *OI*, p. 624.
60 'Communism, the Future of Society', 1869, *BR*, p. 263. In his early writings Blanqui similarly evokes 'an association of free men' as a guiding ideal. See 'Social Wealth Must Belong to Those Who Created It', February 1834, *BR*, p. 53.
61 'Initiation Ceremony of the Society of the Seasons', 1837, *BR*, pp. 67–8.
62 'Philosophical and Political Fragments', 1868-9, *BR*, p. 130.
63 Alternatively, these principles could go under the headings of authority and legitimacy (the assumption that existing orders are not legitimate simply because they exist, and that they are indeed illegitimate if they violate the rights of the people); of association and organization (the assumption that, first, a collective actor is constituted through active assembly and free and equal participation; and that, second, this actor can only become an effective political force through its organization); and of commitment and persistence (the recognition of what is necessary, subjectively, to realize a collective project). Cf. Peter Hallward, 'The Will of the People: Notes towards a Dialectical Voluntarism', *Radical Philosophy*, 155 (May–June 2009), pp. 17–29.
64 'Why There Are No More Riots', 2 February 1834, *BR*, p. 43.

# Chapter 1

1 'Letter to Tessy', 6 September 1852, *BR*, p. 123.
2 'Declaration of the Provisional Committee for Schools', 22 January 1831, *BR*, p. 6.
3 'Philosophical and Political Fragments', October 1853, *BR*, p. 133.
4 'Philosophical and Political Fragments', 1849-50, *BR*, p. 142.
5 'Communism, the Future of Society', 1869, *BR*, p. 265.
6 'Philosophical and Political Fragments', 1868, *BR*, p. 136.
7 'Philosophical and Political Fragments', 1868, *BR*, p. 136. See also *Eternity by the Stars*, 1872, *BR*, pp. 320–1.
8 'Fatal, Fatalism, Fatality', 28 July 1868, *BR*, pp. 186, 191.
9 'Fatal, Fatalism, Fatality', 28 July 1868, *BR*, p. 181.
10 'Philosophical and Political Fragments', 16 April 1868, *BR*, p. 129.
11 'Communism, the Future of Society', 1869, *BR*, p. 265.
12 'Philosophical and Political Fragments', n.d., *BR*, pp. 129–30.
13 Karl Marx, 'Preface (to *A Contribution to the Critique of Political Economy*)', 1859, in *Early Writings*, trans. Rodney Livingstone and Gregor Benton (London: Penguin, 1975). p. 425.

14 'Philosophical and Political Fragments', June 1861, *BR*, p. 129. See also MSS 9586, f. 402 [n.d.].
15 On this comparison, see also Alan B. Spitzer, *The Revolutionary Theories of Louis Auguste Blanqui* (New York: Columbia University Press, 1957), p. 46.
16 Marx, 'Preface (to *A Critique of Political Economy*)', p. 425.
17 Marx, 'Preface (to *A Critique of Political Economy*)', p. 425.
18 'Communism, the Future of Society', 1869, *BR*, p. 265.
19 Auguste Blanqui, 'Point d'Assemblée', 19 November 1870, in *La Patrie en Danger* (Paris: A. Chevalier, 1871), p. 272.
20 'Projet de discours', August 1867, *CS2*, p. 162.
21 Karl Marx, *The Eighteenth Brumaire of Louis Bonaparte* (Moscow: Progress Publishers, 1977), p. 10; translation modified.
22 'Fatal, Fatalism, Fatality', 28 July 1868, *BR*, p. 180.
23 'Philosophical and Political Fragments', 1868–9, *BR*, p. 131. Blanqui rejects Providential design for the same reason: nature is not a 'creation of divine thought', for nature is not a 'creation' but the 'only creator'. Hence 'thought is but one of the most ephemeral creations' of nature (MSS 9590(1), f. 274 [n.d.]).
24 'Athéisme et spiritualisme', 13 December 1880, *ND*, p. 23.
25 'Matter provided humanity with a brain that can be perfected through the reaction that results from thought' ('Philosophical and Political Fragments', 1868–9, *BR*, p. 131).
26 'Fatal, Fatalism, Fatality', 28 July 1868, *BR*, pp. 180–1.
27 'Fatal, Fatalism, Fatality', 28 July 1868, *BR*, p. 186.
28 'Fatal, Fatalism, Fatality', 28 July 1868, *BR*, p. 186.
29 MSS 9590(1), f. 262 [25 August 1868]; 'Fatal, Fatalism, Fatality', 28 July 1868, *BR*, p. 186.
30 'Philosophical and Political Fragments', 1868–9, *BR*, p. 131; emphasis added.
31 MSS 9590(1), f. 156 [8 March 1869].
32 'Communism, the Future of Society', 1869, *BR*, p. 265.
33 'Equality Is Our Flag', 2 February 1834, *BR*, p. 40.
34 'It is through thought that [men] communicate', Blanqui continues, 'through thought that they form one single being. It is through thought that universal solidarity is established, through thought that the interest of one becomes the interest of all – and this interest of all boils down to the interest of the weakest' ('Philosophical and Political Fragments', 1868–9, *BR*, p. 131).
35 MSS 9592(3), ff. 251–2 [n.d.].
36 Jean-Jacques Rousseau, *The Social Contract*, trans. Christopher Betts (Oxford: Oxford University Press, 2008), p. 59.
37 'To build communism it is necessary, simultaneous with the new material foundations, to build the new man and woman. That is why it is very important

to choose the right instrument for mobilizing the masses. Basically, this instrument must be moral in character' (Che Guevara, 'Socialism and Man in Cuba', 1965, in *Che Guevara Reader: Writings on Politics and Revolution*, ed. David Deutschmann (Melbourne: Ocean Press, 2004), p. 217).

38 Che Guevara, 'On the Budgetary Finance System', February 1964, in *Che Guevara Reader*, p. 201.
39 'Philosophical and Political Fragments', n.d. [*c*. 1849], *BR*, p. 129.
40 'Philosophical and Political Fragments', 3 May 1865, *BR*, p. 132; 'Philosophical and Political Fragments', 1868, *BR*, 164. Cf. 'Socialism cannot exist without a change in consciousness resulting in a new fraternal attitude toward humanity' (Che Guevara, 'At the Afro-Asian Conference in Algeria', 24 February 1965, in *Che Guevara Reader*, p. 341).
41 'Fatal, Fatalism, Fatality', 28 July 1868, *BR*, p. 185.
42 MSS 9592(3), f. 220 [n.d.].
43 MSS 9592(3), f. 78 [29 July 1869].
44 'Fatal, Fatalism, Fatality', 28 July 1868, *BR*, p. 188.
45 See 'Fatal, Fatalism, Fatality', 28 July 1868, *BR*, pp. 188, 198.
46 'Fatal, Fatalism, Fatality', 28 July 1868, *BR*, p. 198.
47 MSS 9592(3), f. 307 [n.d.].
48 MSS 9592(3), f. 307 [n.d.].
49 Jean-Jacques Rousseau, *Emile or On Education*, trans. Allan Bloom (London: Penguin, 1991), p. 280.
50 Rousseau, *Emile*, p. 281; Jean-Jacques Rousseau, *Discourse on the Origin of Inequality*, ed. Patrick Coleman, trans. Franklin Philip (Oxford: Oxford University Press, 2009), p. 16.
51 Rousseau, *Social Contract*, p. 91.
52 Rousseau, *Social Contract*, p. 49.
53 MSS 9590(1), f. 278 [n.d.]. Cf. Rousseau, *Social Contract*, Book I, Chapter III.
54 'Philosophical and Political Fragments', March 1870, *BR*, p. 129.
55 Rousseau, 'Discourse on Political Economy', in *Social Contract*, p. 10.
56 'Philosophical and Political Fragments', 1849–50, *BR*, p. 142. Cf. 'As soon as [man] reaches the age of reason, he alone is the judge of how best to look after himself, and thus he becomes his own master' (Rousseau, *Social Contract*, p. 46).
57 'Communism, the Future of Society', 1869, *BR*, p. 267.
58 'Les articles 415 et 416 contre les coalitions', *CS2*, p. 177.
59 'Malfaisance de l'Église', April–May 1865, *ND*, p. 61.
60 'Philosophical and Political Fragments', 25 June 1868, *BR*, p. 132; 'Philosophical and Political Fragments', n.d. [1849–50], *BR*, p. 142.
61 'Communism, the Future of Society', 1869, *BR*, p. 245.
62 'Fatal, Fatalism, Fatality', 28 July 1868, *BR*, p. 192.

63 As Blanqui explains, 'idleness means man as inert, no longer exercising his faculties, degraded to the state of a brute – in short, man ceasing to be man! Intelligence and labour means man exalted by thought, ennobled by the exercise of his power, man mastering all of creation!' ('Social Wealth Must Belong to Those Who Created It', February 1834, *BR*, p. 39). And again: the 'ability' of enlightened thought 'to put right or redress the forces of matter ... distinguishes us from animals, who suffer this force with a passive inertia, incapable of reaction, the powerless playthings of all its manifestations. Animals blindly obey; men defend themselves' ('Philosophical and Political Fragments', 1868–9, *BR*, p. 131).
64 Rousseau, *Emile*, p. 42.
65 'Fatal, Fatalism, Fatality', 28 July 1868, *BR*, p. 187.
66 'Philosophical and Political Fragments', 1868–9, *BR*, p. 131.
67 MSS 9592(3), f. 220 [1868]. See also: 'Men! Leaves! Playthings of the winds, playthings of the passions! But they stand together in solidarity, and are attached to the same trunk: for one this is the tree, for the other it is humanity. The link between leaves is material, the link between humans is moral: consciousness' ('Philosophical and Political Fragments', 11 December 1858, *BR*, p. 133).
68 'Fatal, Fatalism, Fatality', 28 July 1868, *BR*, p. 183.
69 'Philosophical and Political Fragments', 1868–9, *BR*, p. 130.
70 'The Sects and the Revolution', 19 October 1866, *BR*, p. 178.
71 Che Guevara, 'Socialism and Man in Cuba', 1965, in *Che Guevara Reader*, p. 220.
72 'Candide', 3 May 1865, *MF*, p. 248.
73 'The Sects and the Revolution', 19 October 1866, *BR*, p. 178.
74 'Philosophical and Political Fragments', 17 September 1869, *BR*, p. 141.
75 MSS 9590(1), f. 107 [28 April 1870]; 9590(1), f. 193 [19 April 1869]; 'Philosophical and Political Fragments', n.d. [1848–9?], *BR*, p. 165.
76 'One Last Word', 12 February 1871, *BR*, p. 271.
77 'Notes on Positivism', 15 March 1869, *BR*, p. 232.
78 'Philosophical and Political Fragments', August 1867, *BR*, p. 142.
79 '*L'Education fait les esclaves; l'instruction fait les hommes libres*' (MSS 9592(3), f. 222 [n.d.]).
80 MSS 9592(3), f. 74 [8 October 1869].
81 'Philosophical and Political Fragments', n.d. [1849–50], *BR*, p. 142.
82 'Social Wealth Must Belong to Those Who Created It', February 1834, *BR*, pp. 51–2.
83 MSS 9590(1), ff. 153–5 [6 March 1869]. Cf. 'For the Red Flag', 26 February 1848, *BR*, p. 74.
84 MSS 9592(3), f. 150 [21 April 1868].

85 See 'Communism, the Future of Society', 1869, *BR*, p. 264. Or as he similarly writes elsewhere: if the state directed its resources 'to public education and sought to organise a programme of serious, rational teaching, based on science, then in less than ten years the transformation of France would be complete. All the workers, transformed from passive instruments into enlightened citizens, would spontaneously bring into association all their intellectual and physical capacities, and the problem of organising labour in accordance with justice would be resolved' ('Philosophical and Political Fragments', August 1867, *BR*, p. 142).
86 'Communism, the Future of Society', 1869, *BR*, p. 249.
87 'Communism, the Future of Society', 1869, *BR*, p. 249. Cf. 'What, then, is the cause which determines [a man's] will? It is his judgment. And what is the cause which determines his judgment? It is his intelligent faculty, it is his power of judging: the determining cause is himself' (Rousseau, *Emile*, p. 280).
88 Blanqui continues: 'One cannot expect the people to reason about atheism like a thinker. They are not sufficiently educated. But if they were to accept it instinctively, on the basis of brief and general facts, they would be armed for war and would then get to the bottom of things. Without this basis they cannot understand a project of social renewal, a total restructuring of society. They do not suspect that the idea of God is the essential foundation of those [ideas] that weigh down on them. The aristocracy's hatred of atheism, its clinging to religious ideas, should set them on the right path. But they do not pay any attention. And what is more, there are so few of us to advance this thesis! It is totally lacking in spokesmen and encounters nothing but enemies' ('Letter to Blanqui's Supporters in Paris', 18 April 1866, *BR*, p. 174).
89 'Loi qui interdit au peuple la faculté de lire', 2 February, *MF*, p. 103.
90 See 'Première saisie', March 1834, *OI*, pp. 277–9 and 'Attentat contre le peuple', March 1834, *OI*, pp. 280–2.
91 MSS 9592(3), f. 244 [1868].
92 MSS 9587, f. 204 [n.d.]; 'Communism, the Future of Society', 1869, *BR*, pp. 267–8.
93 'Notes on Positivism', 8 April 1869, *BR*, p. 231.
94 'Equality Is Our Flag', 2 February 1834, *BR*, p. 41; MSS 9588(2), f. 540 [1879].
95 'Philosophical and Political Fragments', 2 February 1834, *BR*, p. 143.
96 'Philosophical and Political Fragments', 1868, *BR*, p. 133; MSS 9592(3), f. 244 [1868].
97 'Notes on Positivism', 1 April 1869, *BR*, p. 237; MSS 9592(3), f. 244 [1868].
98 A comparison with 'Western Marxism' might be instructive here. As Perry Anderson argues in his classic survey, the language of a whole sequence of major works on Marxism 'came to acquire an increasingly specialized and inaccessible cast. Theory became, for a whole historical period, an esoteric discipline whose highly technical idiom measured its distance from politics'. Unlike Marx's

persistent concern after 1848 for the lucidity of even his most complex work so as 'to maximize its intelligibility to the working class for which it was designed … the extreme difficulty of language characteristic of much of Western Marxism in the twentieth century was never controlled by the tension of a direct or active relationship to a proletarian audience' (Perry Anderson, *Considerations on Western Marxism* (London: New Left Books, 1976), pp. 53–4).

99 Patrick H. Hutton, *The Cult of the Revolutionary Tradition: The Blanquists in French Politics, 1864–1893* (Berkeley: University of California Press, 1981), p. 164.
100 See Maurice Dommanget, *Les Idées politiques et sociales d'Auguste Blanqui* (Paris: Marcel Rivière, 1957), p. 53.
101 'Philosophical and Political Fragments', 2 February 1850, *BR*, p. 141.
102 See 'Second Petition for the Postponing of Elections', 14 March 1848, *BR*, pp. 75–6; 'Communism, the Future of Society', 1869, *BR*, pp. 261–2.
103 'Communism, the Future of Society', 1869, *BR*, p. 261.
104 'Political and Philosophical Fragments', March 1869, *BR*, p. 155.
105 'Doomed to a bestial existence, and all too happy to receive what their masters deign to leave them of the products of their own labour,' Blanqui continues, 'all [the masses] see in the hand that exploits them is the hand that feeds them' ('Social Wealth Must Belong to Those Who Created It', February 1834, *BR*, p. 51).
106 'Political and Philosophical Fragments', 20 November 1870, *BR*, pp. 132–3.
107 'Letter to Tessy', 6 September 1852, *BR*, p. 123.
108 'Letter to Tessy', 6 September 1852, *BR*, pp. 123–4.
109 'Letter to Tessy', 6 September 1852, *BR*, p. 123.
110 Other readers to note and discuss this issue include Spitzer, *Revolutionary Theories of Louis Auguste Blanqui*, pp. 55–6, 162 and Daniel Bensaïd and Michael Löwy, 'Auguste Blanqui, Heretical Communist', *Radical Philosophy*, 185 (May–June 2014), p. 33.
111 These terms appear side by side in the 'Letter to Maillard', 6 June 1852, *BR*, p. 119.
112 'Report to the Society of the Friends of the People', 2 February 1832, *BR*, pp. 20, 24, 26.
113 'Report to the Society of the Friends of the People', 2 February 1832, *BR*, p. 25. Blanqui is keen to point out that issues of leadership and organization were already apparent during the Restoration, when the people's lack of leaders caused popular disorganization and disorientation to go hand in hand.
114 'Letter to Maillard', 6 June 1852, *BR*, pp. 113–14. See also 'Work, Suffer and Die', c. 1851–2, *BR*, p. 105.
115 Accounting for the failings of 1848, Blanqui would restate essentially the same point regarding the manipulation of the credulous masses by their duplicitous

enemies. 'The real crime was committed by the traitors whom the trusting people had accepted as guides and who then delivered them into the hands of reaction,' he explained ('Warning to the People', 10 February 1851, *BR*, p. 98).

116 For an overview of these groups and traditions, see Eric Hobsbawm, *Primitive Rebels: Studies in Archaic Forms of Social Movement in the Nineteenth and Twentieth Centuries* (London: Abacus, 2017).
117 MSS 9590(1), f. 160 [March 1869].
118 Frederick Engels, 'Introduction', in Karl Marx, *The Class Struggles in France 1848 to 1850* (Moscow: Progress, 1972), p. 22.
119 See, for example, 'Communism, the Future of Society', 1869, *BR*, pp. 267–8. On this point I broadly follow Spitzer's reading in the *Revolutionary Theories of Louis Auguste Blanqui*, pp. 164–5.
120 'Word, Suffer and Die', c. 1851–2, *BR*, p. 105.
121 'Report to the Society of the Friends of the People', 2 February 1832, *BR*, p. 93.
122 'Report to the Society of the Friends of the People', 2 February 1832, *BR*, p. 29.
123 'Auguste Blanqui's Defence Speech at the "Trial of the Fifteen"', 12 January 1832, *BR*, pp. 11–12.
124 'Equality Is Our Flag', 2 February 1834, *BR*, p. 39.
125 'Auguste Blanqui's Defence Speech at the "Trial of the Fifteen"', 12 January 1832, *BR*, p. 12.
126 'Instructions for an Armed Uprising', 1868, *BR*, p. 206.
127 'Philosophical and Political Fragments', 7 February 1856, *BR*, p. 145.
128 'To the Mountain of 1793! To the Pure Socialists, Its True Heirs!', 3 December 1848, *BR*, p. 89.
129 Leon Trotsky, *History of the Russian Revolution*, trans. Max Eastman (London: Penguin, 2017), p. 103.
130 Trotsky, *History of the Russian Revolution*, p. 103.
131 'Philosophical and Political Fragments', 1869, *BR*, p. 145.
132 'Philosophical and Political Fragments', 20 October 1848, *BR*, p. 146.
133 MSS 9590(1), f. 263 [1868].
134 Quoted in Dommanget, *Les idées politiques et sociales d'Auguste Blanqui*, p. 176.
135 'Philosophical and Political Fragments', 19 September 1848, *BR*, p. 145.
136 MSS 9590(2), f. 466 [June 1850].
137 See, for example, MSS 9592(3), f. 71 [29 May 1870].
138 'Communism, the Future of Society', 1869, *BR*, p. 265.
139 Hallward continues: 'the unjust societies in which we live are organized at all levels in such a way as to ensure that the exercise of popular power remains exceptional at best and forgotten at worst. So long as people are discouraged from choosing the path of freedom and insurrection, they will

need encouragement from a committed and reliable vanguard' (Peter Hallward, 'Blanqui's Bifurcations', *Radical Philosophy*, 185 (May–June 2014), p. 36). Here again though the same point applies: for Blanqui what is at stake in the issue of popular power is not simply the choosing of one path or another, and the extent to which this choice can be encouraged or discouraged, so much as the more fundamental consciousness that different paths actually do exist. It is a question of who at present has the capacity to make a choice as to which path is taken, and to take it.

140 Blanqui goes on to note that across all the revolts from December 1830 to September 1831 'one thing remains constant: the idea of destroying the new monarchy did not enter into the people's head' ('Why There Are No More Riots', 2 February 1834, *BR*, pp. 43–4).

141 MSS 9584(2), f. 158 [n.d.].

142 'To the Mountain of 1793! To the Pure Socialists, Its True Heirs!', 3 December 1848, *BR*, p. 90.

143 'To the Mountain of 1793! To the Pure Socialists, Its True Heirs!', 3 December 1848, *BR*, p. 88.

144 'To the Mountain of 1793! To the Pure Socialists, Its True Heirs!', 3 December 1848, *BR*, pp. 88–94.

145 MSS 9590(1), f. 165 [24 March 1869].

146 'Communism, the Future of Society', 1869, *BR*, p. 252.

147 'Projet de discours', August 1869, *CS2*, p. 143.

148 Quoted in Peter McPhee, *Robespierre: A Revolutionary Life* (New Haven, CT: Yale University Press, 2012), p. 112.

149 'Report to the Society of the Friends of the People', 2 February 1832, *BR*, p. 28.

150 'Equality Is Our Flag', 2 February 1834, *BR*, p. 41.

151 Rousseau, *Social Contract*, p. 66.

152 Rousseau, *Social Contract*, p. 66.

153 See, for example, 'Philosophical and Political Fragments', 2 February 1850, *BR*, p. 141.

154 Rousseau, *Social Contract*, p. 75.

155 See Rousseau, *Social Contract*, p. 76; translation modified; 'Instructions for an Armed Uprising', 1868, *BR*, p. 223.

# Chapter 2

1 'Response to the Request for a Toast for a Workers' Banquet', November 1848, *BR*, p. 85.

2 'Report to the Society of the Friends of the People', 2 February 1832, *BR*, p. 20.
3 'Social Wealth Must Belong to Those Who Created It', February 1834, *BR*, p. 53. Cf. 'Qui fait la soupe doit la manger', March 1834, *OI*, p. 293.
4 'Equality Is Our Flag', 2 February 1834, *BR*, p. 39. Blanqui would make a similar point in 1848 when looking back on the radicals of the French Revolution: 'Like Jesus – consoler of the poor, enemy of the powerful – the Mountain loved those who suffer and hated those who cause suffering' ('To the Mountain of 1793! To the Pure Socialists, its True Heirs', 3 December 1848, *BR*, p. 88).
5 'Social Wealth Must Belong to Those Who Created It', February 1834, *BR*, p. 48.
6 'Social Wealth Must Belong to Those Who Created It', February 1834, *BR*, p. 49; 'Qui fait la soupe doit la manger', March 1834, *OI*, p. 291.
7 'Social Wealth Must Belong to Those Who Created It', February 1834, *BR*, pp. 48–9; 'Qui fait la soupe doit la manger', March 1834, *OI*, p. 291.
8 See Henri Comte de Saint-Simon, 'The National or Industrial Party Compared to the Anti-National Party' and 'On the Quarrel between the Bees and the Drones', 1819, in *The Political Thought of Saint-Simon*, ed. Ghita Ionescu (Oxford: Oxford University Press, 1976), pp. 129–37.
9 See Karl Marx, *Capital*, Volume 1, trans. Ben Fowkes (London: Penguin, 1976), Part Eight: So-Called Primitive Accumulation.
10 Marx, *Capital*, Volume 1, p. 928.
11 'Social Wealth Must Belong to Those Who Created It', February 1834, *BR*, p. 49.
12 Blanqui argues that 'from the right to own land the privileged have also assumed the right to own those who make it fertile, considering them to be, in the first instance, the complement to their material property, and, in the final analysis, personal property completely independent of the land' ('Social Wealth Must Belong to Those Who Created It', February 1834, *BR*, p. 49).
13 Slavery is 'the ultimate expression of personal right, and the ultimate expression of the right to property' ('Social Wealth Must Belong to Those Who Created It', February 1834, *BR*, p. 54).
14 'Social Wealth Must Belong to Those Who Created It', February 1834, *BR*, p. 49.
15 'Social Wealth Must Belong to Those Who Created It', February 1834, *BR*, p. 49.
16 'Letter to Maillard', 6 June 1852, *BR*, pp. 118–19.
17 'Social Wealth Must Belong to Those Who Created It', February 1834, *BR*, p. 49.
18 'Philosophical and Political Fragments', July 1870, *BR*, p. 148.
19 'Social Wealth Must Belong to Those Who Created It', February 1834, *BR*, p. 50.
20 'Social Wealth Must Belong to Those Who Created It', February 1834, *BR*, p. 50.
21 'Letter to Maillard', 6 June 1852, *BR*, pp. 118–19.
22 'Social Wealth Must Belong to Those Who Created It', February 1834, *BR*, p. 50.
23 Jean-Jacques Rousseau, *Discourse on the Origin of Inequality*, ed. Patrick Coleman, trans. Franklin Philip (Oxford: Oxford University Press, 2009), p. 66.

24 Rousseau, *Discourse on the Origin of Inequality*, p. 69.
25 'Social Wealth Must Belong to Those Who Created It', February 1834, *BR*, pp. 49–50.
26 Marx, *Capital*, Volume 1, pp. 929–30.
27 'Social Wealth Must Belong to Those Who Created It', February 1834, *BR*, p. 48.
28 'Letter to Maillard', 6 June 1852, *BR*, p. 115.
29 Karl Marx, *The Civil War in France* (Moscow: Foreign Languages Publishing House, n.d.), p. 67. See also Marx, *Capital*, Volume 1, p. 929. Cf. 'Social Wealth Must Belong to Those Who Created It', February 1834, *BR*, pp. 53–4.
30 In some of Marx's more militant political writings the question of property is arguably treated with a notable similarity in register, in unstated analytical assumptions and in proposed political conclusions to those of Blanqui. See, for example: 'The Commune, they exclaim, intends to abolish property, the basis of all civilization! Yes, gentlemen, the Commune intended to abolish that class-property which makes the labour of the many the wealth of the few. It aimed at the expropriation of the expropriators. It wanted to make individual property a truth by transforming the means of production, land and capital, now chiefly the means of enslaving and exploiting labour, into mere instruments of free and associated labour' (Marx, *Civil War in France*, p. 67). That is not to suggest, of course, that one can therefore equate their overall respective treatments of this subject. But a consideration of the intended audiences and aims of any given text is no doubt instructive when it comes to their interpretation and critical analysis.
31 'Social Wealth Must Belong to Those Who Created It', February 1834, *BR*, p. 50.
32 As Jill Harsin explains, in the early 1830s trials were seen as important political interventions: through statements at the trials themselves (which often brought large audiences to the court) and the subsequent pamphlets that reproduced the court proceedings (and seditious articles in the case of press offenses), the republican defendants used the events to publicize their cause and disseminate their ideas. See Jill Harsin, *Barricades: The War on the Streets of Revolutionary Paris, 1830–1848* (Basingstoke: Palgrave, 2002), pp. 52–3.
33 See R. B. Rose, *Gracchus Babeuf: The First Revolutionary Communist* (Stanford, CA: Stanford University Press, 1978), p. 210; Maurice Dommanget, *Auguste Blanqui: Des origines à la revolution de 1848* (Paris: Mouton, 1969), p. 103.
34 'Auguste Blanqui's Defence Speech at the "Trial of the Fifteen"', 12 January 1832, *BR*, p. 9.
35 'Auguste Blanqui's Defence Speech at the "Trial of the Fifteen"', 12 January 1832, *BR*, pp. 9–10.
36 Harsin, *Barricades*, p. 6.
37 'Auguste Blanqui's Defence Speech at the "Trial of the Fifteen"', 12 January 1832, *BR*, p. 11.

38 'Auguste Blanqui's Defence Speech at the "Trial of the Fifteen"', 12 January 1832, *BR*, p. 18.
39 This was how Lafayette described the new regime. Quoted in Pamela Pilbeam, *The 1830 Revolution in France* (London: Macmillan, 1991), p. 84.
40 'Auguste Blanqui's Defence Speech at the "Trial of the Fifteen"', 12 January 1832, BR, p. 10. Cf. Paul-Louis Courier, 'Pièce diplomatique', 1823, in *Œuvres complètes de P.-L. Courier: Tome Premier* (Paris: A. Sautelet, 1830), pp. 365–72.
41 'Auguste Blanqui's Defence Speech at the "Trial of the Fifteen"', 12 January 1832, *BR*, p. 10.
42 Dommanget, *Auguste Blanqui: Des origines à la revolution de 1848*, p. 104. See also Maurice Dommanget, *Auguste Blanqui à Belle-Île* (Paris: Librairie du Travail, 1935), pp. 10–12.
43 Karl Marx and Frederick Engels, *The Communist Manifesto: A Modern Edition* (London: Verso, 2012), pp. 37, 43.
44 Marx, *Civil War in France*, p. 60. (Rather than 'an engine of class despotism', for the last phrase in this sentence I use Engels's alternative rendering in the 1871 German translation.) The impact of the Paris Commune on Marx's thinking on the state is well known. The Commune showed, as Marx wrote in the 1872 preface to the *Manifesto*, that 'the working class cannot simply lay hold of the ready-made state machinery, and wield it for its own purposes' (Quoted in Eric Hobsbawm, 'Introduction', in Karl Marx and Frederick Engels, *The Communist Manifesto: A Modern Edition* (London: Verso, 2012), pp. 13–14, n.10). Daniel Bensaïd and Michael Löwy also note the link between Blanqui and Marx on this score. 'In 1867 Blanqui described the bourgeois state as "a gendarmerie of the rich against the poor". It is, then, as Marx will repeat in light of the Paris Commune, a machine to be smashed' ('Auguste Blanqui, Heretical Communist', *Radical Philosophy*, 185 (May–June 2014), p. 33).
45 V. I. Lenin, 'The State and Revolution', August–September 1917, in *Collected Works*, Volume 25 (Moscow: Progress, 1974), p. 491.
46 'Social Wealth Must Belong to Those Who Created It', February 1834, *BR*, p. 50.
47 'Communism, the Future of Society', 1869, *BR*, p. 244.
48 Blanqui often floats between these terms, as well as the privileged and the rich, to describe those who own the means of production and capital. We return to this issue in Chapter 3.
49 'Social Wealth Must Belong to Those Who Created It', February 1834, *BR*, pp. 50–1.
50 'Social Wealth Must Belong to Those Who Created It', February 1834, *BR*, p. 50. Marx would later argue, in similar terms to Blanqui, that 'even in the state of society most favourable to him, the inevitable consequence for the worker is

overwork and early death, reduction to a mere machine, enslavement to capital'. In capitalist society 'all passions and all activity are lost in *greed*. The worker is only permitted to have enough for him to live, and he is only permitted to live in order to have' ('Economic and Philosophical Manuscripts', 1844, in *Early Writings*, trans. Rodney Livingstone and Gregor Benton (London: Penguin, 1975), pp. 285, 361).

51  For Galtung, structural violence denotes the harm and suffering built into a social structure that cannot be directly traced to an identifiable actor or subject, and that may be inflicted through conditions of work or the uneven distribution of resources within a society where this is objectively avoidable. See Johan Galtung, 'Violence, Peace and Peace Research', *Journal of Peace Research*, 6:3 (1969), pp. 167–91.

52  See 'Aux Royalistes', MSS 9583, f. 115 [9 February 1850].

53  See 'For the Red Flag', 26 February 1848, *BR*, p. 74.

54  'Work, Suffer and Die', *c.* 1851–2, *BR*, p. 104.

55  'To the Mountain of 1793! To the Pure Socialists, its True Heirs!', 3 December 1848, *BR*, p. 88. Or again: 'To read the history of the first Revolution is to read the history of today' ('Letter to Maillard', 6 June 1852, *BR*, p. 114).

56  'The Massacre in Rouen: The Central Republican Society to the Provisional Government', 2 May 1848, *BR*, pp. 80–1.

57  'Philosophical and Political Fragments', 18 January 1859, *BR*, p. 158. As Blanqui similarly noted several decades earlier: 'Think how many massacres have been undertaken since 1805, of all sorts and sizes, in the service of despotism! And yet we only ever hear of 1793 and the guillotine' ('Philosophical and Political Fragments', 19 or 29 September 1831, *BR*, p. 162).

58  'Warning to the People', 10 February 1851, *BR*, p. 98.

59  MSS 9582, f. 232 [26 February 1848].

60  Harsin, *Barricades*, p. 9.

61  'This is not the first time that the executioners act as if they are the victims' ('Auguste Blanqui's Defence Speech at the "Trial of the Fifteen"', 12 January 1832, *BR*, p. 9).

62  'Blanqui's Notes for his Defence at the "Gunpowder Trial"', October 1836, *BR*, p. 62.

63  See 'Auguste Blanqui's Defence Speech at the "Trial of the Fifteen"', 12 January 1832, *BR*, p. 18.

64  The short public declaration issued by the Société des Saisons during the failed coup attempt of 12 May 1839 sheds some light on how these assumptions informed Blanqui's political practice. The document targets the 'tyrant of the Tuileries who laughs at the hunger that gnaws away at the people', declaring that the exploitation and inequality of French society were 'crimes' demanding

punishment ('Appel au peuple de Paris du comité de la Société des Saisons', 12 May 1839, *MF*, p. 129). This understanding of structural violence seems to have justified, in part, the use of insurrectionary violence, for as Harsin notes, carrying out 'violent acts obviously begged the question of legitimacy. Republicans, as the initiators, stressed the prior aggression of the government, which promoted an economic system in which men could not protect their families from starvation' (Harsin, *Barricades*, p. 9).

65 'Philosophical and Political Fragments', 15 January 1859, *BR*, p. 158.
66 'Philosophical and Political Fragments', 1871, *BR*, p. 157.
67 'Equality Is Our Flag', 2 February 1834, *BR*, p. 39.
68 'Social Wealth Must Belong to Those Who Created It', February 1834, *BR*, pp. 52–3; 'Equality Is Our Flag', 2 February 1834, *BR*, pp. 37–8; 'Qui fait la soupe doit la manger', March 1834, *OI*, p. 293. Again we see here that for Blanqui ignorance is at once the cause and consequence of inequality and injustice.
69 'Social Wealth Must Belong to Those Who Created It', February 1834, *BR*, p. 53.
70 'Social Wealth Must Belong to Those Who Created It', February 1834, *BR*, p. 50.
71 'Philosophical and Political Fragments', July 1870, *BR*, p. 148.
72 'Social Wealth Must Belong to Those Who Created It', February 1834, *BR*, p. 52; 'Qui fait la soupe doit la manger', March 1834, *OI*, p. 293.
73 'Social Wealth Must Belong to Those Who Created It', February 1834, *BR*, p. 52.
74 MSS, 9590(2), f. 466 [June 1850]. See also 'La guerre du capital à la révolution', April 1866, *CS2*, p. 55.
75 Patrick H. Hutton, *The Cult of the Revolutionary Tradition: The Blanquists in French Politics, 1864–1893* (Berkeley: University of California Press, 1981), p. 59.
76 MSS 9592(3), ff. 62–3 [2 September 1869].
77 Gustave Tridon, 'La Faim', Monday 19 September 1870, *La Patrie en Danger*. Tridon's political and philosophical essays were praised not only for their intellectual insight but for the power and style of the prose, leading him to be regarded as the 'intellectual spokesman' and 'leading theoretician' of the Blanquist movement (see Hutton, *The Cult of the Revolutionary Tradition*, pp. 28, 164). This article from *La Patrie en Danger*, which explores the sociopolitics of starvation, a major issue that would take on even greater significance as the siege of Paris went on, is perhaps even more notable for having been published on the very day that the siege began.
78 Cf. Eric Hazan, *The Invention of Paris* (London: Verso, 2011), p. 309.
79 Hazan, *Invention of Paris*, p. 309.
80 See 'Lettre Aux Accusés', 11 May 1835, *OI*, p. 306; 'Communism, the Future of Society', 1869, *BR*, p. 244; Hazan, *Invention of Paris*, p. 309.
81 See David Pinkney, *The French Revolution of 1830* (Princeton, NJ: Princeton University Press, 1972), pp. 144, 188; Pilbeam, *1830 Revolution in France*, p. 84.

82 'Auguste Blanqui's Defence Speech at the "Trial of the Fifteen"', 12 January 1832, *BR*, pp. 15–16.
83 'Report to the Society of the Friends of the People', 2 February 1832, *BR*, p. 29.
84 'Letter to Tessy', 6 September 1852, *BR*, p. 121.
85 The so-called *juste milieu* could not conceal the Orléanist government's choice between royalism and republicanism, Blanqui argues, a choice implicit from its conception but one that was becoming increasingly obvious as it consolidated its power and continued to pursue and implement, with even greater rigour, the same reactionary politics inaugurated under the Bourbon Restoration. See 'Report to the Society of the Friends of the People', 2 February 1832, *BR*, pp. 27–8.
86 'We know that the lynxes of monopoly wage this war more through treachery than violence' ('Social Wealth Must Belong to Those Who Created It', February 1834, *BR*, p. 53).
87 Harsin, *Barricades*, p. 28.
88 'Qui fait la soupe doit la manger', March 1834, *OI*, p. 293; 'Social Wealth Must Belong to Those Who Created It', February 1834, *BR*, p. 53. Note the echoes of Rousseau's claim that 'a convention is vain and contradictory if it stipulates absolute authority on one side and limitless obedience on the other' (Jean-Jacques Rousseau, *Social Contract*, trans. Christopher Betts (Oxford: Oxford University Press, 2008), p. 50).
89 'Présentation et but du journal', 2 February 1834, *OI*, pp. 257–8.
90 'Lettre à Adélaïde de Montgolfier', 12 February 1834, *OI*, p. 276. See also 'Lettre à Adélaïde de Montgolfier', 16 July 1831, *OI*, p. 176.
91 'Présentation et but du journal', 2 February 1834, *OI*, p. 258.
92 'Auguste Blanqui's Defence Speech at the "Trial of the Fifteen"', 12 January 1832, *BR*, p. 15.
93 'Report to the Society of the Friends of the People', 2 February 1832, *BR*, p. 28; emphasis in original.
94 MSS 9583, f. 102 [7 February 1850]. See also 'Equality Is Our Flag', 2 February 1834, *BR*, p. 38.
95 Cf. Daniel Bensaïd, '"Leaps! Leaps! Leaps!"', in *Lenin Reloaded: Towards a Politics of Truth*, ed. Sebastian Budgen, Stathis Kouvelakis and Slavoj Žižek (Durham, NC: Duke University Press, 2007), p. 160.
96 MSS 9592(3), ff. 71–2 [1869–70].
97 See 'Auguste Blanqui's Defence Speech at the "Trial of the Fifteen"', 12 January 1832, *BR*, p. 14.
98 Samuel Bernstein, *Auguste Blanqui and the Art of Insurrection* (London: Lawrence and Wishart, 1971), p. 48.
99 Le Nuz, 'Introduction', *MF*, p. 32.
100 'Philosophical and Political Fragments', June 1850, *BR*, p. 155.

101 'Auguste Blanqui's Defence Speech at the "Trial of the Fifteen"', 12 January 1832, *BR*, pp. 13–14.
102 'Auguste Blanqui's Defence Speech at the "Trial of the Fifteen"', 12 January 1832, *BR*, pp. 12–13.
103 Rousseau, 'Discourse on Political Economy', in *Social Contract*, pp. 20–1.
104 MSS 9582, f. 35 [n.d.]; 'Philosophical and Political Fragments', n.d., *BR*, p. 144.
105 Cf. Thomas Bouchet, Vincent Bourdeau et al. (eds), *Quand les socialistes inventaient l'avenir: Presse, théories et experiences, 1825–1860* (Paris: Éditions La Découverte, 2015).
106 'Letter to Maillard', 6 June 1852, *BR*, p. 119; emphasis in original. For Daniel Bensaïd and Michael Löwy, 'Blanqui displays a resolutely practical understanding of the possible' ('Auguste Blanqui, Heretical Communist', *Radical Philosophy*, 185 (May–June 2014) p. 32; translation modified).
107 'Warning to the People', 10 February 1851, *BR*, pp. 99–100.
108 'Tout l'espoir des prolétaires est dans la République', January 1834, *OI*, p. 255. Or again: 'Politics is nothing more than communism's servant' ('Communism, the Future of Society', 1869, *BR*, p. 258).
109 'Equality Is Our Flag', 2 February 1834, *BR*, p. 37.
110 'Equality Is Our Flag', 2 February 1834, *BR*, p. 37. See also 'Democratic Propaganda', 1835, *BR*, pp. 59–60 for a lucid description of the relationship between political means (political rights, electoral reform, universal suffrage) and social ends (the establishment of real equality).
111 'To the Democratic Clubs of Paris', 22 March 1848, *BR*, p. 77. Cf. Bensaïd and Löwy, 'Auguste Blanqui, Heretical Communist', p. 31.
112 See 'Equality Is Our Flag', 2 February 1834, *BR*, pp. 37–41.
113 'Equality Is Our Flag', 2 February 1834, *BR*, pp. 37–9.
114 'Letter to Maillard', 6 June 1852, *BR*, p. 115.
115 'Social Wealth Must Belong to Those Who Created It', February 1834, *BR*, p. 49.
116 'Democratic Propaganda', 1835, *BR*, p. 60.
117 'Democratic Propaganda', 1835, *BR*, pp. 59–60; 'Initiation Ceremony of the Society of the Seasons', 1837, *BR*, p. 67.
118 'Equality Is Our Flag', 2 February 1834, *BR*, p. 38.
119 'Equality Is Our Flag', 2 February 1834, *BR*, p. 38; 'Tout l'espoir des prolétaires est dans la République', January 1834, *OI*, p. 255.
120 MSS 9590(1), f. 170 [14 July 1869]; 'Philosophical and Political Fragments', 1860s, *BR*, p. 164.
121 'Philosophical and Political Fragments', March 1870, *BR*, p. 129.
122 See 'Social Wealth Must Belong to Those Who Created It', February 1834, *BR*, pp. 48, 55.
123 'Notes on Positivism', 15 March 1869, *BR*, p. 232.

124 'Communism, the Future of Society', 1869, *BR*, p. 244.
125 'Instructions for an Armed Uprising', 1868, *BR*, p. 202.
126 MSS 9586, f. 403 [n.d.].
127 See, for example, 'Projet de Discours', August 1867, *CS2*, p. 162; MSS 9587, f. 204 [*c*. 1849].
128 MSS 9592(3), ff. 63–4 [September 1869]; 'Communism, the Future of Society', 1869, *BR*, p. 251.
129 MSS 9590(1), f. 171 [14 July 1869].
130 'Philosophical and Political Fragments', September 1869, *BR*, p. 136.
131 'Philosophical and Political Fragments', 14 July 1869, *BR*, p. 164.
132 Alain Badiou, 'The Idea of Communism', in *The Idea of Communism*, ed. Costas Douzinas and Slavoj Žižek (London: Verso, 2010), p. 9, n.10.
133 Quoted in Jason Barker, 'Translator's Introduction', in Alain Badiou, *Metapolitics*, trans. Jason Barker (London: Verso, 2005), p. xxviii, n.24.
134 'Communism, the Future of Society', 1869, *BR*, p. 251.
135 MSS 9587, f. 359 [8 January 1862].
136 MSS 9592(3), f. 277 [December 1862].
137 'Letter to Maillard', 6 June 1852, *BR*, p. 113.
138 MSS 9590(1), f. 171 [14 July 1869]. Blanqui summarizes: 'We should have nothing in common with the oppressors. Confusion and obscurity are their tactics, their salvation. We must establish a clear dividing line, an impassable dividing line, between us and them. We should share no words with them. Any misunderstanding is always fatal for us, and always to the benefit of the enemy' ('Philosophical and Political Fragments', 14 July 1869, *BR*, p. 139).
139 Acknowledging that the peasantry is alarmed by 'words like *sharing* or *redistribution* and *community*', Blanqui insists that 'this is no reason to remove the word *communism* from the political dictionary, however. Far from it – we must help the country folk get used to hearing it not as a threat but as a hope or expectation' ('Communism, the Future of Society', 1869, *BR*, p. 263; emphasis in original). Cf. Alain Badiou, *The Meaning of Sarkozy*, trans. David Fernbach (London: Verso, 2008).
140 Michael Hardt, 'The Common in Communism', in *The Idea of Communism*, ed. Costas Douzinas and Slavoj Žižek (London: Verso, 2010), p. 131. On this issue see also Jacques Rancière, 'Democracies against Democracy: An Interview with Eric Hazan', in *Democracy in What State?*, trans. William McCuaig (New York: Columbia University Press, 2010), p. 78.
141 'To the Democratic Clubs of Paris', 22 March 1848, *BR*, p. 77.
142 Marx, *Civil War in France*, p. 90. Marx had of course acknowledged in 1848 that 'in depicting the most general phases of the development of the proletariat, we traced the more or less veiled civil war, raging within existing

society, up to the point where that war breaks out into open revolution, and where the violent overthrow of the bourgeoisie lays the foundation for the sway of the proletariat' (Marx and Engels, *Communist Manifesto*, p. 49). It seems that the brutality of the Commune forced Marx to return to and reaffirm this earlier assumption.
143 Walter Benjamin, *The Arcades Project*, ed. Rolf Tiedemann, trans. Howard Eiland and Kevin McLaughlin (Cambridge, MA: Harvard University Press, 1999), pp. 12–13.
144 Eric Hazan, *Paris Sous Tension* (Paris: La Fabrique éditions, 2011), p. 64.

# Chapter 3

1 'Philosophical and Political Fragments', 1867, *BR*, p. 166.
2 'Formulaire de réception de la Société des Familles', 1834, *OI*, p. 299; 'De la législation', 18 August 1831, *OI*, p. 170; 'Social Wealth Must Belong to Those Who Created It', February 1834, *BR*, p. 53.
3 'De la législation', 18 August 1831, *OI*, p. 170.
4 'De la législation', 18 August 1831, *OI*, p. 170.
5 'Auguste Blanqui's Defence Speech at the "Trial of the Fifteen"', 12 January 1832, *BR*, p. 8; *Défense du citoyen Louis Auguste Blanqui devant la Cour d'Assisses* (Paris: Imprimerie de Auguste Mie, 1832), p. 4.
6 'Auguste Blanqui's Defence Speech at the "Trial of the Fifteen"', 12 January 1832, *BR*, p. 13.
7 See 'Democratic Propaganda', 1835, *BR*, p. 59 and 'Initiation Ceremony of the Society of the Seasons', 1837, *BR*, p. 67.
8 'Communism, the Future of Society', 1869, *BR*, p. 251.
9 See, for example, 'Loi qui interdit au peuple la faculté de lire', 2 February 1834, *OI*, p. 273.
10 Saint-Marc Girardin, *Journal des Débats*, Thursday 8 December 1831, p. 1.
11 'Society is divided into two classes, the proletarians and the men of property – this is constantly repeated today' (Antoine Vidal, 'La société est partagée en deux classes...', *L'Écho de la fabrique*, Sunday 29 April 1832, p. 1).
12 'Auguste Blanqui's Defence Speech at the "Trial of the Fifteen"', 12 January 1832, *BR*, p. 16; 'Social Wealth Must Belong to Those Who Created It', February 1834, *BR*, p. 51.
13 'Auguste Blanqui's Defence Speech at the "Trial of the Fifteen"', 12 January 1832, *BR*, p. 17.

14 'Tout l'espoir des prolétaries est dans la République', January 1834, *OI*, p. 253. For information on the authorship of the text, see 'Tout l'espoir des prolétaries est dans la République', January 1834, *OI*, p. 253n.
15 'Tout l'espoir des prolétaries est dans la République', January 1834, *OI*, p. 253; Marx and Engels, *The German Ideology*, 1846, quoted in Michael Löwy, *The Theory of Revolution in the Young Marx* (Chicago, IL: Haymarket Books, 2005), p. 113.
16 'Tout l'espoir des prolétaries est dans la République', January 1834, *OI*, pp. 254–5. See also the claim that past struggles between 'Patriciat and Proletariat' over 'the political and social question' correspond to 'the situation of the European worker' ('L'usure', n.d., *CS1*, pp. 47–8).
17 MSS 9590(2), ff. 370–1 [September 1855].
18 'Auguste Blanqui's Defence Speech at the "Trial of the Fifteen"', 12 January 1832, *BR*, pp. 8, 19.
19 'Formulaire de réception de la Société des Familles', 1834, *OI*, p. 299.
20 'Report to the Society of the Friends of the People', 2 February 1832, *BR*, p. 30.
21 'Formulaire de réception de la Société des Familles', 1834, *OI*, p. 299.
22 'L'aristocratie et le peuple', 23 July 1831, *OI*, p. 167.
23 'Report to the Society of the Friends of the People', 2 February 1832, *BR*, p. 31.
24 'Instructions for an Armed Uprising', 1868, *BR*, p. 239.
25 'Report to the Society of the Friends of the People', 2 February 1832, *BR*, p. 35.
26 See the comments on the British reaction to July 1830 in 'Report to the Society of the Friends of the People', 2 February 1832, *BR*, p. 34.
27 At the very beginning of the speech, for instance, when examining the political conjuncture in France, Blanqui states that 'there is a war to the death between the classes that compose the nation. This truth being fully understood, the truly national party around which all patriots should rally is the party of the masses' ('Report to the Society of the Friends of the People', 2 February 1832, *BR*, p. 20). We see here that social relations and political organization are explicitly framed in national, not international, terms. It is in this sense that the inclusivity of Blanqui's notion of the people often does not seem to extend beyond the French border.
28 See, for example, 'Lettre à Lelewell', 29 February 1832, *OI*, pp. 225–6.
29 Karl Marx and Frederick Engels, *The Communist Manifesto: A Modern Edition* (London: Verso, 2012), p. 49.
30 Marx and Engels, *Communist Manifesto*, p. 58.
31 'Instructions for an Armed Uprising', 1868, *BR*, p. 223.
32 'Report to the Society of the Friends of the People', 2 February 1832, *BR*, p. 21.
33 See Frantz Fanon, *The Wretched of the Earth*, trans. Constance Farrington (London: Penguin Books, 1969), p. 28.

34 This phrase has generated some interest recently by virtue of its evocation in the work of Alain Badiou and Jacques Rancière. See Alain Badiou, *Metapolitics*, trans. Jason Barker (London: Verso, 2005), p. 115.
35 'Report to the Society of the Friends of the People', 2 February 1832, *BR*, p. 24.
36 'Report to the Society of the Friends of the People', 2 February 1832, *BR*, p. 24; translation modified.
37 Here I follow Peter Hallward's claim that using the term 'actor' avoids the problem of a subject's 'underlying submission', as discussed in 'Willing and Able: Political Will and Self-determination', lecture given at the American University in Paris, 10 April 2015.
38 'Saint-Étienne: Lutte entre les fabricants et les ouvriers', December 1849, *CS2*, p. 228.
39 MSS 9591(1), ff. 90, 92 [*c.* 1870?].
40 Jean-Jacques Rousseau, *The Social Contract*, trans. Christopher Betts (Oxford: Oxford University Press, 2008), p. 54.
41 'Report to the Society of the Friends of the People', 2 February 1832, *BR*, p. 25.
42 'Report to the Society of the Friends of the People', 2 February 1832, *BR*, p. 26.
43 Here is this key passage from the 'Report' in full: 'How did it come to pass that such a sudden and fearsome revelation of the power of the masses remained sterile? By what fatality did this revolution made by the people alone, and that should have marked the end of the exclusive reign of the bourgeoisie as well as the advent of popular power, have no other results than establishing the despotism of the middle class, increasing the poverty of the workers and peasants, and plunging France a little deeper into the mud?' ('Report to the Society of the Friends of the People', 2 February 1832, *BR*, p. 24).
44 'Who could have imagined that the revolution would not be a revolution …?' ('Report to the Society of the Friends of the People', 2 February 1832, *BR*, p. 31).
45 'Report to the Society of the Friends of the People', 2 February 1832, *BR*, p. 26.
46 'Report to the Society of the Friends of the People', 2 February 1832, *BR*, p. 24.
47 Roger Garaudy and Arthur Rosenberg quoted in Alan B. Spitzer, *The Revolutionary Theories of Louis Auguste Blanqui* (New York: Columbia University Press, 1957), p. 96.
48 V. P. Volguine, 'Les idées politiques et sociales de Blanqui', in *Textes choisis*, ed. V. P. Volguine (Paris: Éditions Sociales, 1955), pp. 10, 33–4.
49 Samuel Bernstein, *Auguste Blanqui and the Art of Insurrection* (London: Lawrence and Wishart, 1971), pp. 48–9; Volguine, 'Les idées politiques et sociales de Blanqui', p. 15.
50 Bernstein, *Auguste Blanqui and the Art of Insurrection*, p. 49.
51 Philippe Vigier, 'Préface', *OI*, p. 18.

52 Spitzer, *Revolutionary Theories of Louis Auguste Blanqui*, p. 97.
53 Spitzer, *Revolutionary Theories of Louis Auguste Blanqui*, p. 98. For the passage Spitzer is referring to, see 'Auguste Blanqui's Defence Speech at the "Trial of the Fifteen"', 12 January 1832, *BR*, p. 9.
54 Spitzer, *Revolutionary Theories of Louis Auguste Blanqui*, pp. 99–100.
55 'Letter to Maillard', 6 June 1852, *BR*, p. 113. Spitzer cites this passage on *Revolutionary Theories of Louis Auguste Blanqui*, p. 101.
56 Spitzer, *Revolutionary Theories of Louis Auguste Blanqui*, pp. 101–2.
57 Spitzer, *Revolutionary Theories of Louis Auguste Blanqui*, p. 102.
58 Spitzer, *Revolutionary Theories of Louis Auguste Blanqui*, p. 102.
59 'Sociologically,' Spitzer continues, 'the proletarian elements of "this Parisian folk" were not, in the nineteenth century, equivalent to the factory proletariat of an industrial centre such as Lyons. … Although Blanqui saw political promise in the early struggles of the Lyons proletariat, his conception of a revolutionary elite was always focused on the Paris of artisans and intellectuals' (Spitzer, *Revolutionary Theories of Louis Auguste Blanqui*, pp. 165–6).
60 Ernesto Laclau, *On Populist Reason* (London: Verso, 2005), p. 224; emphasis in original. For the earlier critique of 'classism' on which many of these arguments are founded, see Ernesto Laclau and Chantal Mouffe, *Hegemony and Socialist Strategy: Towards a Radical Democratic Politics* (London: Verso, 1985).
61 Laclau, *On Populist Reason*, p. 87.
62 Laclau, *On Populist Reason*, pp. 14, 18–19, 225.
63 Laclau, *On Populist Reason*, p. 183; emphasis in original.
64 Laclau, *On Populist Reason*, pp. 12, 18.
65 The 'act of association produces, in place of the individual persons of every contracting party, a moral and collective body, which is composed of as many members as there are votes in the assembly, and which, by the same act, is endowed with its unity, its common self, its life, and its will'. People will indeed only achieve their collective freedom, Rousseau argues, if they are able 'to create, by combination, a totality of forces sufficient to overcome the obstacles resisting them, to direct their operation by a single impulse, and make them act in unison' (Rousseau, *Social Contract*, pp. 54, 56).
66 See 'Instructions for an Armed Uprising', 1868, *BR*, p. 262.
67 Laclau, *On Populist Reason*, pp. 122, 150.
68 'Philosophical and Political Fragments', 14 July 1869, *BR*, p. 139.
69 'Philosophical and Political Fragments', n.d., *BR*, p. 148.
70 'Philosophical and Political Fragments', n.d., *BR*, p. 153.
71 Laclau, *On Populist Reason*, p. 18. See also pp. 98–9.
72 'Our epoch, the epoch of the bourgeoisie, possesses … this distinctive feature: it has simplified the class antagonisms. Society as a whole is more and more

splitting up into two great hostile camps, into two great classes directly facing each other: bourgeoisie and proletariat' (Marx and Engels, *Communist Manifesto*, p. 35). We might note that some of Blanqui's critics cited above take the Marxist proletariat to mean the 'industrial proletariat' rather than the – much broader – 'class of modern wage labourers who, having no means of production of their own, are reduced to selling their labour power in order to live' (Marx and Engels, *Communist Manifesto*, p. 34, n.3). Marx and Engels's definition, in other words, is in fact far more inclusive than such an emphasis on industrial workers would suggest.

73 Laclau and Mouffe define themselves explicitly against the Jacobin and Marxist paradigms of antagonism (and the Jacobin and Marxist projects more generally), as they conceive them. See Laclau and Mouffe, *Hegemony and Socialist Strategy*, chapters 3 and 4. See also Laclau, *On Populist Reason*, pp. 149–50, 241, 248.
74 See Laclau, *On Populist Reason*, pp. 244–9.
75 *Défense du citoyen Louis Auguste Blanqui devant la Cour d'Assisses* (Paris: Imprimerie de Auguste Mie, 1832), p. 4; Jacques Rancière, *Disagreement: Politics and Philosophy*, trans. Julie Rose (Minneapolis: University of Minnesota Press, 1999), p. 37.
76 Rancière, *Disagreement*, pp. 37–8. See also Jacques Rancière, *Aux bords du politique* (Paris: Gallimard, 2004), pp. 118–19.
77 Rancière, *Disagreement*, p. 38.
78 Rancière, *Disagreement*, pp. 38–9.
79 Rancière, *Disagreement*, p. 35.
80 Rancière, *Disagreement*, p. 37; translation modified.
81 As Rancière notes, 'the wrong [the proletariat's name] exposes cannot be regulated by way of some accord between the parties. It cannot be regulated since the subjects a political wrong sets in motion are not entities to whom such and such has happened by accident, but subjects whose very existence is the mode of manifestation of the wrong' (Rancière, *Disagreement*, p. 39).
82 Léon Favre, 'La fabrique est-elle perdue ?', *L'Écho de la fabrique*, Sunday 22 January 1832.
83 Kristin Ross, 'Democracy for Sale', in *Democracy in What State?* (Columbia University Press: New York, 2010), pp. 90–1.
84 See 'Letter to Maillard', 6 June 1852, *BR*, p. 113.
85 Blanqui, 'La réaction', Monday 19 September 1870, in *La Patrie en Danger*, p. 71.
86 'Lettre à Clemenceau', 1 March 1879, *MF*, p. 394. On this point, see in particular 'The Union of True Democrats', November 1848, *BR*, pp. 83–4.
87 Spitzer, *Revolutionary Theories of Louis Auguste Blanqui*, p. 102. Or similarly, from Bernstein: 'Blanqui called himself a "proletarian", one of 30,000,000 Frenchmen. Of course, neither the term nor the number could withstand

economic analysis. But they were a slide rule with which to set off the ruling class from the nation' (Bernstein, *Auguste Blanqui and the Art of Insurrection*, p. 48).
88  'Letter to Maillard', 6 June 1852, *BR*, p. 113.
89  'Letter to Maillard', 6 June 1852, *BR*, p. 113.
90  'Letter to Maillard', 6 June 1852, *BR*, p. 115.
91  'Letter to Maillard', 6 June 1852, *BR*, pp. 113–14.
92  Daniel Bensaïd is right to note that at times Marx seems to assume that 'the logic of capital itself', through industrial development and the resultant growth, concentration and organization of the working class, will lead to the 'constitution of the proletarians into a ruling class'. So followed the misguided view that 'the political emancipation of the proletariat flowed necessarily from its social development' (Daniel Bensaïd, ' "Leaps! Leaps! Leaps!" ', in *Lenin Reloaded: Towards a Politics of Truth*, ed. Sebastian Budgen, Stathis Kouvelakis and Slavoj Žižek (Durham, NC: Duke University Press, 2007), p. 149).
93  Rancière, *Disagreement*, p. 38.
94  Rancière, *Disagreement*, p. 38; translation modified.
95  See Rancière, *Disagreement*, pp. 23–35, 43. See also Jacques Rancière, *The Ignorant Schoolmaster: Five Lessons in Intellectual Emancipation*, trans. Kristin Ross (Stanford, CA: Stanford University Press, 1991).
96  'Communism, the Future of Society', 1869, *BR*, pp. 249, 250, 264.
97  'Philosophical and Political Fragments', 2 February 1850, *BR*, p. 141.
98  'Auguste Blanqui's Defence Speech at the "Trial of the Fifteen"', 12 January 1832, *BR*, p. 12.
99  'Auguste Blanqui's Defence Speech at the "Trial of the Fifteen"', 12 January 1832, *BR*, p. 12.
100 'Loi qui interdit au peuple la faculté de lire', 2 February 1834, *MF*, p. 104; 'Première Saisie', March 1834, *OI*, p. 279.
101 See 'Attentat contre le peuple', March 1834, *OI*, pp. 281–2.
102 MSS 9590(1), f. 151 [27 February 1869]. Cf. 'Auguste Blanqui's Defence Speech at the "Trial of the Fifteen"', 12 January 1832, *BR*, p. 12.
103 Rancière, *Disagreement*, p. 38.
104 Blanqui repeatedly uses this analogy in the 'Report to the Society of the Friends of the People', 2 February 1832, *BR*, pp. 20–35. He claims that, before July 1830, during the Restoration the people 'remained silent and submitted themselves to the yoke' (p. 21); 'they remained a silent spectator' (p. 22); 'they looked on in silence' (p. 23); the people 'remained silent' and 'had been written off for fifteen years' (p. 23); 'they remained silent and on their guard' (p. 25).
105 'Declaration of the Provisional Committee for Schools', 22 January 1831, *BR*, p. 7.
106 'Présentation et but du journal', 2 February 1834, *OI*, p. 258.

107 'Présentation et but du journal', 2 February 1834, *OI*, pp. 258–9.
108 'Auguste Blanqui's Defence Speech at the "Trial of the Fifteen"', 12 January 1832, *BR*, p. 9.
109 Auguste Blanqui's Defence Speech at the "Trial of the Fifteen"', 12 January 1832, *BR*, pp. 12–13. Blanqui accordingly declares from the outset that the court is illegitimate and that he does not recognize its authority (see pp. 8–9).
110 'Auguste Blanqui's Defence Speech at the "Trial of the Fifteen"', 12 January 1832, *BR*, p. 13.
111 'Auguste Blanqui's Defence Speech at the "Trial of the Fifteen"', 12 January 1832, *BR*, p. 16.
112 'Auguste Blanqui's Defence Speech at the "Trial of the Fifteen"', 12 January 1832, *BR*, p. 12.
113 Johan Galtung notes that 'personal violence may more easily be noticed, even though the "tranquil waters" of structural violence may contain much more violence' ('Violence, Peace and Peace Research', *Journal of Peace Research*, 6:3 (1969), pp. 173–4). Blanqui uses the same analogy – invoking Jean de la Fontaine's fable 'Le Torrent et la Rivère' (1678) he speaks of 'the torrent with a harmless roar and the quiet river that silently swallows you up in its tranquil waters' – in 'Communism, the Future of Society', 1869, *BR*, p. 244.
114 MSS 9581, f. 39 [15 January 1859].
115 'Communism, the Future of Society', 1869, *BR*, p. 244.
116 Read in purely economic terms, Blanqui's critics are right to point out how this fails to capture the social dynamics it seeks to describe, for as Max Weber among others has of course showed, capitalist accumulation is by no means linked to idleness. And although Blanqui uses the term 'idler' less and less over the course of his life, often focusing more on the social relation between those engaged in the production process itself (i.e. the conflict between owners or employers and workers), it does still sometimes appear in his late writings (see, for example, 'L'Armée escalve et opprimée', 31 October 1880, *MF*, p. 418).
117 'Social Wealth Must Belong to Those Who Created It', February 1834, *BR*, p. 48; 'Equality Is Our Flag', 2 February 1834, *BR*, p. 39; 'Qui fait la soupe doit la manger', March 1834, *OI*, p. 291.
118 When reflecting on the French Revolution and its legacy, for example, Blanqui writes that 'only the executioners are pitied, when by chance they succumb, since their job is to be executioners and not victims'. Meanwhile, 'the poor, the people, are destined to be victims' – and 'it is scandalous that they should ever change role' ('Philosophical and Political Fragments', 19 or 29 September 1831, *BR*, p. 162).
119 'Work, Suffer and Die', c. 1851–2, *BR*, p. 104.
120 MSS 9590(1), f. 107 [14 October 1867].

121 'Philosophical and Political Fragments', 1867, *BR*, p. 166.
122 'Philosophical and Political Fragments', 1868–9, *BR*, p. 131.

# Chapter 4

1 'Philosophical and Political Fragments', March 1849, *BR*, p. 135.
2 Jean-Jacques Rousseau, *Emile, or On Education*, trans. Allan Bloom (London: Penguin, 1991), pp. 280–1. Together these principles form the Savoyard Vicar's third article of faith.
3 Rousseau, 'Discourse on Political Economy', in *The Social Contract*, trans. Christopher Betts (Oxford: Oxford University Press, 2008), p. 10; Rousseau, *Social Contract*, pp. 55–6.
4 Perhaps nowhere does Blanqui bring these elements together so clearly as when he writes that equality 'appeals to all virtues and rejects all vices. It kills selfishness and lives on nothing but dedication and devotion: it is through devotion that it unites and brings men together; it is through intelligence alone that it governs them and that it leads them to coordinate their efforts towards a common goal, which is the well-being of all. Finally, it is unity and fraternity that it establishes on earth, just as privilege produces nothing but hatred and isolation' ('Equality Is Our Flag', 2 February 1834, *BR*, p. 38).
5 'Philosophical and Political Fragments', 30 December 1868, *BR*, p. 129.
6 See 'Fatal, Fatalism, Fatality', 28 July 1868, *BR*, p. 181; 'Philosophical and Political Fragments', 1868, *BR*, p. 136.
7 'Report to the Society of the Friends of the People', 2 February 1832, *BR*, p. 33.
8 'Declaration of the Provisional Committee for Schools', 22 January 1831, *BR*, p. 7.
9 As Hallward affirms, 'the practical exercise of will distinguishes itself from mere wish or fantasy through its capacity to initiate a process of genuine "realization"' (Peter Hallward, 'The Will of the People: Notes towards a Dialectical Voluntarism', *Radical Philosophy*, 155 (May–June 2009), p. 25). Here I also draw on Hallward's discussion of the conjunction of *vouloir* and *pouvoir* from 'Willing and Able: Political Will and Self-determination', Lecture given at the American University in Paris, 10 April 2015.
10 'Discours du fabricant-sénateur Comte de Mimeral', February 1866, *CS2*, p. 303.
11 MSS 9586, f. 402 [n.d.]. See also 'Philosophical and Political Fragments', 1868, *BR*, p. 136.
12 'Initiation Ceremony of the Society of the Seasons', 1837, *BR*, p. 67.

13 'Communism, the Future of Society', 1869, *BR*, p. 267. See also the claim that 'Lordly capital is a power that has no counterweight. No force obstructs it' ('Philosophical and Political Fragments', n.d. [c. 1860s?], *BR*, p. 151).
14 'Philosophical and Political Fragments', December 1849, *BR*, p. 152.
15 'Saint-Étienne: Lutte entre les fabricants et les ouvriers', December 1849, *CS2*, p. 226.
16 'Projet de discours', August 1867, *CS2*, p. 153.
17 'The regular destiny of the weak, their providential mission, is to be served up as food for the strong. Society is nothing more than this organised anthropophagy.' Any attempt to protect the weak from the strong is considered 'a revolt against Providence, against the human constitution, an attempt to overthrow the laws of nature' ('Rapport gigantesque de Thiers sur l'assistance publique', 1850, *CS2*, pp. 246–7).
18 'Saint-Étienne: Lutte entre les fabricants et les ouvriers', December 1849, *CS2*, p. 226.
19 'Report to the Society of the Friends of the People', 2 February 1832, *BR*, p. 25.
20 Recall that for Rousseau a general will, 'once declared, is an act of sovereignty and has legal authority' (*Social Contract*, p. 64).
21 'Report to the Society of the Friends of the People', 2 February 1832, *BR*, pp. 24–5.
22 'Why There Are No More Riots', 2 February 1834, *BR*, p. 44.
23 'Report to the Society of the Friends of the People', 2 February 1832, *BR*, p. 24.
24 'L'aristocratie et le peuple', July 1831, *OI*, pp. 167–9.
25 See, for example, MSS 9590(2), ff. 466–7 [June 1850]; 'Letter to Tessy', 6 September 1852, *BR*, p. 124.
26 Peter Hallward, 'Defiance or Emancipation?', *Radical Philosophy*, 183 (January–February 2014), p. 25.
27 'Grève et coopération', October 1867, *CS2*, pp. 166–7; 'Philosophical and Political Fragments', October 1867, *BR*, p. 152.
28 'Philosophical and Political Fragments', October 1867, *BR*, p. 152.
29 After Rousseau, Blanqui recognizes that 'the strength of the people ... is effective only when it is concentrated: it is dissipated and lost when spread out, like the force of gunpowder, which ignites only in the mass, and not when it is scattered on the ground' (Rousseau, *Social Contract*, pp. 115–16).
30 'Philosophical and Political Fragments', 1849, *BR*, p. 150.
31 See MSS 9590(1), f. 87 [16 March 1866].
32 'Auguste Blanqui's Defence Speech at the "Trial of the Fifteen"', 12 January 1832, *BR*, p. 13.
33 'Declaration of the Provisional Committee for Schools', 22 January 1831, *BR*, p. 6.
34 Hallward, 'Will of the People', p. 23.

35 'Philosophical and Political Fragments', August 1867, *BR*, p. 142. The general outline of an emancipated society that is offered in the 'Initiation Ceremony of the Society of the Seasons' again attests to Rousseau's legacy. Indeed, in many ways the text amounts to a more or less faithful restatement of Rousseau's political theory. The overthrow of royalty and the destruction of aristocracy and privilege will, it claims, establish a 'government of the people by the people', that is, a republic founded on equality, imposing on each person equal duties ('To obey the general will, to be devoted to the country and to maintaining fraternity with every member of the nation') and granting them equal rights (the right to life, to work, to existence, to education and to vote). Only those who fulfil their duties to the social body in turn receive rights from it; only those who participate in and thus actively constitute the sovereign authority can be considered citizens (as individuals) and the people (as a collective). The people 'indicate their will' through the law, 'which is nothing other than the expression of the general will', and which is prepared by a chamber of deputies before being submitted to the people for 'approval or rejection'. See 'Initiation Ceremony of the Society of the Seasons', 1837, *BR*, pp. 67–8.
36 'Projet de discours', August 1867, *CS2*, p. 148.
37 'Le luxe', n.d., *CS1*, p. 109.
38 'Communism, the Future of Society', 1869, *BR*, pp. 251, 264.
39 'Communism, the Future of Society', 1869, *BR*, pp. 251–2, 263. And again: 'Individualism is hell for individuals; it takes no account of them and is founded on their systematic destruction. … For an individual, individualism signifies extermination, while communism means the respect, safety and security of every person' ('Notes on Positivism', 15 March 1869, *BR*, p. 232).
40 'What man loses by the social contract is his natural freedom and an unlimited right to anything by which he is tempted and can obtain; what he gains is his civil freedom and the right of property over everything that he possesses' (Rousseau, *Social Contract*, p. 59).
41 Rousseau, *Social Contract*, p. 59.
42 'Qui fait la soupe doit la manger', March 1834, *OI*, p. 295.
43 'Communism, the Future of Society', 1869, *BR*, p. 263.
44 'Equality Is Our Flag', 2 February 1834, *BR*, p. 39.
45 'The Sects and the Revolution', 19 October 1866, *BR*, p. 176.
46 'Communism, the Future of Society', 1869, *BR*, p. 257.
47 'Communism, the Future of Society', 1869, *BR*, p. 252. See also 'On Revolution', 1850, *BR*, p. 97.
48 'Concerning the Clamour against the "Warning to the People"', April 1851, *BR*, p. 103.
49 'Communism, the Future of Society', 1869, *BR*, pp. 255–6.

50 Hallward, 'Will of the People', pp. 20–1, 23.
51 'The Sects and the Revolution', 19 October 1866, *BR*, p. 177.
52 Rousseau, *Social Contract*, p. 54.
53 'Letter to Maillard', 6 June 1852, *BR*, pp. 119–20.
54 'Report to the Society of the Friends of the People', 2 February 1832, *BR*, p. 29.
55 'Report to the Society of the Friends of the People', 2 February 1832, *BR*, p. 31.
56 'Report to the Society of the Friends of the People', 2 February 1832, *BR*, p. 31.
57 'Report to the Society of the Friends of the People', 2 February 1832, *BR*, p. 33. See also 'Lettre à Adelaïde de Montgolfier', 31 July 1832, *OI*, p. 233.
58 'Equality Is Our Flag', 2 February 1834, *BR*, p. 41.
59 'The Massacre in Rouen: The Central Republican Society to the Provisional Government', 2 May 1848, *BR*, p. 80.
60 'Instructions for an Armed Uprising', 1868, *BR*, p. 206.
61 'Warning to the People', 10 February 1851, *BR*, p. 99.
62 'Initiation Ceremony of the Society of the Seasons', 1837, *BR*, p. 69.
63 'Formulaire de réception de la Société des Familles', July–August 1834, *OI*, p. 298.
64 'Malfaisance de l'Eglise', April–May 1865, *ND*, p. 62.
65 'Candide', 3 May 1865, *MF*, p. 247.
66 MSS 9590(1), ff. 162–3 [1869]. For Blanqui, history proves that morality varies 'according to time and place', that its progress is 'more or less slow or fast, but always proportional to the development of enlightenment' (MSS 9592(3), f. 74 [n.d.]).
67 MSS 9590(1), ff. 162–3 [1869]. Morality, Blanqui explains elsewhere, 'the flower of the seed of thought, is nothing other than the more or less powerful expression of the humanitarian instinct that forbids people from mistreating one another and commands them to help one another' ('Philosophical and Political Fragments', 3 May 1865, *BR*, p. 132).
68 'Equality Is Our Flag', 2 February 1834, *BR*, p. 40.
69 'Equality Is Our Flag', 2 February 1834, *BR*, p. 38.
70 MSS 9590(1) f. 181 [14 April 1869]; 'Candide', 3 May 1865, *MF*, pp. 248–9.
71 MSS 9590(1), f. 163 [1869].
72 'Auguste Blanqui's Defence Speech at the "Trial of the Fifteen"', 12 January 1832, *BR*, p. 12.
73 Fidel Castro, 'Second Declaration of Havana', 4 February 1962, in *Fidel Castro Reader*, ed. David Deutschmann and Deborah Shnookal (Melbourne: Ocean Press, 2007), p. 264.
74 'Instructions for an Armed Uprising', 1868, *BR*, p. 207.
75 'Instructions for an Armed Uprising', 1868, *BR*, p. 206. Cf. Machiavelli's rejection of the use of mercenaries and his insistence on the need to raise one's own troops in chapters 12–13 of *The Prince*.

76  MSS 9589, f. 123 [n.d.].
77  'Philosophical and Political Fragments', 21 October 1848, *BR*, p. 163.
78  'Instructions for an Armed Uprising', 1868, *BR*, pp. 206–7. This theme is already present in Blanqui's early writings. In 1831 he claimed that 'the only thing' the enemy fears is 'the energy of their adversaries' ('Lettre à Adelaïde de Montgolfier', 25 August 1831, *OI*, p. 180). In the duel between privilege and equality, he similarly argued three years later, the former 'is unable to fight face-to-face because it feels crushed by the moral superiority of its adversary' ('Equality Is Our Flag', 2 February 1834, *BR*, p. 38).
79  'There is no weapon more powerful than profound conviction and a clear sense of what is to be done' (Fidel Castro quoted in *Cuban Revolution Reader*, ed. Julio García Luis (Melbourne: Ocean Press, 2008), p. 374).
80  See MSS 9592(3), f. 60 [21 September 1869] and 'Response to the Request for a Toast for a Workers' Banquet', November 1848, *BR*, p. 86.
81  'Philosophical and Political Fragments', n.d., *BR*, p. 135.
82  See, for example, 'Auguste Blanqui's Defence Speech at the "Trial of the Fifteen"', 12 January 1832, *BR*, p. 11; 'Equality Is Our Flag', 1834, *BR*, p. 39; 'Philosophical and Political Fragments', March 1849, *BR*, p. 135; 'Instructions for an Armed Uprising', 1868, *BR*, p. 206.
83  'Declaration of the Provisional Committee for Schools', 22 January 1831, *BR*, p. 7.
84  'Equality Is Our Flag', 2 February 1834, *BR*, p. 38.
85  'Deux lettres de Buonarroti', 11 May 1835, *OI*, p. 307.
86  See, for example, 'Blanqui's Notes for his Defence at the "Gunpowder Trial"', October 1836, *BR*, p. 63. Daniel Bensaïd and Michael Löwy highlight Blanqui's atheistic and profane 'revolutionary "religion"' in 'Auguste Blanqui, Heretical Communist', *Radical Philosophy*, 185 (May–June 2014), pp. 29–30.
87  See, for example, 'Blanqui's Notes for his Defence at the "Gunpowder Trial"', October 1836, *BR*, p. 63; 'Concerning the Clamour against the "Warning to the People"', April 1851, *BR*, p. 102; 'Communism, the Future of Society', 1869, *BR*, p. 258.
88  'Equality Is Our Flag', 2 February 1834, *BR*, pp. 40–1.
89  'Letter to Maillard', 6 June 1852, *BR*, p. 117.
90  'Notes on Positivism', 15 March 1869, *BR*, p. 231.
91  MSS 9590(1), f. 193 [16 July 1869].
92  'Notes on Positivism', 8 April 1869, *BR*, p. 241.
93  MSS 9590(1), ff. 267–8 [1868–9]; 'Philosophical and Political Fragments', 1868–9, *BR*, pp. 130–1.
94  'Philosophical and Political Fragments', n.d. [*c*. 1848–50], *BR*, p. 139.
95  MSS 9590(1), f. 153 [6 March 1869].
96  'Projet de discours', August 1867, *CS2*, p. 149.

97   MSS 9590(1), f. 159 [March 1869].
98   Fidel Castro, 'Death of Che Guevara', 1968, in *Cuban Revolution Reader*, p. 203. See also Fidel Castro, *Fidel and Religion: Fidel Castro in Conversation with Frei Betto on Marxism and Liberation Theology* (Melbourne: Ocean Press, 2006).
99   'Declaration of the Provisional Committee for Schools', 22 January 1831, *BR*, p. 7.
100  Rousseau, *Social Contract*, p. 50. See also Etienne De La Boétie, *Discours da la servitude volontaire* (Paris: Librio, 2013).
101  'Athéisme et spiritualisme', 13 December 1880, *ND*, p. 23.
102  'Malfaisance de l'Eglise', April–May 1865, *ND*, p. 62.
103  'Projet de discours', August 1867, *CS2*, p. 158.
104  Alan B. Spitzer, *The Revolutionary Theories of Louis Auguste Blanqui* (New York: Columbia University Press, 1957), pp. 133–4.
105  'First Proclamation', 27 July 1830, *BR*, p. 3.
106  MSS 9592(3), f. 76 [8 September 1869].
107  Le Nuz, 'Introduction', *OI*, pp. 369–70. See 'Initiation Ceremony of the Society of the Seasons', 1837, *BR*, p. 68.
108  'Communism, the Future of Society', 1869, *BR*, p. 248.
109  'Communism, the Future of Society', 1869, *BR*, pp. 249–50.
110  'Communism, the Future of Society', 1869, *BR*, p. 248.
111  'Communism, the Future of Society', 1869, *BR*, p. 248. See also 'Le communisme primitif', April 1869, *CS2*, pp. 72–3 and 'The Sects and the Revolution', 19 October 1866, *BR*, pp. 176–8.
112  'Communism, the Future of Society', 1869, *BR*, p. 264.
113  See in particular the assertion that 'judging by the people's current state of mind, as things stand communism is not exactly knocking at the door. But nothing is so deceptive as a situation, because nothing is so changeable' ('Communism, the Future of Society', 1869, *BR*, pp. 263–4), which serves as the epigraph for Quelques agents du Parti imaginaire, 'Préface: A un ami', *MF*, p. 9. Similarly, even when Blanqui writes that communism 'is the revolution itself' he goes on to add that communism 'cannot impose itself suddenly, no more the day after than the day before its victory' ('Communism, the Future of Society', 1869, *BR*, p. 258).
114  'Communism, the Future of Society', 1869, *BR*, p. 259.
115  'Social Wealth Must Belong to Those Who Created It', February 1834, *BR*, p. 49.
116  'Democratic Propaganda', 1835, *BR*, p. 60.
117  'Les apologies de l'usure', n.d., *CS1*, p. 145.
118  MSS 9590(1), f. 107 [14 October 1867]; 'Projet de discours', August 1867, *CS2*, pp. 160–1.

119  Michael Hardt, 'Introduction: Thomas Jefferson, or, The Transition of Democracy', in Thomas Jefferson, *The Declaration of Independence*, ed. Michael Hardt (London: Verso, 2007), p. xvi. The point of departure here is Lenin's claim that 'human nature as it is now', which 'cannot do without subordination, control, and "managers"', is, as Hardt summarizes, 'trained to be subservient and passive' (pp. x, xvi).
120  Hardt, 'Introduction: Thomas Jefferson, or, The Transition of Democracy', p. viii.
121  Hardt, 'Introduction: Thomas Jefferson, or, The Transition of Democracy', pp. ix–xi.
122  Hardt, 'Introduction: Thomas Jefferson, or, The Transition of Democracy', p. xi.
123  Hardt, 'Introduction: Thomas Jefferson, or, The Transition of Democracy', pp. xix–xx.
124  Hardt, 'Introduction: Thomas Jefferson, or, The Transition of Democracy', p. xv.
125  Hardt, 'Introduction: Thomas Jefferson, or, The Transition of Democracy', p. xx.
126  MSS 9590(1), f. 107 [28 April 1870].
127  'Philosophical and Political Fragments', 1869, *BR*, p. 145.
128  'Philosophical and Political Fragments', 7 February 1856, *BR*, p. 145.
129  MSS, 9590(1), ff. 106–7 [14 October 1867]. See also 'Philosophical and Political Fragments', n.d. [1848–9?], *BR*, p. 165.
130  Hardt, 'Introduction: Thomas Jefferson, or, The Transition of Democracy', pp. x–xi.
131  Niccolò Machiavelli, *The Prince*, trans. Peter Bondanella (Oxford: Oxford University Press, 2005), p. 22.
132  'Communism, the Future of Society', 1869, *BR*, p. 250.
133  'Communism, the Future of Society', 1869, *BR*, p. 258.
134  'Notes on Positivism', 15 March 1869, *BR*, p. 232.
135  Blanqui is therefore completely at odds with Hardt's claim that, according to Jefferson's conception of 'self-transformation', 'when people participate actively in government, deciding on all the matters that concern them, either directly or by instructing their delegates up to the highest levels of government, they are transformed. There is no great instructor that teaches [the people] the necessary lessons. The process of transition is a self-training in the capacities of self-rule. Through practice they develop the skills, knowledges, and habits necessary for self-government and, in the process, a new humanity is created' (Hardt, 'Introduction: Thomas Jefferson, or, The Transition of Democracy', pp. xx, xxii).
136  Marx, 'Concerning Feuerbach' ['Theses on Feuerbach'], 1845, in *Early Writings*, trans. Rodney Livingstone and Gregor Benton (London: Penguin, 1975), p. 422.
137  'Projet de discours', August 1867, *CS2*, p. 154.
138  'Projet de discours', August 1867, *CS2*, pp. 155–6.

139 'Projet de discours', August 1867, *CS2*, p. 154. One finds similar accounts elsewhere: 'Darkness does not vanish in twenty-four hours. It is the most tenacious of all our enemies. Twenty years may not be enough to usher in complete daylight. Enlightened workers already know through experience that ignorance is the principal – and, we might even say, the sole – obstacle to the development of associations. The masses do not understand them and are mistrustful. ... Nevertheless, the obvious benefits of association will soon become clear in the eyes of all the industrial proletariat once the government is working for enlightenment, and they will quickly rally to the cause. The countryside poses a far greater problem, however. First, ignorance and suspicion prey far more on cottages than on workshops. Second, the motivating forces of necessity and self-interest that might lead the peasant towards association are not as strong' ('Communism, the Future of Society', 1869, *BR*, pp. 262–3).

140 'Projet de discours', August 1867, *CS2*, p. 157; emphasis in original.

141 'Communism, the Future of Society', 1869, *BR*, p. 262.

142 'The will of the people is a matter of material power and active empowerment, before it is a matter of representation, authority or legitimacy' (Hallward, 'Will of the People', p. 22). Cf. 'The construction of a "people" would be impossible without the operation of mechanisms of representation' (Ernesto Laclau, *On Populist Reason* (London: Verso, 2005), p. 161).

143 Hallward, 'Will of the People', p. 23.

144 Hallward, 'Will of the People', p. 23.

145 See Rousseau's similarly paternalistic analogies in *Social Contract*, pp. 46, 50.

146 Rousseau, *Social Contract*, p. 66.

147 Rousseau, *Social Contract*, p. 75.

148 'Wise men who try to address the common people not in its own language, but in theirs, cannot make themselves understood. But there are innumerable ideas which cannot be translated into the language of the people' (Rousseau, *Social Contract*, p. 78).

149 Rousseau, *Social Contract*, p. 78.

150 Rousseau, *Social Contract*, p. 78.

151 Rousseau, 'Discourse on Political Economy', pp. 9–10.

152 'Public education, following rules prescribed by the government, and controlled by officers established by the sovereign, is therefore one of the fundamental principles of the popular or legitimate form of government. If children are brought up in common on terms of complete equality, if they are imbued with the laws of the state and the maxims of the general will, and instructed to respect them above everything, if they are surrounded with examples and objects that unceasingly speak to them of the tender mother who provides for them, of the incalculable gifts they receive from her and the gratitude they

owe her in return – we cannot doubt that they will learn in this way to cherish each other like brothers, to want nothing except what is wanted by society, to replace the sterile and empty chattering of the sophists by the actions of men and citizens, and one day to become the defenders and fathers of their country, whose children they have been for so long' (Rousseau, 'Discourse on Political Economy', p. 23).

153 If, Rousseau explains, '[men] are trained early enough to consider their individual selves only in relation to the body of the state, and to see their own existence, so to speak, only as a part of its existence, they may finally come to identify themselves to some extent with the greater whole, to feel that they are members of their home country, to have towards it those supreme feelings that every man living in isolation has only towards himself, to raise their souls constantly to this higher level, and so transform the dangerous inclination towards self-love, the source of all our vices, into a sublime virtue. ... It is from the first moment of life that we must learn how to be worthy to live; and since we participate from birth in the rights of citizens, it is at the instant of our birth that the exercise of our duties should begin' (Rousseau, 'Discourse on Political Economy', pp. 22–3).

154 Rousseau, 'Discourse on Political Economy', p. 24.

155 Rousseau, *Social Contract*, pp. 79–80.

156 Rousseau, *Social Contract*, pp. 76–7.

157 'Initiation Ceremony of the Society of the Seasons', 1837, *BR*, p. 68. In this evocation of a force capable of administering 'heroic remedies' one might suggest certain echoes of Rousseau's depiction of the legislator as 'a man extraordinary in every respect', 'a mind of a superior kind' taking 'decisions of [a] higher reason, beyond the scope of average men' (Rousseau, *Social Contract*, pp. 76–8).

158 'Initiation Ceremony of the Society of the Seasons', 1837, *BR*, p. 68.

159 Not only do the workers and students of Paris represent the nation as a whole, however – they may in fact do so *in spite of* the workers and peasants of the provinces who numerically comprise the majority of the nation. Why? Because these groups remain under the sway of clerical domination and therefore, in their mis-educated ignorance, are manipulated into acting as the agents of reaction. 'The workers who are devoted to the emancipation of the masses,' Blanqui writes, 'know all too well that neither force nor dexterity amount to intelligence'; they know that any claims to the contrary, 'that manual skills are of equal worth to cerebral power', seek to suppress this very power ('Communism, the Future of Society', 1869, *BR*, p. 265). For Blanqui, then, to be 'properly informed' is, first, to understand the strength and significance of one's own enlightened thought as the basis of one's capacity for conscious volition in the

cause of emancipation; and, second, it is to devote oneself to the emancipation of all, to those who remain uninformed and, therefore, oppressed.
160 'The Sects and the Revolution', 19 October 1866, *BR*, p. 177.
161 Rousseau, *Social Contract*, p. 46.

## Chapter 5

1 'Notes on Positivism', 1 April 1869, *BR*, p. 235.
2 See MSS 9592(3) f. 384 [n.d.] and 'Philosophical and Political Fragments', n.d., *BR*, pp. 129–30.
3 'Philosophical and Political Fragments', 3 May 1865, *BR*, p. 132.
4 Although never clearly defined, in this context by 'philosophy' Blanqui seems to mean a broadly coherent system of thought that influences or determines social relations and political structures, and which produces moral norms and guiding principles for human behaviour and social life more generally.
5 MSS 9592(3) ff. 384–5 [n.d.].
6 Alan B. Spitzer, *The Revolutionary Theories of Louis Auguste Blanqui* (New York: Columbia University Press, 1957), p. 44.
7 MSS 9590(1), ff. 187–8 [23 April 1869].
8 MSS 9590(1), ff. 187–9 [23 April 1869].
9 MSS 9590(1), ff. 187–8 [23 April 1869]. On this point see also 'Les apologies de l'usure', n.d., *CS1*, p. 145.
10 'Notes on Positivism', 8 April 1869, *BR*, p. 239.
11 'Notes on Positivism', 15 March 1869, *BR*, pp. 232–3.
12 'Communism, the Future of Society', 1869, *BR*, p. 265.
13 'Notes on Positivism', 15 March 1869, *BR*, p. 232.
14 'Communism, the Future of Society', 1869, *BR*, p. 243.
15 'Communism, the Future of Society', 1869, *BR*, p. 243.
16 'Notes on Positivism', 15 March 1869, *BR*, p. 232; 'Candide', 3 May 1865, *MF*, p. 248.
17 See MSS 9590(1), f. 157 [March 1869].
18 'Le communisme primitif', March 1870, *CS2*, p. 74.
19 'Notes on Positivism', 15 March 1869, *BR*, p. 232.
20 'Notes on Positivism', 1 April 1869, *BR*, p. 235.
21 'Les apologies de l'usure', n.d., *CS1*, p. 146.
22 'Les apologies de l'usure', n.d., *CS1*, p. 146.
23 See Le Nuz, 'Introduction', *OI*, p. 89 and 'Introduction', *OI*, p. 250. See also Spitzer, *Revolutionary Theories of Louis Auguste Blanqui*, pp. 98, 102 and

Maurice Dommanget, *Auguste Blanqui à Belle-Île* (Paris: Librarie du Travail, 1935), pp. 10, 12.

24 See in particular 'Auguste Blanqui's Defence Speech at the "Trial of the Fifteen"', 12 January 1832, *BR*, p. 9.

25 Blanqui's analysis might be summarized as follows. France's capitulation in 1814–15 was the work of the bourgeois class who, as ever more concerned with material self-interest than freedom, opened their arms to France's foreign enemies and supported the Restoration in order to bring an end to a war that was beginning to hinder commerce. Under Louis XVIII, the bourgeoisie entered into an alliance with the upper classes – émigrés, nobles and big landowners who supported the Bourbons – in return for the Charter and the Chamber of Deputies. The bourgeois continued to support the reactionary and repressive Restoration happily, Blanqui is keen to point out, until Charles X's attempts from 1825 to re-establish the nobility's supremacy and return to the principles of the *ancien régime* led to a struggle between the upper and middle classes. The bourgeoisie began to gain greater power through their growing dominance in the Chamber of Deputies, posing a threat to a government that ultimately ruled in the name of the upper class. For the people, meanwhile, this was a period of political retreat. Disorganized and demoralized in the face of the foreign invasion and having lost faith in the cause of liberty, the events of 1815 caused the people to fall silent and submit to their oppressors – the middle and upper classes. But they had certainly not resigned themselves to this fate, as soon became clear in the summer of 1830. See 'Report to the Society of the Friends of the People', 2 February 1832, *BR*, pp. 21–3.

26 'Report to the Society of the Friends of the People', 2 February 1832, *BR*, p. 20.

27 'Report to the Society of the Friends of the People', 2 February 1832, *BR*, p. 23.

28 M. Ralea quoted in Spitzer, *Revolutionary Theories of Louis Auguste Blanqui*, p. 135; translation modified.

29 'Letter to Blanqui's Supporters in Paris', 18 April 1866, *BR*, p. 174.

30 See Spitzer, *Revolutionary Theories of Louis Auguste Blanqui*, chapter 7.

31 'Speech at the Prado', 25 February 1848, *BR*, p. 73.

32 'Letter to Blanqui's Supporters in Paris', 18 April 1866, *BR*, pp. 174–5.

33 Spitzer's conclusion is instructive: 'The record of his failures would certainly seem to indicate a persistent indifference to the objective revolutionary potentialities of his time. Paradoxically, this conclusion is contradicted by the details of his revolutionary career. In *every* political crisis after 1839 with which we connect Blanqui, we find that he actually attempted to postpone the violent consummation of the movements he had helped to organize because the immediate circumstances were not propitious for a revolution' (Spitzer, *Revolutionary Theories of Louis Auguste Blanqui*, p. 145).

34 Jill Harsin, *Barricades: The War on the Streets of Revolutionary Paris, 1830-1848* (Basingstoke: Palgrave, 2002), pp. 106-7, 110-11. Cf. 'As it is clear that new writings from a republican perspective, and with the goal we have just indicated, would be the object of perpetual harassment, however moderate they might be, we have resolved to thwart the relentless efforts of the police. What is important to us above all is to enlighten the masses, but trials, imprisonments and fines would soon destroy our efforts, despite all the perseverance that patriotism might inspire in us' ('Democratic Propaganda', 1835, *BR*, p. 60).

35 'Philosophical and Political Fragments', 12 July 1879, *BR*, p. 135.

36 'Les apologies de l'usure', n.d., *CS1*, p. 136. See also 'L'economie politique sans morale', March 1870, *CS2*, p. 58.

37 Karl Marx and Frederick Engels, *The Communist Manifesto: A Modern Edition* (London: Verso, 2012), p. 45.

38 'Declaration of the Provisional Committee for Schools', 22 January 1831, *BR*, p. 7.

39 'Auguste Blanqui's Defence Speech at the "Trial of the Fifteen"', 12 January 1832, *BR*, p. 19.

40 'Report to the Society of the Friends of the People', 2 February 1832, *BR*, p. 30. Cf. 'Fatal, Fatalism, Fatality', 28 July 1868, *BR*, p. 181, where Blanqui disparages this very phrase – 'The march of progress is inevitable, irresistible! Nothing can stop it!' – on the basis of its appeal to a form of positivist fatalism.

41 'Equality Is Our Flag', 2 February 1832, *BR*, p. 38; 'Social Wealth Must Belong to Those Who Created It', February 1834, *BR*, p. 53.

42 See 'Social Wealth Must Belong to Those Who Created It', February 1834, *BR*, pp. 53-4; 'Qui fait la soupe doit la manger', March 1834, *OI*, p. 294.

43 'Social Wealth Must Belong to Those Who Created It', February 1834, *BR*, p. 55.

44 'We know that our projects are dismissed as utopias,' Blanqui continues. 'But history offers us a guarantee of ... the infallible realisation of these utopias' ('Equality Is Our Flag', 2 February 1832, *BR*, pp. 36-7. See also 'Social Wealth Must Belong to Those Who Created It', February 1834, *BR*, p. 54).

45 'Social Wealth Must Belong to Those Who Created It', February 1834, *BR*, p. 54.

46 'Equality Is Our Flag', 2 February 1834, *BR*, p. 39. See also the similar assertion that 'if the right to property were destined to triumph, a bleak future indeed would appear before us' ('Social Wealth Must Belong to Those Who Created It', February 1834, *BR*, p. 54).

47 'Equality Is Our Flag', 2 February 1834, p. 37.

48 'Equality Is Our Flag', 2 February 1834, p. 37.

49 As Spitzer notes with regard to 1789: 'All Frenchmen who devoted themselves to human progress were, for Blanqui and many others, but the executors of the testament of the great Revolution and at the same time its heirs' (Spitzer, *Revolutionary Theories of Louis Auguste Blanqui*, p. 121).

50 'Communism, the Future of Society', 1869, *BR*, p. 243; emphasis added.
51 As Hobsbawm then summarizes: 'Historical change through social praxis, through collective action, is at its core' (Eric Hobsbawm, 'Introduction', in Karl Marx and Frederick Engels, *The Communist Manifesto: A Modern Edition* (London: Verso, 2012), p. 27).
52 'Democratic Propaganda', 1835, *BR*, p. 60.
53 Cf. Che Guevara's assertion that the 'favourable circumstances' for revolution are 'consciousness of the necessity of change and confidence in the possibility of this revolutionary change' ('Guerrilla Warfare: A Method', September 1963, in *Che Guevara Reader: Writings on Politics and Revolution*, ed. David Deutschmann (Melbourne: Ocean Press, 2004), p. 75).
54 'Social Wealth Must Belong to Those Who Created It', February 1834, *BR*, p. 54.
55 Marx and Engels, *Communist Manifesto*, p. 35.
56 See Daniel Bensaïd and Michael Löwy, 'Auguste Blanqui, Heretical Communist', *Radical Philosophy*, 185 (May–June 2014), p. 28.
57 Che Guevara, 'Political Sovereignty and Economic Independence', 20 March 1960, in *Che Guevara Reader*, p. 102. See also Jon Lee Anderson, *Che Guevara: A Revolutionary Life* (London: Bantam, 2010), p. 191.
58 Frantz Fanon, *The Wretched of the Earth*, trans. Constance Farrington (London: Penguin Books, 1969), p. 37.
59 Hobsbawm, 'Introduction', p. 28.
60 'Débats parlementaires de février sur l'enseignement', n.d., *ND*, pp. 54–5. In the decades following 1848 Blanqui would reiterate this need to 'sound the alarm' against the imminent threat of reaction. See, for example, 'Concerning the Clamour against the "Warning to the People"', April 1851, *BR*, p. 101, MSS 9587, f. 378 [1862] and MSS 9588(2), f. 541 [25 September 1879]. Walter Benjamin was particularly taken by this idea, highlighting Blanqui's 'firm resolve to snatch humanity at the last moment from the catastrophe looming at every turn' (Walter Benjamin, *The Arcades Project*, ed. Rolf Tiedemann, trans. Howard Eiland and Kevin McLaughlin (Cambridge, MA: Harvard University Press, 1999) p. 339). See also Michael Löwy, *Fire Alarm: Reading Walter Benjamin's 'On the Concept of History'*, trans. Chris Turner (London: Verso, 2005).
61 Régis Debray, *Revolution in the Revolution?*, trans. Bobbye Ortiz (Harmondsworth: Penguin, 1968), p. 24.
62 'Response to the Request for a Toast for a Workers' Banquet', November 1848, *BR*, p. 86.
63 'Auguste Blanqui's Defence Speech at the "Trial of the Fifteen"', 12 January 1832, *BR*, p. 17.
64 'Fatal, Fatalism, Fatality', 28 July 1868, *BR*, p. 180.
65 'Philosophical and Political Fragments', 1868, *BR*, p. 136.

66 'Notes on Positivism', 8 April 1869, *BR*, p. 241.
67 'It need only call itself a *science*,' Blanqui continues, 'to adopt this universally respected name, for it to become immediately sacrosanct' ('Notes on Positivism', 1 April 1869, *BR*, pp. 233–4). On Blanqui's opposition to this 'alliance of science and order', see also Jacques Rancière, 'The Radical Gap: A Preface to Auguste Blanqui, *Eternity by the Stars*', *Radical Philosophy*, 185 (May–June 2014), p. 21.
68 'Notes on Positivism', 1 April 1869, *BR*, p. 233.
69 'Fatal, Fatalism, Fatality', 28 July 1868, *BR*, p. 179.
70 'Notes on Positivism', 8 April 1869, *BR*, p. 239.
71 'Notes on Positivism', 8 April 1869, *BR*, p. 239.
72 'Notes on Positivism', 1 April 1869, *BR*, p. 235.
73 'Les apologies de l'usure', n.d., *CS1*, p. 136.
74 'Letter to Maillard', 6 June 1852, *BR*, pp. 115–16; 'Warning to the People', 10 February 1851, *BR*, pp. 99–100; 'Concerning the Clamour against the "Warning to the People"', April 1851, *BR*, p. 103.
75 MSS 9590(2), f. 465 [June 1850].
76 MSS 9590(2), f. 465 [June 1850].
77 'Philosophical and Political Fragments', 19 or 29 September 1831, *BR*, p. 162.
78 'Philosophical and Political Fragments', 1868, *BR*, p. 136.
79 'Notes on Positivism', 1 April 1869, *BR*, p. 235.
80 'Communism, the Future of Society', 1869, *BR*, p. 254. And again: 'A battle is lost? … Inevitable! … Liberty is annulled? Again inevitable … Blood is running in the streets, cities are in flames, a nation is destroyed? … Inevitable, always inevitable. No need for tears. There is nothing to say. Nothing could be done. It was the inevitable march of Humanity, and since, incidentally, Humanity is progressing, so then everything is for the best. If Humanity breaks a leg along the way and lies moaning on its bed for a millennium or so, what does it matter? The broken leg was a necessary part of its development' ('Fatal, Fatalism, Fatality', 28 July 1868, *BR*, p. 180).
81 'Communism, the Future of Society', 1869, *BR*, p. 254.
82 History, Engels continues, '"possesses *no* immense wealth", it "wages *no* battles". It is *man*, real living man, that does all that, that possesses and fights; "history" is not a person apart, using man as a means to achieve *its own* particular aims; history is *nothing but* the activity of man pursuing his aims' (Karl Marx and Frederick Engels, *The Holy Family, or Critique of Critical Critique*, trans. R. Dixon (Moscow: Foreign Languages Publishing House, 1956), p. 125; emphasis in original). Cf. Daniel Bensaïd, *Marx for Our Times* (London: Verso, 2009). p. 10.
83 MSS 9581, f. 39 [15 January 1859]. See also the similar assertion from 1831 that what is at stake in the continual insistence on the violence of 1793 over

the (far greater) violence of the royalist counter-revolutionary massacres of 1805–30 is not the question of violence at all. Rather, it is the assumption 'that the executioners are pitied, when by chance they succumb, since their job is to be executioners and not victims; that the poor, the people, are destined to be victims, and that it is scandalous that they should ever change role' ('Lettre à [Adelaïde de Montgolfier]?', 19 or 29 September 1831, *OI*, p. 585).
84  MSS 9581, f. 39 [15 January 1859].
85  'Blanqui's Defence Speech at the "Trial of the Fifteen"', 12 January 1832, *BR*, pp. 17–18.
86  'Communism, the Future of Society', 1869, *BR*, p. 255.
87  MSS 9581, f. 40 [15 January 1859].
88  See in particular Miguel Abensour, *Les Passages Blanqui: Walter Benjamin entre mélancolie et révolution* (Paris: Sens & Tonka, 2013), pp. 19–20, 45 and Miguel Abensour and Valentin Pelosse, *Libérer l'Enfermé* (Paris: Sens & Tonka, 2014), p. 17.
89  Abensour, *Les passages Blanqui*, pp. 40–1; Peter Hallward, 'Blanqui's Bifurcations', *Radical Philosophy*, 185 (May–June 2014), p. 40.
90  Benjamin, 'Paris, Capital of the Nineteenth Century: Exposé of 1939', in *The Arcades Project*, p. 26.
91  Benjamin, *Arcades Project*, p. 339.
92  *Eternity by the Stars*, 1872, *BR*, p. 281; hereafter *ES*.
93  'This absolute certainty of the infinity of the world, together with its incomprehensibility,' Blanqui acknowledges, 'constitutes one of the most irritating provocations that torments the human mind' (*ES*, p. 282). As Hallward notes, this was a typical assumption prior to Georg Cantor's pioneering work on the infinite (see 'Blanqui's Bifurcations', p. 38).
94  *ES*, p. 284.
95  *ES*, p. 299.
96  *ES*, p. 303.
97  *ES*, pp. 287, 307.
98  *ES*, p. 310.
99  As was noted both soon after the text's initial publication and again more recently, Blanqui here overlooks the extent to which these combinations of elements might themselves form new elements and thereby create new material forms. See Hallward, 'Blanqui's Bifurcations', p. 39.
100  *ES*, pp. 284–5, 311–12.
101  *ES*, p. 307.
102  *ES*, p. 307.
103  *ES*, p. 300.
104  *ES*, pp. 302, 305.

105 *ES*, p. 303.
106 *ES*, p. 311.
107 *ES*, p. 313.
108 *ES*, p. 316.
109 *ES*, pp. 325, 327.
110 *ES*, pp. 317–18.
111 *ES*, p. 319.
112 *ES*, p. 322.
113 *ES*, p. 315.
114 *ES*, p. 320.
115 'One Last Word', 12 February 1871, *BR*, p. 271.
116 *ES*, pp. 320–1. Blanqui made a similar argument three years earlier: 'Millions of intelligences, of diverse abilities, are constantly locked in struggle upon the battlefields of life. What can the immanent and immutable forces of matter have in common with this confused whirlwind of wills, which are more fluid than water and whose perpetual conflicts hurl masses of human beings this way and that, in a thousand divergent directions?' ('Fatal, Fatalism, Fatality', 28 July 1868, *BR*, p. 181). On this point I follow Spitzer's reading, which highlights the 'tremendous significance' of this 'but' for Blanqui's 'entire social and political philosophy'. See Spitzer, *Revolutionary Theories of Louis Auguste Blanqui*, p. 39.
117 *ES*, p. 318.
118 Hallward shows how the strict division between 'volition and fate' is what distinguishes Blanqui's notion of eternal return from that of Nietzsche – hence the error, which dates back to Benjamin and has persisted ever since, of aligning the two. See Hallward, 'Blanqui's Bifurcations', pp. 41–2.
119 MSS 9592(3), f. 181 [*c.* 1860s?].
120 *ES*, p. 315.
121 'Everything that you could have been in this world, you actually are somewhere else. In addition to the whole course that one lives, from birth to death, on a great number of Earths, one's life also unfolds, on other planets, in many thousands of different editions' (*ES*, p. 316).
122 *ES*, p. 317.
123 *ES*, pp. 328, 317.
124 *ES*, p. 315. Spitzer's succinct gloss on this passage is cogent. 'This is a purely a posteriori fatality,' he notes. 'At every moment man is offered many alternatives. In choosing one he abandons the others forever – that is, commits himself to a particular consequence – but each specific choice is the product of the individual will' (Spitzer, *Revolutionary Theories of Louis Auguste Blanqui*, p. 44).

125 At the beginning of section VII of the text, 'Analysis and Synthesis of the Universe', Blanqui concedes that 'we are authorised at this point to make use of obscure language, since here the question itself becomes obscure' (*ES*, p. 308).

126 Geffroy, *L'Enfermé*, p. 403. (Recall that the 'Taschereau document' of 1848 accused Blanqui of betraying his former comrades of May 1839 in exchange for a reduced prison sentence.) 'My entire appeal,' Blanqui told his sister, 'my entire defence was in this work' (quoted in *Instructions pour une prise d'armes, L'Eternité par les astres et autres texts*, eds. Miguel Abensour and Valentin Pelosse (Paris: Sens & Tonka, 2000), p. 378). But could this not be the result of him wanting the text to be read and taken seriously first and foremost as a scientific work? Sincerely believing he had unlocked the secrets of the universe, it seems little wonder that he would place his hopes on these insights to save him from further imprisonment and the grave mental and physical suffering it caused him. And in any case, at the trial itself Blanqui was no less combative in the face of his accusers and their 'monarchical ideas' (see Alain Decaux, *Blanqui l'Insurgé* (Paris: Librairie Académique Perrin, 1976), pp. 593–4).

127 See Benjamin, *Arcades Project*, p. 111. Following Benjamin, Frank Chouraqui claims that, in composing this 'consolation for a life of missed opportunities and for a world that shall never come to be what it ought to', 'the hard-nosed activist turned speculative prophet' bids a 'final farewell to revolution' (Frank Chouraqui, 'At the Crossroads of History: Blanqui at the Castle of the Bull', in *Eternity by the Stars*, trans. Frank Chouraqui (New York: Contra Mundum Press, 2013), pp. 22, 30). See also Bernstein's assertion that Blanqui's text 'was proof of diligent effort to banish himself as far as possible from earth and politics' (Samuel Bernstein, *Auguste Blanqui and the Art of Insurrection* (London: Lawrence and Wishart, 1971), p. 342).

128 See Maurice Dommanget, *Blanqui, La Guerre de 1870-1871 et La Commune* (Paris: Éditions Domat-Montchrestien, 1947), pp. 145–7. Blanqui also explicitly states in *Eternity* itself that he has been pondering such questions for several decades. 'As far back as thirty years ago,' he reveals, 'I had already begun to suspect that our planet must exist in thousands of copies, because of the infinity of celestial bodies. Yet this opinion remained simply a matter of instinct and intuition, one based solely on the fact of the *infinite*' (*ES*, pp. 312–13).

129 In another letter two days later, Blanqui described *Eternity* as his 'only remedy' for the appalling physical and moral suffering he endured as a result of material and intellectual deprivation (see Dommanget, *Blanqui, La Guerre de 1870-1871 et La Commune*, p. 144). In light of this personal correspondence, Dommanget suggests that, 'unable to engage in politics', Blanqui 'would engage in astronomy. Unable to wander around on earth, he would wander around in the sky'. And again: 'After the philosophical hiatus of *Eternity by the Stars*, Blanqui

decided to resume the struggle, to pursue his ideal of social transformation' (Dommanget, *Blanqui, La Guerre de 1870–1871 et La Commune*, pp. 145, 155). However, I would argue the contrary: just as Blanqui never separates philosophy from politics, theory from practice, there is no division between Blanqui the astronomer and Blanqui the political theorist. Where the separation between the eternal universe and human politics occurs in the text itself only serves to return Blanqui – as he does in final sections – to the political concerns of our world with greater force and urgency.

130 Dommanget, *Blanqui, La Guerre de 1870–1871 et La Commune*, pp. 138–9.
131 *ES*, p. 286.
132 *ES*, p. 299.
133 MSS 9588(2), f. 458 [12 July 1879].
134 MSS 9588(2), f. 459 [15 July 1879].
135 Benjamin, *Arcades Project*, pp. 25, 112, 939.
136 Hallward, 'Blanqui's Bifurcations', pp. 36, 40.
137 Benjamin, *Arcades Project*, pp. 111–12.
138 Benjamin, *Arcades Project*, pp. 25, 112.
139 Benjamin, *Arcades Project*, pp. 26, 113. Cf. Abensour and Pelosse, *Libérer l'Enfermé*, p. 33
140 Benjamin, *Arcades Project*, p. 15.
141 Benjamin, *Arcades Project*, p. 15; Abensour and Pelosse, *Libérer l'Enfermé*, p. 53; Abensour, *Les Passages Blanqui*, pp. 38, 56.
142 See the readings of Abensour and Chouraqui in particular.
143 Benjamin, *Arcades Project*, p. 460.
144 Benjamin, *Arcades Project*, p. 119.
145 Benjamin, *Arcades Project*, p. 339.
146 Quoted in Bensaïd and Löwy, 'Auguste Blanqui, Heretical Communist', p. 28.
147 MSS, 9592(3), f. 161 [24 June 1868].
148 'Philosophical and Political Fragments', 1868, *BR*, p. 136.
149 'Philosophical and Political Fragments', 1871, *BR*, p. 158.
150 Benjamin, *Arcades Project*, pp. 25–6.
151 'Warning to the People', 10 February 1851, *BR*, p. 99.
152 'Auguste Blanqui's Defence Speech at the "Trial of the Fifteen"', 12 January 1832, *BR*, p. 12.
153 'Declaration of the Provisional Committee for Schools', 22 January 1831, *BR*, p. 6. See also 'Auguste Blanqui's Defence Speech at the "Trial of the Fifteen"', 12 January 1832, *BR*, p. 13.
154 Gustave Tridon, 'La Faim', *La Patrie en Danger*, Monday 19 September 1870.
155 'Auguste Blanqui's Defence Speech at the "Trial of the Fifteen"', 12 January 1832, *BR*, p. 13.

156  Peter Hallward, 'Communism of the Intellect, Communism of the Will', in *The Idea of Communism*, ed. Costas Douzinas and Slavoj Žižek (London: Verso, 2010), p. 112.
157  *ES*, p. 327.
158  *ES*, p. 328.
159  *ES*, pp. 327–8.
160  Hobsbawm, 'Introduction', p. 27.

# Conclusion

1  Antonio Gramsci, 'State and Civil Society', in *Selections from the Prison Notebooks*, ed. and trans. Quintin Hoare and Geoffrey Nowel Smith (London: Lawrence and Wishart, 1971), p. 249.
2  'Like Machiavelli, [Gramsci] is a theorist of how societies should be founded or transformed, not of constitutional details' (Eric Hobsbawm, 'Gramsci', in *How to Change the World: Tales of Marx and Marxism* (London: Abacus, 2012), p. 331).
3  'Communism, the Future of Society', 1869, *BR*, pp. 245–6.
4  Jean-Jacques Rousseau, *The Social Contract*, trans. Christopher Betts (Oxford: Oxford University Press, 2008), p. 46.
5  Gustave Geffroy, *L'Enfermé* (Paris: Bibliothèque Charpentier, 1919), pp. 333–4.
6  Frederick Engels, 'Engels to Vera Zasulich', 23 April 1885, online at marxists.org.
7  'Letter to Blanqui's Supporters in Paris', 18 April 1866, *BR*, p. 172.
8  'Why There Are No More Riots', 2 February 1834, *BR*, p. 47.
9  'Politics becomes permanent action and gives birth to permanent organisations,' Antonio Gramsci writes, by contrast, in one particularly instructive passage, 'precisely in so far as it identifies itself with economics. But it also distinct from it, which is why one may speak separately of economics and politics, and speak of "political passion" as of an immediate impulse to action which is born on the "permanent and organic" terrain of economic life but which transcends it' ('The Modern Prince', in *Selections from the Prison Notebooks*, pp. 139–40).
10  'Auguste Blanqui's Defence Speech at the "Trial of the Fifteen"', 12 January 1832, *BR*, p. 13.
11  'Philosophical and Political Fragments', n.d., *BR*, p. 148.
12  'Blanqui's Notes for his Defence at the "Gunpowder Trial"', October 1836, *BR*, p. 63.
13  'Posterity', writes Rancière, 'has preferred to retain the reassuring image of an unrepentant conspirator who was regrettably ignorant of the laws of history'

(Jacques Rancière, 'The Radical Gap: A Preface to Auguste Blanqui, *Eternity by the Stars*', *Radical Philosophy*, 185 (May–June 2014), p. 25).
14  Rancière, 'Radical Gap', p. 25.
15  'Philosophical and Political Fragments', 7 April 1860, *BR*, p. 167.
16  'Philosophical and Political Fragments', 7 April 1860, *BR*, p. 167.
17  Perry Anderson, *Spectrum: From Right to Left in the World of Ideas* (London: Verso, 2007), p. xvii.
18  Blanqui's own words on the Hébertists are worth remembering here: 'If it is good to avoid their faults and flaws, nevertheless their qualities should serve as an example to follow. They were heroic; the least we can do is not treat them as ignoble' ('Philosophical and Political Fragments', 1871, *BR*, pp. 159–60).
19  This became particularly clear in 2011–12, when various forms of occupations and encampments sprung up in various public spaces across Europe, North Africa and North America.
20  'Instructions for an Armed Uprising', 1868, *BR*, p. 206.

# Bibliography

## Works by Blanqui

### Unpublished manuscripts

Bibliothèque Nationale de France, Papiers philosophiques d'Auguste Blanqui, Nouvelles acquisitions françaises 9578–98.

### Newspapers

*Le Libérateur* (1834).
*Les Veillées du peuple* (1849).
*Candide* (1866).
*La Patrie en Danger* (1870).
*Ni Dieu, Ni Maitre* (1880–1).

### Books and pamphlets

*Aux Étudiants en médecine et en droit*, Paris: Fournier, 1830.
*Défense du citoyen L. A. Blanqui devant la Cour d'Assises*, Paris: Imprimerie Auguste Mie, 1832. [This text was also published in Société des Amis du Peuple, *Procès des Quinze*, Paris: Imprimerie de Auguste Mie, 1832.]
*Propagande démocratique*, Paris: Imprimerie de L. E. Herhran, 1835. [Co-authored with Louis-Ambroise Hadot-Desages.]
*Réponse du Citoyen Auguste Blanqui*, Paris: Imprimerie d'Ad. Blondeau, 1848.
*Parisiens !*, Paris: Blondeau, n.d. [1848] [Address signed 'Auguste Blanqui, donjon de Vincennes, 15 septembre 1848'.]
*Départ des prisonniers de Vincennes, leurs adieux au peuple. Les dernières paroles des citoyens Barbès, Raspail, Blanqui et Huber, adressées au président de la République Louis-Napoléon*, Paris: Galerie Richer, 1849.

*Histoire du Mont-Saint-Michel comme prison d'État, avec les correspondances inédites des citoyens Armand Barbès, Auguste Blanqui, Martin-Bernard, Flotte, Mathieu d'Epinal, Béraud, etc.*, edited by Fulgence Girard, Paris: P. Permain, 1849.

*Foi et science ou la sainte mixture du R. P. Gratry*, Brussels: D. Brismée, 1866. [Published under the pseudonym Suzamel.]

*La Patrie en Danger*, Paris: A. Chevalier, 1871.

'Introduction', in Gustave Tridon, *Les Hébertistes*, Brussels: Imprimerie de J.H Briand, 1871), pp. 1–11. [Published anonymously.]

*Un dernier mot*, Paris: Châtelain, 1871.

*L'Éternité par les astres*, Paris: Librairie Germer Baillière, 1872.

*L'Armée esclave et opprimée*, Paris: Imprimerie du Passage de l'Opéra, 1880.

## Posthumous publications

*Critique Sociale: 2 vols*, Paris: Félix Alcan, 1885.

'Lettre à Maillard', *Le Cri du Peuple*, 1, 2, 3 October 1885.

'Lettres Inédites d'Auguste Blanqui', *Les Lettres*, 7 (6 August 1906), pp. 445–518.

*Science et foi*, Conflans-Sainte-Honorine: L'Idée Libre, 1925.

*Ni Dieu, ni maître ! critique matérialiste*, Conflans-Sainte-Honorine: L'Idée Libre, 1925.

*Instructions pour une prise d'armes*, Le Militant Rouge, 11, 12; 1, 2 (November, December 1926; January, February 1927), pp. 242–5, 281–286, 15–17, 63–75. [Published across four editions.]

'Notes inédites de Blanqui sur Robespierre', edited by Albert Mathiez, in Mathiez, *Girondins et Montagnards*, Paris: Firmin-Didot, 1930, pp. 220–38.

*Ni Dieu ni Maître ! Les plus belles pensées athéistes et anticléricales d'Auguste Blanqui*, edited by Maurice Dommanget, Herblay: L'Idée Libre, 1954.

*Textes choisis*, edited by V. P. Volguine, Paris: Éditions Sociales, 1955.

*Lettres familières d'Auguste Blanqui et du docteur Louis Watteau*, edited by Maurice Paz, Marseille: Institut historique de Provence, 1976.

*Ecrits sur la Révolution: Œuvres complètes 1 textes politiques et lettres de prison*, edited by Arno Münster, Paris: La Galilée, 1977.

*Œuvres I: Des origines à la Révolution de 1848*, edited by Dominique Le Nuz, Nancy: Presses Universitaires de Nancy, 1993.

*Instructions pour une prise d'armes, L'Eternité par les astres et autres texts*, edited by Miguel Abensour and Valentin Pelosse, Paris: Sens & Tonka, 2000 [1973].

*L'Éternité par les astres*, preface Jacques Rancière, Paris: Les Impressions nouvelles, 2002.

*Instructions pour une prise d'armes*, Nantes: Ars Magna, 2006.

*Maintenant, il faut des armes*, edited by Dominique Le Nuz, Paris: La fabrique éditions, 2007.

*Le communisme, avenir de la société*, preface Roger Martelli, Paris: Le Passager Clandestin, 2008.

*Auguste Blanqui et sa famille: correspondance, 1807–1918*, edited by Gilles Feyel et Jean-Paul Lelu, Chartres: Société archéologique d'Eure-et-Loire, 2009.

'Eternity According to the Stars', translated by Matthew A. Anderson, *New Centennial Review*, 9:3 (Winter 2009), pp. 3–60.

*Instructions pour une prise d'armes*, preface Elsa Guillalot, Grenoble: Éditions cent pages, 2009.

*Ni Dieu, Ni Maître*, preface Maurice Dommanget, Brussels: Éditions Aden, 2009.

*Critique Sociale: Fragments et Notes*, preface Gérald Dittmar and Éric Dussert, Paris: Éditions Dittmar, 2012.

*Qui fait la soupe doit la manger suivi de Instructions pour une prise d'armes*, Paris: Éditions d'Ores et déjà, 2012.

*Auguste Blanqui face à ses juges*, Saint-Didier: Éditions l'Escalier, 2013.

*Eternity by the Stars*, translated by Frank Chouraqui, New York: Contra Mundum Press, 2013.

*Qui a du fer a du pain et autres textes*, Saint-Didier: Éditions l'Escalier, 2013.

*The Blanqui Reader*, edited by Peter Hallward and Philippe Le Goff, London: Verso, 2018.

# Works on Blanqui

## Biographies

Bernstein, Samuel, *Auguste Blanqui and the Art of Insurrection*, London: Lawrence and Wishart, 1971.

Dommanget, Maurice, *Auguste Blanqui: Des origines à la révolution de 1848*, Paris: Mouton, 1969.

Decaux, Alain, *Blanqui l'Insurgé*, Paris: Librairie Académique Perrin, 1976.

Dommanget, Maurice, *Auguste Blanqui à Belle-Île*, Paris: Librarie du Travail, 1935.

Dommanget, Maurice, *Blanqui, La Guerre de 1870–1871 et La Commune*, Paris: Éditions Domat-Montchrestien, 1947.

Dommanget, Maurice, *Un drame politique en 1848: Blanqui et le document Taschereau*, Paris: Les Deux Sirènes, 1948.

Dommanget, Maurice, *Blanqui et l'opposition révolutionnaire à la fin du Second Empire*, Paris: Armand Colin, 1960.

Dommanget, Maurice, *Blanqui*, Paris: EDI, 1970.

Dommanget, Maurice, *Auguste Blanqui au début de la III$^{ème}$ République*, Paris: Mouton, 1971.

Dommanget, Maurice, *Auguste Blanqui et la révolution de 1848*, Paris: Mouton, 1972.

Geffroy, Gustave, *L'Enfermé*, Paris: Bibliothèque Charpentier, 1919.

Greene, Doug Enaa, *Communist Insurgent: Blanqui's Politics of Revolution*, Chicago, IL: Haymarket, 2017.

Paz, Maurice, *Un révolutionnaire professionel, Auguste Blanqui*, Paris: Fayard, 1984.

Stewart, Neil, *Blanqui*, London: Gollancz, 1939.

## Other studies

Abensour, Miguel, *Les Passages Blanqui: Walter Benjamin entre mélancolie et révolution*, Paris: Sens & Tonka, 2013. [First published as 'W. Benjamin entre mélancolie et révolution. Passages Blanqui', in *Walter Benjamin et Paris*, edited by Heinz Wismann, Paris: Editions du Cerf, 1986, pp. 219–48.]

Abensour, Miguel, and Valentin Pelosse, *Libérer l'Enfermé*, Paris: Sens & Tonka, 2014. [First published as 'Libérer l'Enfermé (en guise de postface)', in *Instructions pour une prise d'armes, L'Eternité par les astres et autres texts*, edited by Miguel Abensour and Valentin Pelosse, Paris: Editions de la Tête de Feuille, 1973, pp. 201–30.]

Bensaïd, Daniel, and Michael Löwy, 'Auguste Blanqui, Heretical Communist', *Radical Philosophy*, 185 (May–June 2014), pp. 26–35.

Castille, Hippolyte, *L.A. Blanqui*, Paris: F. Sartorius, 1857.

Chouraqui, Frank, 'At the Crossroads of History: Blanqui at the Castle of the Bull', in *Eternity by the Stars*, translated by Frank Chouraqui, New York: Contra Mundum Press, 2013, pp. 1–62.

Costa, Charles da, *Les Blanquistes*, Paris: Marcel Rivière, 1912.

Dommanget, Maurice, *Les Idées politiques et sociales d'Auguste Blanqui*, Paris: Marcel Rivière, 1957.

Hallward, Peter, 'Blanqui's Bifurcations', *Radical Philosophy*, 185 (May–June 2014), pp. 36–44.

Hallward, Peter, 'Preface: Blanqui Our Contemporary?', in *The Blanqui Reader*, edited by Peter Hallward and Philippe Le Goff, London: Verso, 2018, pp. xvii–xxiv.

Hutton, Patrick H., *The Cult of the Revolutionary Tradition: The Blanquists in French Politics, 1864–1893*, Berkeley: University of California Press, 1981.

Johnstone, Monty, 'Marx, Blanqui and Majority Rule', in *Socialist Register 1983*, edited by Ralph Miliband and John Saville, London: Merlin, 1983, pp. 296–318.

Le Goff, Philippe, 'Introduction', in *The Blanqui Reader*, edited by Peter Hallward and Philippe Le Goff, London: Verso, 2018, pp. xxv–xxxv.

Le Nuz, Dominique, 'Introduction', in *Maintenant, il faut des armes*, edited by Dominique Le Nuz, Paris: La fabrique éditions, 2007, pp. 29–44.

Malon, Benoît, 'Blanqui socialiste', *Revue Socialiste*, 50 (February 1889), pp. 288–301.

Marty, André, *80e anniversaire de la Commune de Paris: Quelques aspects de l'activité de Blanqui*, Paris: Société des Amis de Blanqui, 1951.

Marty, André, *Auguste Blanqui, un révolutionnaire des temps d'orage*, Paris: Éditions du Centenaire de la Commune de Paris, 1971.

Mason, Edward S., 'Blanqui and Communism', *Political Science Quarterly*, 44:4 (December 1929), pp. 498–527.

Mauclair, Camille, 'Blanqui et l'énergie présente', *Mercure de France*, 23:93 (September 1897), pp. 440–9.

Mirecourt, Eugène de, *Blanqui*, Paris: Chez L'Auteur, 1857.

Molinier, Sylvain, *Blanqui*, Paris: Presses Universitaires de France, 1948.

Münster, Arno, 'Introduction', in *Ecrits sur la Révolution: Œuvres complètes 1 textes politiques et lettres de prison*, edited by Arno Münster, Paris: La Galilée, 1977, pp. 9–58.

Paz, Maurice, 'Clemenceau, Blanqui's Heir: An Unpublished Letter from Blanqui to Clemenceau Dated 18 March 1879', *Historical Journal*, 16:3 (1973), pp. 604–15. [See also D. R. Watson, 'Clemenceau and Blanqui: A Reply to M. Paz', *Historical Journal*, 21:2 (1978), pp. 387–97.]

Pillon, F., 'Le socialisme d'Auguste Blanqui', *La Critique Philosophique*, 4 (1888), pp. 61–75, 126–37.

Pompery, Edouard de, *Blanquisme et opportunisme*, Paris: Auguste Ghio, 1879.

Quelques agents du Parti imaginaire, 'Préface: A un ami', in *Maintenant, il faut des armes*, edited by Dominique Le Nuz, Paris: La fabrique éditions, 2007, pp. 9–28.

Rancière, Jacques, 'The Radical Gap: A Preface to Auguste Blanqui, *Eternity by the Stars*', *Radical Philosophy*, 185 (May–June 2014), pp. 19–25.

Silvestre, Théophile, *Blanqui, étude historique*, Paris: Librairie Poulet-Malassis, 1862.

Simon, François, *Louis-Auguste Blanqui en Anjou. Essai de vulgarisation de l'histoire locale*, Angers: Coopérative Imprimerie Angevine, 1939.

Société d'histoire de la révolution de 1848 et des révolutions du XIXe siècle, *Blanqui et les blanquistes*, Paris: SEDES, 1986.

Spitzer, Alan B., *The Revolutionary Theories of Louis Auguste Blanqui*, New York: Columbia University Press, 1957.

Vigier, Philippe, 'Préface', in *Œuvres I: Des origines à la Révolution de 1848*, edited by Dominique Le Nuz, Nancy: Presses Universitaires de Nancy, 1993, pp. 9–19.

Volguine, V. P., 'Les idées politiques et sociales de Blanqui', in *Textes choisis*, edited by V. P. Volguine, Paris: Éditions Sociales, 1955, pp. 7–68.

Wassermann, Suzanne, *Les Clubs de Barbès et de Blanqui en 1848*, Genève: Mégariotis Reprints, 1978.

Zévaès, Alexandre, *Auguste Blanqui, patriote et socialiste français*, Paris: M. Rivière, 1920.

## Other works consulted

Anderson, Jon Lee, *Che Guevara: A Revolutionary Life*, London: Bantam, 2010.

Anderson, Perry, *Considerations on Western Marxism*, London: New Left Books, 1976.

Anderson, Perry, *Spectrum: From Right to Left in the World of Ideas*, London: Verso, 2007.

Badiou, Alain, *Metapolitics*, translated by Jason Barker, London: Verso, 2005.

Badiou, Alain, *The Meaning of Sarkozy*, translated by David Fernbach, London: Verso, 2008.

Badiou, Alain, 'The Idea of Communism', in *The Idea of Communism*, edited by Costas Douzinas and Slavoj Žižek, London: Verso, 2010, pp. 1–14.

Benjamin, Walter, *The Arcades Project*, edited by Rolf Tiedemann, translated by Howard Eiland and Kevin McLaughlin, Cambridge, MA: Harvard University Press, 1999.

Benjamin, Walter, *Illuminations*, edited by Hannah Arendt, translated by Harry Zorn, London: Pimlico, 1999.

Bensaïd, Daniel, '"Leaps! Leaps! Leaps!"', in *Lenin Reloaded: Towards a Politics of Truth*, edited by Sebastian Budgen, Stathis Kouvelakis and Slavoj Žižek, Durham, NC: Duke University Press, 2007, pp. 148–63.

Bensaïd, Daniel, *Marx for Our Times*, London: Verso, 2009.

Boétie, Étienne de la, *Discours da la servitude volontaire*, Paris: Librio, 2013.

Bouchet, Thomas, Vincent Bourdeau, et al. (eds), *Quand les socialistes inventaient l'avenir: Presse, théories et experiences, 1825–1860*, Paris: Éditions La Découverte, 2015.

Buonarroti, Philippe, *Conspiration pour l'Égalité dite de Babeuf*, edited by Jean-Marc Schiappa et al., Paris: Éditions la ville brûle, 2014.

Castro, Fidel, *Fidel and Religion: Fidel Castro in Conversation with Frei Betto on Marxism and Liberation Theology*, Melbourne: Ocean Press, 2006.

Castro, Fidel, *Fidel Castro Reader*, edited by David Deutschmann and Deborah Shnookal, Melbourne: Ocean Press, 2007.

Chevalier, Louis, *Classes laborieuses et classes dangereuses*, Paris: Éditions Perrin, 2007.

Collingham, H. A. C., *The July Monarchy: A Political History of France 1830–1848*, London: Longman, 1988.

Debray, Régis, *Revolution in the Revolution?*, translated by Bobbye Ortiz, Harmondsworth: Penguin, 1968.

Derfler, Leslie, *Paul Lafargue and the Founding of French Marxism, 1842–1882*, Cambridge, MA: Harvard University Press, 1991.

Draper, Hal, *The 'Dictatorship of the Proletariat' from Marx to Lenin*, New York: Monthly Review Press, 1987.

Engels, Frederick, 'The Programme of the Blanquist Fugitives from the Paris Commune', 26 June 1874, https://www.marxists.org/archive/marx/works/1874/06/26.htm (accessed 9 April 2015).

Engels, Frederick, 'Introduction', in Karl Marx, *The Class Struggles in France 1848 to 1850*, Moscow: Progress, 1972, pp. 5–26.

Fanon, Frantz, *The Wretched of the Earth*, translated by Constance Farrington, London: Penguin Books, 1969.

Galtung, Johan, 'Violence, Peace and Peace Research', *Journal of Peace Research*, 6:3 (1969), pp. 167–91.

García Luis, Julio (ed.), *Cuban Revolution Reader*, Melbourne: Ocean Press, 2008.

Girardin, Saint-Marc, *Souvenirs et réflexions politiques d'un journalise*, Paris: Michel-Lévy frères, 1859.

Gramsci, Antonio, *Selections from the Prison Notebooks*, edited and translated by Quintin Hoare and Geoffrey Nowel Smith, London: Lawrence and Wishart, 1971.

Guevara, Ernesto Che, *Che Guevara Reader: Writings on Politics and Revolution*, edited by David Deutschmann, Melbourne: Ocean Press, 2004.

Hallward, Peter, 'The Will of the People: Notes towards a Dialectical Voluntarism', *Radical Philosophy*, 155 (May–June 2009), pp. 17–29.

Hallward, Peter, 'Communism of the Intellect, Communism of the Will', in *The Idea of Communism*, edited by Costas Douzinas and Slavoj Žižek, London: Verso, 2010, pp. 111–30.

Hallward, Peter, 'Defiance or Emancipation?', *Radical Philosophy*, 183 (January–February 2014), pp. 21–32.

Hallward, Peter, 'Willing and Able: Political Will and Self-determination', Lecture given at the American University in Paris, 10 April 2015.

Hardt, Michael, 'Introduction: Thomas Jefferson, or, The Transition of Democracy', in Thomas Jefferson, *The Declaration of Independence*, edited by Michael Hardt, London: Verso, 2007, pp. vii–xxv.

Hardt, Michael, 'The Common in Communism', in *The Idea of Communism*, edited by Costas Douzinas and Slavoj Žižek, London: Verso, 2010, pp. 131–44.

Harsin, Jill, *Barricades: The War on the Streets of Revolutionary Paris, 1830–1848*, Basingstoke: Palgrave, 2002.

Hazan, Eric, *The Invention of Paris*, London: Verso, 2011.

Hazan, Eric, *Paris Sous Tension*, Paris: La Fabrique éditions, 2011.

Hegel, G. W. F., *The Philosophy of History*, Mineola, New York: Dover, 1956.

Heine, Heinrich, *French Affairs: Letters from Paris*, Volume 2, translated by Charles Godfrey Leland, New York: United States Book, 1893.

Hobsbawm, Eric, *How to Change the World: Tales of Marx and Marxism*, London: Abacus, 2012.

Hobsbawm, Eric, 'Introduction', in Karl Marx and Frederick Engels, *The Communist Manifesto: A Modern Edition*, London: Verso, 2012, pp. 1–28.

Hobsbawm, Eric, *Primitive Rebels: Studies in Archaic Forms of Social Movement in the Nineteenth and Twentieth Centuries*, London: Abacus, 2017.

Hugo, Victor, *Œuvres complètes de Victor Hugo. Vol. 25: Choses Vues I*, Paris: Ollendorff, 1913.

Hugo, Victor, *The Memoirs of Victor Hugo*, translated by John W. Harding, London: William Heinemann, 1899.

Hunt, Richard, *The Political Ideas of Marx and Engels. Vol. 1: Marxism and Totalitarian Democracy, 1818–1850*, London: Macmillan, 1975.

Laclau, Ernesto, and Chantal Mouffe, *Hegemony and Socialist Strategy: Towards a Radical Democratic Politics*, London: Verso, 1985.

Laclau, Ernesto, *On Populist Reason*, London: Verso, 2005.

Lenin, V. I., 'What Is to Be Done?', March 1902, in *Collected Works*, Volume 5, Moscow: Progress, 1960, pp. 347–529.

Lenin, V. I., 'The Dual Power', April 1917, in *Collected Works*, Volume 24, Moscow: Progress, 1974, pp. 38–41.

Lenin, V. I., 'The State and Revolution', August-September 1917, in *Collected Works*, Volume 25, Moscow: Progress, 1974, pp. 385–498.

Löwy, Michael, *Fire Alarm: Reading Walter Benjamin's 'On the Concept of History'*, translated by Chris Turner, London: Verso, 2005.
Löwy, Michael, *The Theory of Revolution in the Young Marx*, Chicago, IL: Haymarket Books, 2005.
Luxemburg, Rosa, 'Blanquism and Social Democracy', June 1906, https://www.marxists.org/archive/luxemburg/1906/06/blanquism.html (accessed 9 April 2015).
Machiavelli, Niccolò, *The Prince*, translated by Russell Price, Cambridge: Cambridge University Press, 1988.
Machiavelli, Niccolò, *The Prince*, translated by George Bull, London: Penguin, 2003.
Machiavelli, Niccolò, *The Prince*, translated by Peter Bondanella, Oxford: Oxford University Press, 2005.
Marx, Karl, *The Civil War in France*, Moscow: Foreign Languages Publishing House, n.d..
Marx, Karl, *The Class Struggles in France 1848 to 1850*, Moscow: Progress, 1972.
Marx, Karl, *Early Writings*, translated by Rodney Livingstone and Gregor Benton London: Penguin, 1975.
Marx, Karl, *Capital*, Volume 1, translated by Ben Fowkes, London: Penguin, 1976.
Marx, Karl, *The Eighteenth Brumaire of Louis Bonaparte*, Moscow: Progress, 1977.
Marx, Karl, and Frederick Engels, *The Holy Family, or Critique of Critical Critique*, translated by R. Dixon, Moscow: Foreign Languages Publishing House, 1956.
Marx, Karl, and Frederick Engels, 'Introduction to the Leaflet of L.A. Blanqui's Toast Sent to the Refugee Committee', 1851, in *Marx and Engels Collected Works*, Volume 10, London: Lawrence and Wishart, 1978, p. 537.
Marx, Karl, and Frederick Engels, *The Communist Manifesto: A Modern Edition*, London: Verso, 2012.
McPhee, Peter, *Robespierre: A Revolutionary Life*, New Haven, CT: Yale University Press, 2012.
Pilbeam, Pamela, *The 1830 Revolution in France*, London: Macmillan, 1991.
Pinkney, David, *The French Revolution of 1830*, Princeton, NJ: Princeton University Press, 1972.
Rancière, Jacques, *The Ignorant Schoolmaster: Five Lessons in Intellectual Emancipation*, translated by Kristin Ross, Stanford, CA: Stanford University Press, 1991.
Rancière, Jacques, *Disagreement: Politics and Philosophy*, translated by Julie Rose, Minneapolis: University of Minnesota Press, 1999.
Rancière, Jacques, *Aux bords du politique*, Paris: Gallimard, 2004.

Rancière, Jacques, 'Democracies against Democracy: An Interview with Eric Hazan', in *Democracy in What State?*, translated by William McCuaig, New York: Columbia University Press, 2010, pp. 76–81.

Rose, R. B., *Gracchus Babeuf: The First Revolutionary Communist*, Stanford, CA: Stanford University Press, 1978.

Ross, Kristin, 'Democracy for Sale', in *Democracy in What State?*, New York: Columbia University Press, 2010, pp. 82–99.

Rousseau, Jean-Jacques, *Emile, or On Education*, translated by Allan Bloom, London: Penguin, 1991.

Rousseau, Jean-Jacques, *The Social Contract*, translated by Christopher Betts, Oxford: Oxford University Press, 2008.

Rousseau, Jean-Jacques, *Discourse on the Origin of Inequality*, edited by Patrick Coleman, translated by Franklin Philip, Oxford: Oxford University Press, 2009.

Saint-Simon, Henri Comte de, *The Political Thought of Saint-Simon*, edited by Ghita Ionescu, Oxford: Oxford University Press, 1976.

Sand, George, *Letters of George Sand*, Volume 2, translated by Raphaël Ledos de Beaufort, New York: Cosimo, 2009.

Spitzer, Alan B., *Old Hatreds and Young Hopes: The French Carbonari against the Bourbon Restoration*, Cambridge, MA: Harvard University Press, 1971.

Toqueville, Alexis de, *Recollections: The French Revolution of 1848*, edited by J. P. Mayer and A. P. Kerr, translated by George Lawrence, New Brunswick: Transaction, 1987.

Tridon, Gustave, *Les Hébertistes*, Brussels: Imprimerie de J. H. Briand, 1871.

Trotsky, Leon, *History of the Russian Revolution*, translated by Max Eastman, London: Penguin, 2017.

# Index

action *see* collective action; political action; voluntary action
actor(s) 47, 83–112
 collective 19, 90, 98, 100, 103, 115, 144, 154, 186–7, 190–1, 197 n.63
 conscious and voluntary 33
 versus an instrument 32
 political (*see* political actors)
 versus subject 90
adventurism 1, 12, 13, 20, 21, 132, 154
agency 22, 52, 95, 154, 190–1
 collective 33, 41
 human 14, 116, 147, 159, 163, 180
 political 19, 83, 87, 88, 143, 186, 190
Anderson, Perry 191, 201–2 n.98
aristocracy 37, 50, 57, 64, 67, 72, 86, 87, 89, 92, 97–8, 107, 158, 188, 201 n.88, 222 n.35
association 17–19, 32, 74, 77, 78, 216 n.65
 collective 120–1, 151
 communism and enlightenment 34–7, 138–9, 151
 political 120, 179
 social 152, 179
 voluntary act of 97, 113, 143–4
'astronomical hypothesis' 167–71, 172, 182
atheism 37, 201 n.88

Babeuf, Gracchus 2, 3, 4, 61
Badiou, Alain 3, 79, 80, 215 n.34
Ballanche, Pierre-Simon 104
barbarism 58, 67, 151, 161, 179, 181, 182
Belle-Île (island) 1, 8, 164, 176
Benjamin, Walter 11, 13, 14, 21, 81, 147, 153, 167–8, 175–9, 189, 232 n.60
Bernstein, Samuel 92, 95, 193 n.13, 217 n.87, 236 n.127
Blanc, Louis 2, 8, 14, 75
Blanqui, Louis-Auguste
 an authoritarian elitist 45–6
 birth of 6

critics of 217 n.72, 219 n.116
death of 10
duty, conception of 124–7
education of 6
engagement–imprisonment–liberation 7–10
failure of 1, 7, 9, 12, 16
illness of 7, 8, 10
impact of 1830 revolution on 6–7
imprisonment 1, 7–8, 10, 164, 167–8, 176
a neo-Jacobin thinker 2–3, 13, 14
opinions about 10–13
a political revolutionist 195 n.33
popular unity concept 101
an orator 1, 10
in revolutionary politics, position of 2–6
rise to prominence 1–2, 7
supporters/followers 8, 9, 69, 126, 180
a writer 2, 9, 10, 14 (*see also* Blanqui's writings)
Blanqui's political theory 2, 14–15, 22, 106, 114, 123, 139, 157, 184–7
Blanqui's politics 2, 20, 51, 144, 162, 178, 189
 basic principles of 49
 Benjamin's claims on 168
 conflictual nature of 55–6, 100
 divisive logic of 102
 limitations/shortcomings of 21, 107, 114
Blanqui's project 2, 3, 21, 31, 88, 107, 113, 160
 ambiguities in 28
 analysis of 15–20
 foundation of 26, 184
 humanism of 65
 philosophy, role in 148–9, 155, 184, 229 n.4, 237 n.129
 politics of principles 56, 76, 81
 primacy of Paris 137
 shortcomings/limitations of 20, 26–7, 154

strengths of 27, 154
structural tensions within 40–1
Blanqui's writings 45, 79, 93, 107, 147, 160, 177, 190, 196 n.50
   accusation of apostasy in 128
   on conscious volition 30–1 (*see also* conscious volition)
   dichotomous antagonism in 46
   moral tenor to 28
   political (non-)subjectivity in 106
   on property 61 (*see also* property)
   on revolutionary transition 136, 139
   Rousseau, reference in 18
   style of 38–9
   on the universe 169–71 (*see also* 'astronomical hypothesis')
   on violence 65–6
'Blanquism' 1, 2, 12, 13, 185, 195 n.36
'blind multitude' 51, 141, 143
Bonaparte, Louis-Napoleon 8, 9, 11, 40, 41, 49, 71, 101, 106, 161, 164
Bourbon Restoration 6, 210 n.85
bourgeoisie 10, 12, 16, 48, 81, 87, 101, 102, 217–18 n.72
   commercial 62
   definition of 93–4
   educated 44
   exploitation of people 43, 62–5, 92
   intellectuals 46–7
   struggle of the masses against the 66–70, 90
   usurpers 117–18
brain/'brain', the 130
   cerebral transformation 28, 152
   education and the 23, 114
   of France 48 (*see also* June Days revolt (1848))
   and human progress 149–50
   intelligence as product of 184 (*see also* intelligence)
   and thought 27–8, 129, 198 n.25
   unity within multiplicity 32
   and will 29, 32
Britain 87, 88
Buonarroti, Philippe 3–4, 44, 128

Cabet, Etienne 15, 47, 74, 121
*Candide* (newspaper) 38
canuts (silk weavers) revolt 35, 68, 85
capitalism 13, 28, 46, 63, 92, 98, 156, 159–60, 188
Carbonari, the 3, 6, 44
Castille, Hippolyte 11
Castro, Fidel 8, 126, 129, 161
Charles X 3, 43, 117, 153, 230 n.25
church/Church, the 31, 34, 40, 51, 64
civil war 47, 57–70, 153
   Blanqui's concept of 56, 65
   property and 57–61
   between rich and poor 61–2, 66, 67, 71, 111
   revolution and repression 65–70
   the state and 61–5
*Civil War in France, The* 63, 206 n.30, 207 n.44, 212–13 n.142
class cooperation 69, 71
class struggle 12, 13, 93–5, 102, 154
*Class Struggles in France* 10
Clemenceau, Georges 101
clerical teaching 35, 51
collective action 15, 18–20, 39, 49, 50, 95, 119, 123, 144, 152, 154, 190, 192, 232 n.51
collective will 13, 52, 96, 113–14, 115, 117, 118, 119, 139, 144
commitment 20, 53, 81
   principled 8, 21, 55, 56, 84, 112
communism 10–11, 12, 46, 78, 80, 121, 128–9, 132–3, 144, 159, 198–9 n.37
   association and enlightenment 34–7, 138–9, 151
   and enlightenment 40, 133, 139, 152
   for equality 120, 132
   barriers to 34
   revolutionary 11, 60
'Communism, the Future of Society' 64, 78, 133, 151, 193 n.7, 197 n.60, 201 nn.85–7, 233 n.80
*Communist Manifesto* 38, 63, 88, 98, 157, 159–60, 207 n.44, 217 n.72
Comte, Auguste 14, 38, 162, 166
conflict 47, 55–82
   Blanqui's concept of 55–6, 60
   civil war 57–70 (*see also* civil war)
   class 71, 153–4

between enlightenment and
    ignorance 36–7
political 69, 70, 94
between privilege and equality 35
in property matters 57–61 (*see also*
    property)
social 22, 48, 64, 73, 75, 87, 158
of wills 114–16
conscious volition 5, 120, 126, 127,
    133, 183–4
Blanqui's notion of 20, 114, 139,
    141, 143–4
capacity for 30–1, 228 n.159
collective 33, 113, 154
exercise of 31–2, 150, 184
gap between knowledge and
    ignorance 20
individual 32–3
meaning of 14–15
political subjectivation and 103, 106–7
voluntarism as 23 (*see also* voluntarism)
consciousness
class 28
collective 26, 32, 49
constitutive and primary 4
enlightened 20, 21, 30, 31, 45, 48, 49
human 14–15, 147, 149–50
ideas and 26, 132–3
intellectual 23, 52
intelligence and 21–2, 44–5, 139, 149,
    151, 154
political 21, 28, 36, 37, 39, 52
popular 39, 51, 117, 185
self- 150, 151
social 26
working-class 156–7
conspiracy 155, 156, 157, 185, 195 n.36
    *see also* conspiratorial actions;
    conspiratorial politics
conspiratorial actions 1, 7, 8, 12, 13, 185
conspiratorial politics 20, 44, 45, 155–6
*Contribution to the Critique of Political
    Economy, A* 26
counter-revolution 40, 48–9, 66, 71, 101,
    123, 124, 135, 137, 191, 234 n.83
coups
August 1870 1, 44, 155
May 1839 1, 7, 44
December 1851 11, 41, 164

Courier, Paul-Louis 18, 62
*Critique Sociale* 9, 140

Debray, Régis 161
deception/deceit 77, 126
    and duplicity 4
    and manipulation 37, 71, 124, 132, 150
    and oppression 127
    of people 35, 50, 51
    property seizure by 57, 59
déclassés 5, 44
'Defence Speech' 61, 62, 67, 73–4, 84, 85–6,
    92–4, 99, 108, 153, 157–8, 179
democracy 45, 63, 78–80, 134–9, 188
democrats 92, 101, 102, 135
despotism 13, 63, 91, 164, 207 n.44, 208
    n.57, 215 n.43
determinism 147, 154
    anti- 21, 161
    economic 20
    historical 14, 27, 152, 162, 163, 164
    positivist 164, 165–6
devotion 12, 31, 41, 53, 114, 124–5, 127–8,
    144, 159, 180, 188, 220 n.4
*Discourse on Political Economy* 142, 227–8
    nn.152–3
dictatorship
    Parisian 45, 136, 137–8, 185
    of the proletariat 10, 135, 138–9
domination 19, 32, 70, 89, 112
    and exploitation 4, 79, 90, 184, 190
    of labour by capital 116
    mis-education and 34–5, 64–5
    religious 5
    social 132
    structural 60
Dommanget, Maurice 13, 63, 193 n.13, 194
    n.19, 236 n.128, 236–7 n.129
dualism 4–5, 24–5, 27, 172
duty 46, 124–7

education 20, 39, 136
    and the brain 23, 114
    emancipatory 34–7
    enlightened 34, 125–6
    equality of 34, 104, 125–6
    and ideas 34
    individual 33
    and intelligence 33 (*see also* intelligence)

mass 5, 9
mis- 34, 41, 45, 51, 64, 126, 140, 184
political 36, 142
politics of (mis) 33–42
popular (*see* popular education)
press as means of 37–9
for progress 5, 33–4, 150
public/of the public 140, 201 n.85, 227–8 n.152
and social change 33, 34
elections 39–40, 66
elite 47, 62, 127
enlightened 45, 105, 144, 184
intellectual 38, 125
non- 50, 141
revolutionary 44, 46, 143, 216 n.59
elitism 52, 141, 195 n.34
anti-democratic 12
authoritarian 1, 45–6
vanguardist 139
emancipation 120, 121, 152
collective 140, 190
education and 34–7
egalitarian 8
and enlightenment 34, 35
intellectual 21, 35, 41, 51
of the masses by workers 49, 228 n.159
oppression and 5, 49
self- 20, 52, 53
social 38, 41, 74, 96, 107, 112
of society 34, 133, 222 n.35
universal 88
of the workers 76
empowerment 43, 88, 120, 143, 183
active 100, 187, 227 n.142
collective 6, 105
direct 18
dis- 76, 90, 123, 154, 187, 191
material 112
political 96
popular (*see* popular empowerment)
proletariat 100, 187
Engels, Friedrich 12, 46, 38, 86, 88, 121, 153, 161, 233 n.82
enlightened consciousness 20, 21, 30, 31, 45, 48, 49, 114, 136–7, 173, 184
enlightened instruction 23, 28, 34, 52, 125, 127, 139, 184–5
enlightened intelligence 21, 114, 139, 184–5

enlightened thought 28, 45, 51, 52, 77, 88, 105, 113, 114, 125, 143, 183, 200 n.63, 228 n.159
enlightenment
association and communism 34–7, 138–9, 151
communism and 40, 133, 139, 152
emancipation and 34, 35
and ignorance 34–7, 56, 193 n.7
individual 23, 32–3
intellectual 125
lack of 136
mass 39, 132–3
popular 5, 38, 51, 105, 107, 151
public 38, 50
and revolution 39–42
stifling of 35, 51
universal/universality of 36, 37, 40, 104, 132, 133, 139
and will 30
enslavement 17, 31, 41, 48–9, 51, 58, 63, 68, 79, 90, 101, 162, 184 *see also* servitude
equality 2, 5, 18, 28, 40, 56, 71, 72, 157–61 *see also* inequality
education for 34, 104, 125–6
and freedom 78–82
of intelligence 104–5
and justice 4, 34, 76–8, 179–80, 191
movement for 47
principle of 74, 75, 159
social 3, 187
universal 84
*Eternity by the Stars* 10, 21, 24, 147–8, 168–9, 172, 174, 175–8, 180–2, 187, 236–7 n.129
Eudes, Emile 9
Europe 1, 8, 46, 87–8, 123, 150, 154, 239 n.19
exclusion 84, 86, 97, 103, 107, 108, 111, 144, 164, 179, 186, 187, 192
exploitation
by the bourgeoisie 43, 62–5, 92
capitalist 98, 118
domination and 4, 79, 90, 184, 190
ignorance and 5
and inequality 59, 111, 132, 208 n.64
of the masses 17, 35–6, 46, 57–8, 62–5, 166

Fanon, Frantz 13, 89, 161, 187
fatalism 147, 162–5, 171–4, 190, 231 n.40
Ferry, Jules 72–3
first principles 53, 56, 70, 72, 76–82
Fourier, Charles 15, 24, 47, 74, 121, 149
France 1, 9, 13, 45, 48, 63, 71, 74, 75, 76 *see also* Paris
   Brittany 8, 10
   Château de Taureau prison 10, 168
   groupings in 3, 153–4
   massacre in Rouen 66
   Mont Saint-Michel prison 7, 176
   Paris as the political vanguard of 46–7
   people as true representative of 87–9 (*see also* people, the)
   Puget-Théniers 6
   slavery in 58 (*see also* enslavement; servitude)
freedom 9, 11, 15
   collective realization of 5, 19, 47, 150
   democracy with 78–80
   equality and 78–82
   of people 45, 47, 56, 58–9
   of press 37–9, 106
   Rousseau's views on 30–1, 113, 130
   universal 74
   volition and 30–1, 119, 120
French Revolution 2–4, 13, 47, 66, 67, 153, 166, 205 n.4, 219 n.118
Franco-Prussian War 9, 69

Galtung, Johan 65, 208 n.51, 219 n.113
Garibaldi, Giuseppe 11
Geffroy, Gustave 7–8, 175, 185, 196 n.50, 236 n.126
general will 17, 19, 51–2, 113, 115, 120, 141–3, 196 n.58, 221 n.20, 222 n.35, 227 n.152
*German Ideology, The* 86
Girardin, Saint-Marc 85
Gramsci, Antonio 13, 15, 183, 196 n.43, 238 n.9
*Guerrilla Warfare* 38, 232 n.53
Guevara, Che 8, 13, 29, 33, 38, 129, 161, 180, 187, 232 n.53

Hallward, Peter 49, 118, 121, 141, 176, 180, 203–4 n.139, 215 n.37, 220 n.9, 234 n.93, 235 n.118

Hardt, Michael 81, 134–6, 138, 185, 212 n.140, 226 n.119, 226 n.135
Haussmann, Baron 49
Hazan, Eric 69–70, 81
Heine, Heinrich 11
historical change 27, 147–51, 154, 160, 182, 232 n.51
historical necessity 5, 19, 21, 24, 152, 162, 167, 187, 189
history 147–82
   'astronomical hypothesis' 167–8, 172, 182
   equality or catastrophe 157–61
   eternity, meaning of 175–7
   fatalism 147, 162–5, 171–4
   finite and the infinite 168–71
   historical materialism 153–7, 178
   human (*see* human history)
   philosophical primacy 148–52
   poverty of positivism 161–2
   and progress 147, 149–52, 159–61, 164, 168, 178–82
   tradition of the oppressed 165–7
Hobsbawm, Eric 159–60, 182, 232 n.51
Hugo, Victor 11–12
human action 83, 129–30, 159, 160, 182
human history 19, 38, 162–3, 166, 177, 182, 183
   contingency of 181, 189
   fatalism and 163
   human agency, role in 14, 159–60
   philosophical primacy and 148, 149
   principle of property 58 (*see also* property)
   volition and 154, 172–3 (*see also* volition)
human realm 24–5, 30, 115
humanity 51, 57, 58, 67, 77, 198 n.25, 199 n.40, 200 n.67, 226 n.135, 232 n.60
   as agent of change 149
   choice between 'socialism or barbarism' 161, 182
   collective 27–8, 31, 110
   definition 25, 26, 28
   free volition as characteristic of 130–1
   morality and 125–6
   printing press as benefit to 38 (*see also* newspapers; press)
   progress and 178–9, 233 n.80 (*see also* progress, human)

realization through voluntary action 32
social arrangements of 148, 149, 152, 162, 182, 189
transformation of 133–4
and the universe 171–3, 176, 177
Hutton, Patrick 39

idealism 26, 156
idea(s) 4, 47, 72, 75, 96, 126–7, 149
communicability of 38
and consciousness 26, 132–3
education and 34
intelligence and 51, 60, 137, 147, 182
making of mankind 25–6
revolutionary 8, 11
social relations, basis of 60
ignorance 20, 31, 68, 76, 77, 86–7, 88, 105, 126, 131, 137
causative factors of 34–5, 45, 50–1
credulous 52
enlightenment and 34–7, 56, 193 n.7
and exploitation 5
and oppression 40, 41
popular 5, 36, 133
religion as a cause for 45, 50–1, 140
voluntarist 189
Imperial regime 9, 101
impoverishment 34, 41, 64, 76, 85, 91, 108, 111
individualism 78, 79–80, 120, 159, 222 n.39
inequality 17, 18, 56, 71, 101, 110–11, 158, 193 n.7
cerebral 37
exploitation and 59, 111, 132, 208 n.64
and injustice 60, 61, 65, 70, 104, 111, 128, 160, 209 n.68
intellectual 105
material 108
political 108
in property matters 59–62, 65, 68
social 78, 102
injustice 56, 69, 70, 179
economic 5
inequality and 60, 61, 65, 70, 104, 111, 128, 160, 209 n.68
law and 74
and oppression 37, 67, 131, 165
resistance to 118
social 165, 166, 180

*Instructions for an Armed Uprising* 9, 16, 47, 87, 124, 175, 177, 223 n.75, 224 n.78
insurrections 42, 66–7, 122, 195 n.36, 203–4 n.139, 209 n.64 *see also* Revolutions
1792 (August) 3, 47
1793 (May) 3, 47
1827 (November) 1
1830 (July) 47, 82, 89–91
1832 (June) 36
1834 (April) 36, 66
1839 (May) 7, 36
1848 (February) 47
1870
August 9
October 1, 10
intellectuals 5, 46, 47, 143, 216 n.59
intelligence 23–53, 60
Blanqui's dualism 24–5 (*see also* dualism)
and consciousness 21–2, 44–5, 139, 149, 151, 154
education and 33, 34–7 (*see also* education)
enlightened 21, 114, 139, 184–5
equality of 104–5
and ideas 51, 60, 137, 147, 182
individual and the collective 32–3
human 28, 33, 51, 149, 151, 184
mankind is thought 25–7
materialism, transformation, volition 27–32
politically decisive 23, 107
politics of (mis)education 33–42
revolution of the intellect 24–33
superior 52, 88, 141
*Internationale, The* 89

Jacobins 3, 13, 18, 47, 94–5, 187, 217 n.73
Jacotot, Joseph 104
Jefferson, Thomas 134, 135–6, 144–5, 185, 226 n.119, 226 n.135
*Journal des Débats* 85, 86
July Monarchy 6, 8, 61, 70, 72, 122, 155
July Revolution 6, 42, 123 *see also* 'Three Glorious Days', July 1830
June Days revolt (1848) 7, 48, 69, 81, 161
*juste milieu* 71, 72, 76, 210 n.85

justice 2, 4, 5, 56, 67 *see also* injustice
  education for 34, 125–6
  equality and 4, 34, 76–8, 179–80, 191
  principle of 30
  social 17, 47, 74, 108, 163, 165

*La Patrie en Danger* (newspaper) 9, 38, 101, 209 n.77
*La Philosophie positive* 163
labour 85, 92, 95, 99, 102, 109–10
  dominiation of 116
  fruits of 57, 59, 84, 111
  instruments of 57–8, 59, 64, 78, 79
  and land 57–9
  servitude of 57–9 (*see also* servitude)
Laclau, Ernesto 83, 95–9, 103, 112, 135, 141, 216 n.60, 217 n.73
Lafargue, Paul 9, 12, 194 n.19, 194 n.32
*Le Libérateur* (newspaper) 38, 57, 71–2, 76, 77, 86, 93, 107, 158
Le Nuz, Dominique 73
leadership 42–53, 192
  Blanqui's conception of 46–7
  enlightened 51, 69
  function/role of 47, 118
  intellectual 11, 43
  leaders and popular forces 42–4 (*see also* popular forces)
  militant forms of 91
  and organization 42, 43, 202 n.113
  political 11, 43, 117
*L'Écho de la fabrique* 101, 213 n.11
Ledru-Rollin, Alexandre 2, 8, 75, 122
legislators 52, 73, 84, 141–5, 228 n.157
*L'Enfermé* ('The Prisoner') 7–8, 13, 236 n.126
Lenin, V. I. 3, 13, 8, 48, 63, 134–6, 138, 187, 195 n.37, 226 n.119
'Letter to Maillard' 8, 75, 93, 101, 196 n.45
Louis XVIII 3, 230 n.25
Louis-Philippe 6, 36, 71, 72, 86, 123, 155
Luxemburg, Rosa 3, 12, 13, 161
Lyon 35, 68, 69, 81, 85, 101, 216 n.59

Machiavelli, Niccolò 15–17, 74, 91, 138, 183, 196 n.43, 196 n.50, 223 n.75
manipulation 6, 113, 187, 202 n.115
  deceit and 37, 71, 124, 132, 150
  of material by man 25

  miseducation and 34–7, 45
  opportunism and 4, 79
  reactionary 34, 36
mankind 25–7, 31, 149
Marx, Karl 2, 15, 27, 38, 63, 81, 86, 88, 121, 153, 161
  on communist revolution 60
  on materialism 26
  primitive accumulation theory 57–8, 59
  on socialism 10–11
  writings 206 n.30
Marxism 25, 201–2 n.98
Marxists 13, 92, 94, 217 n.72, 217 n.73
mass/masses, the 28 *see also* people, the
  emancipation of, by workers 49, 228 n.159
  enslavement of 41, 162, 184 (*see also* enslavement)
  exploitation of 17, 35–6, 46, 57–8, 62–5, 166
  impoverishment of 34, 41, 76, 85, 91, 108, 111
  insurgent force of 14, 43, 47–8, 75, 82, 100
  misinformation and misleading of the 34–5
  mobilization 1, 52, 74, 122, 123, 186
  poverty of 17, 35–6, 58, 62–3
  power of 6, 91, 215 n.43
  propaganda 12, 44, 155
  struggle against the bourgeoisie 66–70, 90
materialism 9, 28, 62, 129, 162
  historical 153–7, 178
  versus idealism 26
  versus spiritualism 31
middle class 46, 106, 153, 166–7, 215 n.43, 230 n.25
Mirecourt, Eugène de 11
monarchy 40, 41, 118, 137, 204 n.140 see *also* July Monarchy
  absolute 45
  constitutional 43
  hereditary, opposition to 117
  monarchical 71
  republican 6, 71
morality 4, 18, 29, 38, 125–7, 129–31, 144, 148, 150, 173, 223 nn.66–7
Michel, Louise 11
Mountain, the 49–50, 205 n.4

Napoleon III *see* Bonaparte, Louis-Napoleon
National Convention of 1792–4 49–51
neutrality 56, 71–2, 76, 82, 186
newspapers 9, 37–8, 39, 69, 72, 101, 106, 107, 180 *see also individual newspapers*
*Ni Dieu, Ni Maître* (newspaper) 10, 38
Noir, Victor 9

oligarchy 80, 96, 188
opportunism 4, 14, 56, 186
oppressed, the 47, 61, 68, 87, 106, 134, 143
  capacity of 15–16, 41
  emancipation of 112
  multitude 28, 108
  'Newspaper of the Oppressed' 72, 107 (*see also Le Libérateur* (newspaper))
  against oppressors 56, 66, 98, 112, 153, 161
  tradition of 165–7
  types of 37
oppression 15, 32, 36, 47, 68, 71, 96, 116, 134, 143, 166 *see also* violence
  clerical teaching leading to 35, 51
  and deceit 127
  emancipation and 5, 49
  ignorance and 40, 41
  injustice and 37, 61, 67, 131, 165
  monarchical or feudal 33
  political 132
  press's role against 37–9
  resistance to 118–19
  structural 64, 119
oppressors 16, 36, 41, 56, 59, 65, 66, 69, 80, 98, 112, 153, 161, 212 n.138, 230 n.25
organization 42–53
  of people 1, 5, 44–7
  political 12, 15–16, 20
  revolutionary 44
  social 17
Orléanist regime 1, 37, 71, 106

Paris 5, 7, 87–9
  dictatorship of 45, 136, 137–8, 185
  *grands travaux* 49
  insurgent 47–53
  intellectual primacy of 48
  Necker prison hospital 9
  political primacy of 47, 48, 137
  political vanguard of France 46–7
  Prussian siege of 1–2, 10, 69, 172
  Saint-Pélagie prison 8
  workers in 46, 49, 88, 94, 157–8, 228–9 n.159 (*see also* workers/working class)
Paris Commune (1871) 9, 10, 13, 168, 175, 195 n.33, 207 n.44
Parisian dictatorship 45, 136, 137–8, 185
peasants 58, 62, 67–8, 86, 87, 94, 109, 212 n.139, 215 n.43, 227 n.139, 228 n.159
people, the 1, 5, 21 *see also* mass/masses, the
  Blanqui's conception of 87–9
  deception of 35, 50, 51
  depoliticization of 123
  empowerment of 100, 187, 227 n.142
  enlightened minority 45–6
  enslavement of 31, 51, 58, 63, 68 (*see also* enslavement)
  freedom of 45, 47 (*see also* freedom)
  ignorance of 34–5, 45–6, 50–1
  insurgent force of 14, 43, 47–8, 75, 82, 100
  lack of political education 36
  life based on thinking and ideas 25–6
  oppressed 15–16, 41, 96, 134, 143
  passivity of 36, 41, 45, 52
  power of 49, 89–90, 145, 164
  revolutionary elite and the 44–7
  and the rich (*see* rich and poor)
  self-rule of 18, 40, 45, 134–8, 143, 226 n.135
  stupefaction of 35 (*see also* stupefaction (*abrutissement*))
  working class (*see* proletariat/proletarians; workers/working class)
philosophy 24, 29, 182
  governing of society 25
  political, of Rousseau 17–19
  primacy of 148–52
  role in Blanqui's project 148–9, 155, 184, 229 n.4, 237 n.129

plebeians/plebs 61, 85–6, 110, 137–8 see also mass/masses, the; people, the
political action 118, 150, 155, 179, 185, 196 n.43
   Blanqui's conception of 20, 26–7, 46–7, 89–92
   collective 14, 60, 74, 90, 98, 144, 182, 187, 189–90, 192
   decisive 15, 49, 52, 112, 160, 184
   enlightened consciousness as determinant of 49
   justice and 30
   organized 105, 121, 189
   Rousseauist approach to 19
   uninformed 113
political actors 42, 50, 84–7, 89, 110, 112, 114, 186–7
   collective 126, 183
   Laclau's notion of 96–7
   voluntary 21, 143
political agency 19, 83, 87, 88, 143, 186, 190
political censorship 7, 107
political force 4, 20, 46, 49, 115, 124, 156, 186, 197 n.63
political militancy 191, 192
political power 38, 55, 103, 192
   collective 23
   seizure and retaining of 15, 16, 52, 74, 132, 134, 164
   will, imposition of 115
political primacy 15–16, 47, 48, 88
political repression 44, 155
political strategy 19–20, 192
political struggle 70, 87, 96, 154, 157, 161, 165, 179, 189, 195 n.37
   emancipation and 36, 74
   driving factor of 31–2
   in human self-transformation 150
   militant 61
   temporalities of 147
   and volition 116, 122, 129–30, 144
political subjectivity 23, 28, 108, 120
political temporality 19
political theory 2, 14–15, 22, 70, 106, 114, 123, 139, 157, 184–7
politics
   of action 5–6, 15
   of Blanqui (see Blanqui's politics)
   conspiratorial 20, 44, 45, 155–6
   elitist conception of 52
   emancipatory 13, 22, 111, 116, 119, 134, 180
   as faith 128–30
   militant 15, 27, 61, 157, 182, 190, 206 n.30
   of (mis)education 33–42
   of pen 5–6
   primacy of 4, 147–8, 154
   of principled conviction 8, 72, 76, 186
   revolutionary (see revolutionary politics)
   Rousseau's conception of 28–9
popular disempowerment 123, 154
popular education 33, 34, 39, 40–2, 44, 45, 105, 120, 135, 136, 139, 140, 179
popular empowerment 2, 13, 15, 20, 75, 90, 123, 184, 187, 191, 192
   direct 73, 119, 141
popular forces 15, 19, 43–4, 49, 50, 74, 92, 118, 127, 186–7
popular government 115, 142
popular mobilization 12, 21, 43, 113, 118–19, 185–6, 188, 192
popular power 2, 82, 118, 143, 155, 187, 188, 192, 203–4 n.139, 215 n.43
   collective force and 89–91, 96, 97
   containment of 6
   egalitarian 18–19
   fear of 46
   obstacles and resistance to 122, 123
   struggle for 14
popular self-determination 119, 191
popular transformation 105, 135–6
popular victory 42–3, 90, 97, 122, 164
positivism 14, 161–3, 189
post-revolutionary transition 45, 114, 131–2, 144
power
   absolute 116, 120
   balance of 9, 89
   class 6, 64
   collective 16, 32, 49, 89–90, 112, 117, 119
   hegemonic 52, 115, 138
   illegitimate 131, 179–80
   intellectual 38, 143
   of the masses 6, 91, 215 n.43
   material 96, 227 n.142

of the people 49, 89–90, 145, 164
political (*see* political power)
popular (*see* popular power)
of the proprietors 61–2
revolutionary 143
seizure of 13, 36, 40, 45, 75, 119, 120
state 4, 44, 55, 63, 74, 138
transitional 45, 131, 143, 184
press 16, 36, 64 *see also* newspapers
popular 37, 51
freedom of 37–9, 106
restriction of 37, 41–2
*Prince, The* 15, 16, 196 n.43, 196 n.50
principle of legitimacy 46, 71
privileged, the 17, 41, 44, 57–9, 61–4, 68, 70, 84–5, 95–6, 108–9, 111, 167, 180, 188, 205 n.12
progress
collective 33
education for 5, 33–4, 150
history and 147, 149–52, 159–61, 164, 168, 178–82
human 21, 32, 34, 38, 147, 178–9, 231 n.49, 233 n.80
social 5, 152, 159, 160, 179, 182, 187
proletariat/proletarians 10–11, 14, 21, 43, 46, 48, 71, 77, 81, 217–18 n.72 *see also* workers/working class
alliance with the 'Mountain' 49–50
Blanqui's 83–4, 91–2, 94, 95, 99–104, 106, 108, 111–12, 154, 186–7
versus democrat 101, 102
dictatorship of 10, 135, 138–9
empowerment of 100, 187
exclusion of 84, 86, 103
slaves of the bourgeoisie 63 (*see also* enslavement; servitude)
social rights of the 81–2
starvation of 108–9, 111 (*see also* starvation)
'subjectification' 100, 103
untold suffering of work 108–12
property 57–61
Blanqui's analysis of 18, 21
crtitique of 57, 59–60, 78
inequality in 59–62, 65, 68
principle of 58, 158
private 17, 59, 60–1, 68, 70, 77
right to 57, 58, 78, 205 n.13, 231 n.46

seizure of land 57–9
usurpation of 57–9, 61
Protot, Eugène 9
Proudhon, Pierre-Joseph 2, 193 n.16
Provisional Government (1848) 1, 8, 36, 75, 208 n.56, 223 n.59
Prussia 1–2, 9, 10, 69, 172
putchism 1, 13, 45–6, 154–5

Rancière, Jacques 83, 98–100, 103–10, 112, 215 n.34
realism 15, 16, 17, 132–4, 138
red flag, abandonment of 36 *see also* Revolutions, 1848 (February)
religion 9, 35, 44–5, 128–9, 133, 162, 224 n.86
'Report to the Society of the Friends of the People' 42–3, 87, 92, 153, 202 n.113, 210 n.85, 214 n.27, 215 n.43, 218 n.104, 231 n.40
repression 6, 19, 35, 38, 48, 49, 51, 65–8, 125, 139, 175
military 68
political 44, 155
royalist 165
state 65, 110, 185
republicanism 2, 13–14, 46, 72, 155, 210 n.85
republicans 4, 8, 62, 71, 75, 101, 124–5, 153–4, 158, 209 n.64
*Réveil* (newspaper) 69
revolution 5, 7, 8, 12, 16, 87 *see also* insurrections; Revolutions
civil war and 65–70
communist 60
counter- (*see* counter-revolution)
enlightenment and 39–42
of the intellect 24–33
political 123–4, 133, 134, 195 n.33
proletarian 81–2
social 73, 133
revolutionary party 8, 41–2, 161–2, 164, 190
revolutionary politics 1, 2, 5–6, 7, 43, 44, 45–6, 49, 89, 94, 99, 135, 189
revolutionary transition 45, 105, 114, 131–6, 144, 184–5
Revolutions *see also* insurrections
1789 3, 13

1830 (July) 1, 6–7, 36, 89–91, 153
  (*see also* 'Three Glorious Days',
  July 1830)
1848 (February) 7, 36, 41, 47, 81,
  123, 155
Rigault, Raoul 9
rich and poor 35, 48, 61–2, 67, 84, 86, 92,
  97–8, 102, 106, 110, 111, 115–16,
  122, 188
riots 1, 7, 65 *see also* insurrections;
  Revolutions
Robespierre, Maximilien 13, 18, 28, 47,
  48, 50, 51
Rome 58, 85–6
Ross, Kristin 101
Rousseau, Jean-Jacques 15, 50, 51–2,
  120, 122
  on collective political action 90
  conception of politics 28–9
  critique of property 57, 59
  on freedom 30–1, 113, 130
  general will concept 17, 19, 141–2 (*see
    also* general will)
  on law and injustice 74
  on the legislator 142–3
  political philosophy of 17–19
  on popular government 142
  on popular power 18–19
  *Second Discourse* 17
  on unity 97
royalism 46, 210 n.85
royalist(s) 71, 73, 153–4, 234 n.83
  moderate 3
  repression 165
  'terror' 66
  ultra- 3

Saint-Just, Louis Antoine de 13, 56
Saint-Simon, Henri Comte de 15, 24, 57,
  109, 121, 205 n.8
sans-culottes 3
schools 34, 39, 64
science 25, 35, 129, 140, 148, 162–3, 181,
  201 n.85, 233 n.67
Second Empire 8, 49, 64, 69, 79, 162
self-determination 215 n.37, 220 n.9
  collective 21, 40–1, 42, 74, 113, 117,
    144, 152
  popular 119, 191

socio-political 5
  voluntary 31, 130, 184–5
self-emancipation 20, 28, 185
self-government 137–8, 226 n.135
self-transformation 28, 136, 139, 150,
  226 n.135
servitude 17, 36, 40, 56, 73, 77, 80 *see also*
  enslavement
  of labour 57–9, 68
  unconscious 45, 49
  voluntary 130–1
social arrangements 18, 29, 78, 148, 149,
  152, 162, 182, 184, 188, 189
social change 40, 50, 83, 132
  education and 33, 34
  due to philosophical change 26, 148, 182
  radical 14, 55, 182, 185, 187, 190, 192
social contract 17, 29, 222 n.40
*Social Contract, The* 18, 30, 51, 142,
  196–7 n.58
social justice 17, 47, 74, 108–9, 163, 165
social reforms 73, 155
social relations 4, 11, 26. 34, 40, 44, 55,
  57, 60, 62, 98, 119, 188, 214 n.27,
  229 n.4
social revolution 73, 133
social transformation 39, 47, 52–3, 75,
  76, 118, 132–4, 148, 158, 164, 185,
  237 n.129
socialism 12, 13–15, 74, 129, 156, 199 n.40
  enlightened 6, 42
  practical 15, 75
  revolutionary 10, 42, 75
  utopian 14, 15, 24
Société des Saisons 7, 44, 208–9 n.64
Société Républicaine Centrale 7, 66, 76
sovereignty 111, 117, 196–7 n.58, 221 n.20
  popular 18, 46, 71, 124
spiritualism 31, 129, 131
Spitzer, Alan 93–5, 102, 131, 149, 154–5,
  216 n.59, 217 n.87, 230 n.33, 231
  n.49, 235 n.116, 235 n.124
starvation 35, 64, 67, 69, 70, 108–9, 111,
  180, 209 n.64, 209 n.77
state, the
  capitalist 63–4
  church and the 40, 51
  civil war and 61–5
  power of 4, 44, 55, 63, 74, 138

struggle
    class 12, 13, 93–5, 102, 153–4
    political (*see* political struggle)
    popular 95, 187–8
    social 31, 70
    sociopolitical 21, 23, 51
stupefaction (*abrutissement*) 31, 35, 51, 130, 115, 184
suffering 35, 50, 59, 64–5, 70, 71–2, 74, 87, 164–7, 187, 195 n.33, 205 n.4
    material 86, 128
    mental and physical 236 n.126
    passive 110–11
    physical and moral 236 n.129
    social 163
    violence and 67–8, 158, 208 n.51
    of work 108–12
superstition 35, 134

Taschereau document 7, 175, 236 n.126
taxes 61, 62, 73, 151
teleology 165, 166, 189
temporality 19, 114, 138, 144, 145, 189–90
Terror (of 1793–94), the 66, 67, 165, 166
thought/thinking
    brain and 27–8, 129, 198 n.25
    collective 32
    conscious 96, 115, 139, 150
    enlightened (*see* enlightened thought)
    human 4, 23, 24, 27, 29, 114, 149–50, 182
    mankind and 25–7
    political 2, 22
    and volition 29–32, 36
'Three Glorious Days', July 1830 1, 6, 89–91, 117, 131, 187
Tkachev, Pyotr 11
Toqueville, Alexis de 11
'Trial of the Fifteen' 61, 99, 157
Tridon, Gustave 9, 69, 126, 180, 196 n.50, 209 n.77
*Trois Glorieuses*, the *see* 'Three Glorious Days', July 1830
Trotsky, Leon 15, 48, 195n.36

universal suffrage 39–40, 73, 136, 211 n.110
upper class 106, 153, 230 n.25
usurpation 43, 57–9, 61, 77, 81, 84, 117, 118, 145
usurpers 57, 59, 81, 84, 117–18

utopia/utopianism 2, 10, 14, 15, 24, 47

Vallès, Jules 9
vanguard(s) 20, 37, 52, 87, 155
    enlightened 105
    political 46–7
    revolutionary 44–7, 48, 143
victims 35, 45, 64, 66–7, 69, 80, 110, 131, 166, 173, 219 n.118, 234 n.83
victory 56, 157–61, 179
    popular 42–3, 90, 97, 122, 164
Vigier, Philippe 93, 102
violence 30, 64, 71, 90, 115–16, 130, 166, 210 n.86, 233–4 n.83
    insurrectionary 66–7, 209 n.64
    political 62
    structural 65, 208 n.51, 209 n.64, 219 n.113
    and suffering 67–8, 158, 208 n.51
    against workers 57, 58, 59, 65–6
Volgin, V. P. 92, 94, 95
volition 21, 22, 113–45
    collective 32, 114, 117–21, 131–2
    conflict of wills 114–16
    conscious (*see* conscious volition)
    free 130
    and freedom 30–1, 119, 120
    human 29, 116, 172
    moral duty and 124–7
    obstacles and resistance, overcoming of 121–4
    politics as faith 128–30
    thought and 29–32, 36
    transition and transformation 134–41 (*see also* revolutionary transition)
    unconscious 30
    voluntary servitude 130–1
Voltaire 18, 38
voluntarism 23, 115, 130–1, 152, 156, 158, 177, 180, 187–8
voluntary action 20, 21, 23, 30, 32, 90, 112, 114, 139, 183–4, 187

wage slavery 58, 59, 63, 64
war
    art of 16
    Church against devotion and intelligence 31
    civil (*see* civil war)

Prussian 1–2, 9, 10, 69, 172
social 64, 65, 67
'Warning to the People' 8, 16, 175, 177, 203 n.115, 232 n.60
will 3, 4, 5 *see also* freedom; volition
   brain and 29, 32
   collective (*see* collective will)
   conflict of 114–16
   conscious 114–15
   enlightenment and 30
   free 18, 29, 30, 32, 121
   general (*see* general will)
   political 117, 119
workers/working class 10, 31, 37, 97, 156, 167, 202 n.98, 207 n.44, 218 n.92
   *see also* proletariat/proletarians
   'advanced' 28
   condition in Orléanist France 86
   cooperatives and associations of 140
   emancipation of the 76
   enlightened 186, 227 n.139
   exploitation and slavery 64–5 (*see also* exploitation; enslavement)
   impoverished 84, 112, 187 (*see also* impoverishment)
   masses' emancipation, devotion to 49, 228 n.159
   oppressed 47, 61, 66, 68 (*see also* oppression)
   Parisian 46, 49, 88, 94, 157–8, 228–9 n.159
   ribbon 116
   servitude of labour 57–9
   silk 85, 101 (*see also* canuts (silk weavers) revolt)
   tax system and 61, 62
   as victims 64, 66–7 (*see also* victims)
   violence against 57, 58, 59, 65–6

Žižek, Slavoj 135, 218 n.92

www.ingramcontent.com/pod-product-compliance
Lightning Source LLC
Chambersburg PA
CBHW072135290426

44111CB00012B/1876